THE STATES AND THE NATION SERIES, of which this volume is a part, is designed to assist the American people in a serious look at the ideals they have espoused and the experiences they have undergone in the history of the nation. The content of every volume represents the scholarship, experience, and opinions of its author. The costs of writing and editing were met mainly by grants from the National Endowment for the Humanities, a federal agency. The project was administered by the American Association for State and Local History, a nonprofit learned society, working with an Editorial Board of distinguished editors, authors, and historians, whose names are listed below.

Utah

A Bicentennial History

Charles S. Peterson

W. W. Norton & Company, Inc.

New York

American Association for State and Local History

Nashville

To Betty

Copyright © 1977
American Association for State and Local History
Nashville, Tennessee

Published and distributed by W. W. Norton & Company, Inc.
500 Fifth Avenue
New York, New York 10036

Library of Congress Cataloguing-in-Publication Data

Peterson, Charles S
    Utah: a Bicentennial history.

    (The States and the Nation series)
    Bibliography: p.
    Includes index.
    1. Utah—History. I. Title. II. Series.
F826.P48   979.2   77-2726
ISBN 0–393–05629–5

Printed in the United States of America
1 2 3 4 5 6 7 8 9 0

Contents

Illustrations

5824

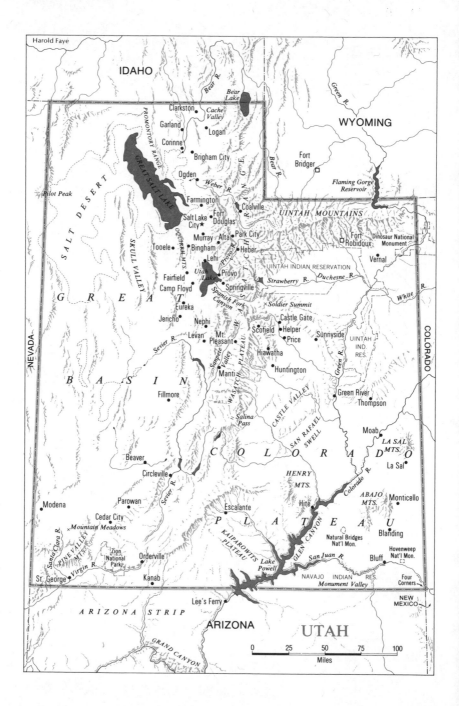

Harold Faye

IDAHO

WYOMING

Bear *R.*

Bear
Lake

Clarkston
Cache
Valley

Garland
Logan

Corinne

Green R.

Brigham City

Bear *R.*

Fort
Bridger

Ogden

Flaming Gorge
Reservoir

Weber R.

Pilot Peak

Farmington

UINTAH MOUNTAINS

SALT DESERT

PROMONTORY RANGE

GREAT SALT LAKE

Salt Lake
City

Fort
Douglas

Coalville

Murray Alta

Park City

Fort
Robidoux

Dinosaur National
Monument

Tooele

Bingham

Heber

Vernal

OQUIRRH MTS.

SKULL VALLEY

Lehi

Provo R.

UINTAH INDIAN RESERVATION

White R.

Fairfield

*Utah
Lake*

Provo

Springville

Strawberry *R.*

Duchesne R.

Camp Floyd

*Spanish Fork
Canyon*

G   R   E   A   T

Eureka

Soldier Summit

WASATCH PLATEAU

SALT DESERT

Jericho

Nephi

Castle Gate

Scofield Helper

Sunnyside

UINTAH
IND.
RES.

Levan

Mt.
Pleasant

Price

Hiawatha

B   A   S   I   N

SANPETE VALLEY

Manti

Huntington

Green R.

Fillmore

CASTLE VALLEY

Green River

Thompson

NEVADA

Salina
Pass

*SAN RAFAEL
SWELL*

Moab

LA SAL
MTS.

Beaver

C   O   L   O   R   A   D   O

La Sal

Circleville

Sevier R.

HENRY
MTS.

Colorado R.

ABAJO
MTS.

Monticello

Modena

Parowan

Escalante

Hite

Cedar City

Mountain Meadows

P   L   A   T   E   A   U

*KAIPAROWITS
PLATEAU*

Natural Bridges
Nat'l Mon.

Blanding

Santa Clara R.

*PINE VALLEY
MTS.*

Zion
National
Park

Orderville

GLEN CANYON

Lake
Powell

San Juan R.

Hovenweep
Nat'l Mon.

Bluff

Virgin R.

St. George

Kanab

NAVAJO   INDIAN   RES.
Monument Valley

Four
Corners

Lee's Ferry

NEW
MEXICO

ARIZONA   STRIP

ARIZONA

UTAH

GRAND CANYON

0   25   50   75   100

Miles

COLORADO

Invitation to the Reader

IN 1807, former President John Adams argued that a complete history of the American Revolution could not be written until the history of change in each state was known, because the principles of the Revolution were as various as the states that went through it. Two hundred years after the Declaration of Independence, the American nation has spread over a continent and beyond. The states have grown in number from thirteen to fifty. And democratic principles have been interpreted differently in every one of them.

We therefore invite you to consider that the history of your state may have more to do with the bicentennial review of the American Revolution than does the story of Bunker Hill or Valley Forge. The Revolution has continued as Americans extended liberty and democracy over a vast territory. John Adams was right: the states are part of that story, and the story is incomplete without an account of their diversity.

The Declaration of Independence stressed life, liberty, and the pursuit of happiness; accordingly, it shattered the notion of holding new territories in the subordinate status of colonies. The Northwest Ordinance of 1787 set forth a procedure for new states to enter the Union on an equal footing with the old. The Federal Constitution shortly confirmed this novel means of building a nation out of equal states. The step-by-step process through which territories have achieved self-government and national representation is among the most important of the Founding Fathers' legacies.

The method of state-making reconciled the ancient conflict between liberty and empire, resulting in what Thomas Jefferson called an empire for liberty. The system has worked and remains unaltered, despite enormous changes that have taken place in the nation. The country's extent and variety now surpass anything the patriots of '76 could likely have imagined. The United States has changed from an agrarian republic into a highly industrial and urban democracy, from a fledgling nation into a major world power. As Oliver Wendell Holmes remarked in 1920, the creators of the nation could not have seen completely how it and its constitution and its states would develop. Any meaningful review in the bicentennial era must consider what the country has become, as well as what it was.

The new nation of equal states took as its motto *E Pluribus Unum*—"out of many, one." But just as many peoples have become Americans without complete loss of ethnic and cultural identities, so have the states retained differences of character. Some have been superficial, expressed in stereotyped images— big, boastful Texas, "sophisticated" New York, "hillbilly" Arkansas. Other differences have been more real, sometimes instructively, sometimes amusingly; democracy has embraced Huey Long's Louisiana, bilingual New Mexico, unicameral Nebraska, and a Texas that once taxed fortunetellers and spawned politicians called "Woodpecker Republicans" and "Skunk Democrats." Some differences have been profound, as when South Carolina secessionists led other states out of the Union in opposition to abolitionists in Massachusetts and Ohio. The result was a bitter Civil War.

The Revolution's first shots may have sounded in Lexington and Concord; but fights over what democracy should mean and who should have independence have erupted from Pennsylvania's Gettysburg to the "Bleeding Kansas" of John Brown, from the Alamo in Texas to the Indian battles at Montana's Little Bighorn. Utah Mormons have known the strain of isolation; Hawaiians at Pearl Harbor, the terror of attack; Georgians during Sherman's march, the sadness of defeat and devastation. Each state's experience differs instructively; each adds understanding to the whole.

The purpose of this series of books is to make that kind of understanding accessible, in a way that will last in value far beyond the bicentennial fireworks. The series offers a volume on every state, plus the District of Columbia—fifty-one, in all.

Each book contains, besides the text, a view of the state through eyes other than the author's—a "photographer's essay," in which a skilled photographer presents his own personal perceptions of the state's contemporary flavor.

We have asked authors not for comprehensive chronicles, nor for research monographs or new data for scholars. Bibliographies and footnotes are minimal. We have asked each author for a summing up—interpretive, sensitive, thoughtful, individual, even personal—of what seems significant about his or her state's history. What distinguishes it? What has mattered about it, to its own people and to the rest of the nation? What has it come to now?

To interpret the states in all their variety, we have sought a variety of backgrounds in authors themselves and have encouraged variety in the approaches they take. They have in common only these things: historical knowledge, writing skill, and strong personal feelings about a particular state. Each has wide latitude for the use of the short space. And if each succeeds, it will be by offering you, in your capacity as a *citizen* of a state *and* of a nation, stimulating insights to test against your own.

James Morton Smith
General Editor

Utah

1

A Process of Becoming

AMERICAN states and the territories from which they grow are created by the acts of statesmen. Rules regulating the creative process are prescribed and in varying degree fulfilled. Petitions and constitutions are drafted. Politicians contend and orators argue. Time draws on and finally with the flourish of a pen a state is born.

But in a deeper way states are realized long before organic acts add legal stature to the characteristics of being. The raw stuff exists from time immemorial, "unstoried, artless, unenhanced." [1] In the beginning, it is a matter of geography and nature—nothing more. Then, in one of the wonders of statecraft, human experience unfolds to fill the void. A tradition evolves—an exploration here, a river crossing there, an outpost, and a time of starving and tragedy. So it goes. A region has come to be.

For Utah the American experience began with the Spanish Padres Dominguez and Escalante. Strangely enough it began in 1776, in the dusty miles of one of the West's great explorations. During the three quarters of a century that followed, the processes by which Utah was defined progressed sufficiently to provide a number of guidelines to help Congress as it created the

---

1. Robert Frost, "The Gift Outright," *Complete Poems of Robert Frost* (New York: Henry Holt and Company, 1949), p. 467.

3

territory in the great Compromise of 1850. Extending from the 37th parallel on the south to the 42nd on the north, the new territory embraced most of modern Nevada, half of Colorado, and about an eighth of Wyoming. Harried by the momentous problems of slavery and assimilation of the Mexican Cession, Congress responded to the strongest determinants and the surest definitions. It rejected two solutions less responsive to geography and less sensitive to lines already laid down by emerging regional traditions. A Mormon proposal for a vast state to be called Deseret was ignored, as was a proposal from President Zachary Taylor.

The fact that the lines Congress laid out made good sense depended in part upon conditions external to Utah. The territory was in effect created from leftovers after Congress had met regional interests more deeply entrenched in the national consciousness. To the west lay California, by 1850 a password on every man's lips, its image indelibly marked by the Gold Rush. To the north was Oregon, a territory since two years past, secured in American tradition by long sparrings with England. New Mexico, newly won but set apart by a venerable past, lay south. And to the east stood the wall of the Continental Divide, backed by Kansas, now caught in the strife that led to the Civil War. Thus Utah Territory was the land beyond, filling-stuff for a continent and obstacle to a nation's travels, at once America's most internal and its most remote province. It was the odds and ends of creation. Drought was general, good soil limited, climate uninviting. Two great physiographic provinces—the Colorado Plateau and the Great Basin—dominated the territory. Similar in immensity, aridity, and ruggedness, they were distinctive otherwise. The Plateau articulates outward to the Gulf of Mexico, to the Pacific, and to the world. The Basin drains in upon itself and articulates directly with nothing. The Plateau is rugged and colorful almost beyond description, and has been a land without water, although one of the nation's great drainage systems courses through its canyon troughs. The Basin can boast no similar water flow but is nevertheless the site of Utah's watered valleys and, of course, the Great Salt Lake and its salt deserts.

Utah Territory was also a land of mountains. The grandest portions of the Rockies were within its original bounds, and the fronts of the Wasatch Range guard the cities of the modern state. Along the northeastern boundary the Uinta Mountains extend east and west, out of kilter in a land of north–south ranges. Farther west the serried spines of the Great Basin's desert mountains haze off toward the grand crest of the Sierra Nevada.

For sojourners of the early nineteenth century, Utah country was an enigma. They had been conditioned to expect river systems to originate in the highlands and fall to the sea. There was no precedent for an inward-working drainage system. The realization that such a throwback of creation did exist occasioned wonder nationally, wonder well expressed by John C. Frémont when he described the phenomenon in the mid-1840s.

> [It is] a novelty in our country, and excites Asiatic, not American ideas. Interior basins, with their own systems of lakes and rivers, and often sterile, are common enough in Asia. . . . But in America such things are new and strange, unknown and unsuspected, and discredited when related. But I flatter myself that what is discovered, though not enough to satisfy curiosity, is sufficient to excite it, and that subsequent explorations will complete what has been commenced.[2]

Events outpaced even Frémont's fond anticipation. In three years exploration had passed to settlement, and in six years Frémont's strange land had become part of the nation, as America rushed to encompass the West.

As spectacular as it was, this rush rested upon a process of becoming that had been in motion at least since 1776. The very forces that complicated and slowed Utah's recognition as a region make its discovery and rediscovery during the seventy years after the American Revolution one of the nation's great adventures.

History provides few more clearly defined firsts than the Dominguez–Escalante exploration of 1776 does for Utah. Indeed, as a point of beginning the famed expedition of the New

2. John C. Frémont, *The Exploring Expedition to the Rocky Mountains, Oregon and California* (Buffalo, N.Y.: Geo. H. Bergy & Co., 1841), p. 414.

Mexican padres belongs to Utah in a special way. Parts of the other Four-Corner states—New Mexico, Colorado, and Arizona—through which the trail of the padres looped had long been within the realm of Spanish influence. But earlier Spanish thrusts had apparently penetrated Utah only in 1765 and then briefly, leaving it the repository of mystery and wondrous tales.[3]

A belated Spanish surge brought the Utah country within range of New Mexico in 1776. The first California missions had recently been established. To further their growth and secure their defense, efforts began in the early 1770s to connect California with San Xavier del Bac, near present Tucson, and with Santa Fe. The connection with San Xavier del Bac had been opened by early 1776. Attention then turned to the country between New Mexico and California. Father Francisco Garces, one of history's great loners, came by a direct route from the west and arrived at Oraibi, the westernmost of the Hopi villages, on July 2.

To Francisco Atanasio Dominguez and Silvestre Velez de Escalante fell the task of exploring from the east. Unlike Garces, they gathered a retinue, small though it was. In addition to Bernardo Miera y Pacheco, a doughty and gifted soldier who served as cartographer, they employed nine men and two young Indian guides, making a full complement of fourteen. They departed from Santa Fe on July 29, 1776, after missing a projected departure date of July 4, which had it been kept would have given the expedition a symbolic harmony almost poetic in character.

From the time of their departure, the padres noted resources and prospects for missions and carefully recorded trail data. A special interest in Utah Lake and the Laguna Indians who lived by it appears early in their journal. With two Laguna guides provided by a Ute tribe in western Colorado, they proceeded northwest to the Green River near the present Dinosaur National

3. For an account of the recent discovery of the records of an expedition to the southeastern corner of Utah, see Donald Cutter, "Prelude to a Pageant in the Wilderness," *Western Historical Quarterly* 8 (January 1977): 5–14.

Monument. From the Green River they turned south and west to Spanish Fork Canyon, which they followed into Utah Valley on September 23. Comparing Utah Valley to the Valley of Mexico, the padres promised to return and settle among its Indians. They noted but did not visit the Great Salt Lake.

Still intent on reaching California, they hurried south on September 25. Early snows persuaded Dominguez and Escalante that to push on to the west was folly, and, after casting lots to convince Miera (whose mind was set on California), they turned homeward. The group wandered through some of the most rugged country in the West before they reached the Colorado River on November 7, at a place known since as the Crossing of the Fathers. The river behind them, they hurried on, reaching Santa Fe early in the new year.

Their journey was an important achievement. They had traveled nearly 2,000 miles in five months, produced a truly remarkable diary, and drawn a map that has both illuminated and confused Utah's geography. They had recognized the importance of the Wasatch Front and generally measured the natural characteristics of Utah. In addition, they had laid to rest a number of myths and raised up a few to replace them. Legends about a country of giants and rich cities were now acknowledged to be impossible. Also disproved were rumors of descendants of parties strayed from the Coronado expedition and mysterious Spaniards supposed to have penetrated the country from some other direction.

Perhaps more significant than myths laid to rest were myths perpetuated in new and altered forms. Miera's work proved especially fruitful in this respect. The old soldier drafted several versions of his map, which laid the groundwork for an accurate grasp of Utah's geography. Unfortunately it also confused the Green River, called the San Buenaventura, with the Sevier and showed the Green flowing, not to the Colorado River, but into a lake at the western extremity of the mapped area. By themselves these were serious mistakes, but Miera compounded error when he indicated that the Great Salt Lake drained west toward the Pacific. During the next seventy years, Miera's San Buenaventura and his west-draining sea afflicted in one form or another virtually every map of the American West, including one of vast influence which the great Alexander von Humboldt published in 1811 as part of his famed *Political Essay on the Kingdom of New Spain*. One effect was to perpetuate in different form the age-old myth that a waterway extended across the continent to the Orient. Another was to confuse and complicate the relationship of the four great drainage systems that did exist in the West, suggesting that the Missouri, the Columbia, the Colorado, and the Rio Grande all sprang from a continental eminence within a relatively small area. The process of eliminating the unnatural offspring of Miera's San Buenaventura River occupied two generations of explorers and mapmakers from half a dozen countries and culminated a mere half-decade before Utah became a territory.

With geography in mind, it is easy to follow Bernard DeVoto's thinking that the grand tour of the padres was "all arroyos, gulches, canyons, mesas, mountainsides, ridges, labyrinths, mazes, rock slides." [4] It was this, indeed, but fortunately it was more. It was also an introduction to the natives of the Colorado Plateau and the Great Basin, a primer in the tradition of a people whose lifestyle and character had already set the region apart.

Escalante's diary and the Miera map reveal a grasp of tribal relations that covers a vast area extending in three directions from the modern borders of Utah. In addition they provide a more detailed portrait of tribal groupings within the state. In the south the Hopis were well known, as were the Cosninas (Coconino Indians?) south of the Grand Canyon. In a great arc to the north ranged various horse and buffalo cultures designated collectively as the Comanches. Shown to control all of northeastern Utah were Comanche Yamparicas (Shoshonis?). Miera's map notes that they were so "nimble at horseback riding" that they had become the "Señores and owners of all lands of the Zibolos." [5] Although Escalante and Dominguez met no Coman-

4. Bernard DeVoto, *The Course of Empire*, Sentry Edition (Cambridge: The Riverside Press, 1962), p. 292.

5. A copy of Miera's map accompanies Herbert Eugene Bolton, *Pageant in the Wilderness: The Story of the Escalante Expedition to the Interior Basin, 1776, Including the*

ches, they saw their sign and shared the dread that the Yutas held for them. They also noted, but did not see, tribes north and west of Utah Lake (Gosiutes?), reported to be gentle and primitive and to speak a language like the Comanches.

Central to the vast ethnographic pattern thus sketched were the Yutas. As Escalante applied it, the name was a lingual designation. All the Indians encountered in Utah and Colorado spoke dialects of the same language and were consequently termed a single "kingdom divided into five provinces, known by the common name Yutas." [6]

In western Colorado the explorers identified three Yuta tribes: the Muhuaches, the Tabehuaches, and the Sabuaganas. All lived in roving bands and possessed horse and buffalo cultures. The Lagunas of Utah Valley emerged in the Escalante diary as peaceful, sedentary, and impoverished, and as eminently promising candidates for conversion. Their range of activity was restricted by the Comanches, but they had previously hunted in the canyons to the north and east of Utah Valley and several had been found as distant as western Colorado. To the south, in west-central Utah, the Spanish came upon the Yutas Barbones, Indians with beards like the "hermits of Europe." [7] Likely the source of vague reports that bearded Spaniards inhabited the new country, these Indians proved to be even more fearful and poverty-stricken than the Lagunas. Still further south lived a race of Yutas even more apprehensive than the bearded Indians. These Escalante called Yutas Cobardes or the cowards. A related province was that of the Payuchis (Southern Paiutes?). Known in New Mexico before 1776, the Payuchis inhabited a strip of wild country adjacent to the Colorado River along the Utah–Arizona border of today.

During the decades that followed the Dominguez–Escalante mission, white contacts multiplied. Few whites saw as compre-

---

Diary and Itinerary of Father Escalante Translated and Annotated (Salt Lake City: Utah Historical Society, 1940).

6. Bolton, *Pageant in the Wilderness*, p. 227; see also *The Dominguez–Escalante Journal: Their Expedition through Colorado, Utah, Arizona, and New Mexico in 1776*, trans. Fray Angelico Chavez, ed. Ted J. Warner (Provo: Brigham Young University Press, 1976), pp. 102, 188–189.

7. Bolton, *Pageant in the Wilderness*, p. 189.

hendingly as the padres; but the lore growing from a thousand encounters, confusing though it often was, helped to identify the country. This process of contact is not easily traced but came in general to deal with the Utes, the Paiutes, and the Gosiutes, each of whom belonged to the larger Shoshonean family.

By the 1840s the name "Ute" was apparently applied to Escalante's group from southwestern Colorado to his bearded Indians—the Pavante Utes of pioneer times. Even the Pavante and San Pitch groups on the western periphery of the Utes had become equestrian and enjoyed the power over pedestrian relatives that mobility provided. They lived in tribal groups and ranged broadly from fairly well-defined base localities. With buffalo becoming extinct they depended more and more upon small game and trade with the advancing whites. Trade caravans and emigrants were often forced to pay tribute, and the hapless Paiutes and Gosiutes were pillaged and bullied. Mountain men found the Utes to be brave and candid, less inclined to war and theft than most mountain tribes, but also often found them to be among the world's most accomplished beggars. As trapper Warren Angus Ferris expressed it, they made an art of begging, plying it with "incorrigible pertinacity," not for the property itself but "for the honor of having obtained it in that mode." [8] Power to govern appears to have been associated with mobility and wealth rather than with inherited right.

Few demonstrate this pattern more completely than the famed Chief Walker. Said to have come to influence by merit of wealth, Walker had long dealt in slaves as well as furs and horses and extorted a "blackmail salary" from whites and Indians alike.[9] His movement and that of similar bands was a major element in traffic over the Old Spanish Trail and in the commerce that sustained the earliest trading posts in Utah.

8. Warren Angus Ferris, *Life in the Rocky Mountains: A Diary of Wanderings on the Sources of the Rivers Missouri, Columbia, and Colorado from February, 1830, to November, 1835,* ed. Paul C. Phillips (Denver: Old West Publishing Co., 1940), p. 311.

9. Entry of Thomas L. Kane, The Journal History of the Church of Jesus Christ of Latter-day Saints, March 26, 1850, Historical Department, Church of Jesus Christ of Latter-day Saints, Salt Lake City, Utah (hereafter cited as Church Historical Department).

Walker was capable of doing things in the grand style, as when he joined the notorious trapper Pegleg Smith to steal thousands of California horses. Later he maneuvered with Brigham Young to maintain and advance personal interests. In the mid-1840s Walker was introduced to the reading public by John C. Frémont, who encountered his band on the Sevier River waiting to "levy their usual tribute upon the great California caravans." According to Frémont, they were "robbers of a higher form" who seized what they wished but affected purchase by "giving something nominal in return." [10] During the next decade Walker appeared repeatedly as a colorful and significant figure in travel books. Thus in his own time he came near being "Mr. Utah," his name and reputation helping fix the attention of Americans upon his tribe and the country.

Along with Nevada and parts of northern Arizona, Utah was distinguished as the homeland of the Gosiutes and Paiutes, Indians so destitute and so primitive that whites long accustomed to primitive tribes often noted their comparative backwardness. Known collectively by the derisive term Diggers, these two tribes were often confused. Both were of Shoshonean stock, but they inhabited different localities and had different lingual and tribal relationships. The Gosiutes occupied the salt desert west of the Great Salt Lake and resembled the Shoshonis of southern Idaho and Wyoming in language and culture. The Paiutes occupied the south extremities of the Great Basin and the canyonlands of the Colorado Plateau in Utah's far south and extended south into northern Arizona and west into Nevada and California.

The basic orientation of both groups has been described as "gastric." [11] So common was starvation that all institutions and activities were organized toward the food quest, which was conducted by small family groups. This way of life allowed few luxuries. Horses were used, if at all, for food. Huts of sage-

---

10. Frémont, *Exploring Expedition,* p. 396.
11. Julian H. Steward, *Basin-Plateau Aboriginal Socio-Political Groups,* Bureau of American Ethnology Bulletin 120 (Washington, D.C.: Government Printing Office, 1938), p. 46.

brush or willows, along with holes and cliff overhangs, provided shelter. Few villages or bands existed. As essential as was
the family to their economy, they often sacrificed weak
members to the slave trade—which resulted in a society marked
by few women, children, or aged.

Contact with whites and Indians rendered aggressive by white
influences contributed further to the unhappy lot of the Gosiutes
and Paiutes. During this contact period they were systematically
ravaged for slaving purposes. Few proved capable of migration,
and those carried off to captivity often fell prey to disease or
were observed to simply "pine away and . . . die in grief for
the loss of their native deserts." [12] After 1840 both tribes were
drawn from their food-gathering patterns to the emigrant trails
of the Great Basin, where they begged and picked up any animal untended for the moment or shot and poisoned others. Even
the most enlightened observers held them to be outlandish and
strange, the "Arabs of the New World." [13]

Thus Escalante's picture of gentle Indian groups each in its
own place changed rapidly after 1776. Utes became warlike and
mobile, exploiting and disturbing the more primitive societies.
Some of these became highwaymen themselves, quite capable
of preying on emigrant livestock. On the other hand, all the
Utah Indians proved less fierce than the Apaches to the south
and the Blackfeet in the north. Ute interest in trade and the sim-
plicity of Paiute and Gosiute culture gave bounds to the country
and invited white penetration.

The medium through which Utah's aboriginal past met the future of America was the mountain man. A romantic anomaly of
frontier democracy, the mountain man was at once hero and
delinquent, distant wayfarer and expectant capitalist, recluse
and publicist, alien and native. Although his campfires flickered
only briefly in the second quarter of the nineteenth century, they
lighted the nation's approach to the West. Mountain men were
few in number—by recent estimates, 3,000. Certainly no more
than 300 operated in Utah country at a given time. Yet they

12. William J. Snow, "Indians and Spanish Slave Trade," *Utah Historical Quarterly*
2 (July 1929): 79.
13. Frémont, *Exploring Expedition,* p. 391.

were a diverse lot and approached the region from three directions. From Oregon came Peter Skene Ogden and the Hudson's
Bay Company brigades. From St. Louis came Jedediah Smith,
Jim Bridger, and others of William H. Ashley's company. From
New Mexico came the Taos trappers, including Étienne Provost, Antoine Robidoux, and Kit Carson. For Utah the fruit of
their effort was discovery; for America it was a sense of territory that enveloped the West.

Echoes of the age-old yearning for a passageway to the Orient
had beckoned Spanish explorers and confused map makers.
With the 1824 discovery of South Pass, a gentle gap through the
Rockies, the passageway was fixed and Utah was placed on a
great national road. Although trappers employed by John Jacob
Astor had apparently picked their way through South Pass more
than a decade before, Jedediah Smith has received credit for the
effective discovery in the spring of 1824. It was a high moment
in the history of Utah. Soon missionaries and Oregon-settlers,
Mormons and gold-seekers would pour through its open portal.
But before they came, South Pass was front door to William H.
Ashley's men. For them it opened to the unspoiled trapping
grounds of the Great Salt Lake region, to a country of friendly
Indians, and to a brief time of quick profits and the high adventure of discovery.

Within two years the Ashley men had engulfed the region and
laid bare its secrets, except for the enigma of the Great Basin itself, and were well on their way to exhausting its trapping
streams. The upper affluents of the Green River were fully
explored. Ashley himself floated its plunging course in 1825,
breaking from its canyon gates at Split Mountain into the Uinta
Basin not far from Escalante's path. Others spread to the Bear
River, followed its loop north from the Uinta Mountains; marveled at the brilliant and shifting blues of Bear Lake, backwater
of the Bear River "navelled in the hills" of the Wasatch Range;
and welcomed the protecting embrace of Willow Valley—soon
renamed Cache Valley—which became a famous wintering
grounds in the years after 1824.[14]

For the Ashley men the discovery of the Great Salt Lake

14. Ferris, *Life in the Rocky Mountains,* p. 44.

climaxed the drama of exploration. Rumored as early as 1688, when Baron Lahontan told of a salten sea 300 leagues in circumference, and reported but unseen by Escalante, the Great Salt Lake became the region's chief distinguishing feature. Claims to prior discovery are numerous. One account places discovery in 1822 and attributes it to Louis Vasquez, later partner to Jim Bridger. Another gives credit to the brooding Dane John H. Weber, who reported in later life that he had found the lake in 1823. But among the Ashley men, Jim Bridger usually takes priority. Hardly more than a boy, Bridger followed the Bear River in 1824–1825 from a Cache Valley camp to the Salt Lake, which, with youthful confidence, he judged to be an arm of the Pacific. This misconception was dispelled during the spring of 1826, when four men coasted the lake's mudflat peripheries. About the same time, other Ashley men explored the Provo River, Utah Lake, and the mountains immediately to its southeast.

However, other discoverers challenged the Ashley men for priority. The Hudson's Bay Company's Snake Country expedition came from the Northwest in 1825, while several parties had pushed north from New Mexico the year before in response to reports that an 1823 party had made good profits. At the head of one of the New Mexico companies in 1824 was Étienne Provost, who explored Provo River and probably discovered the Great Salt Lake in the late fall, anticipating Bridger by several months. A band of Snake Indians massacred part of Provost's party in the vicinity of the Salt Lake, whereupon he retreated to the Uinta Basin for the winter. He headed west again in the spring of 1825, meeting Peter Skene Ogden at the head of the Snake Country expedition in Weber Canyon on May 23.

Ogden had left the Flathead Post northwest of modern Missoula on December 20, with instructions to explore south to the Spanish or Colorado River. Trapping as he went, he reached the Bear River north of Preston, Idaho, on April 26. Dour and fretful, he continued south through Cache Valley, finding few beaver and much evidence of American trappers. Crossing into Weber Canyon, he encountered a large party of Americans under a noisy nationalist named Johnson Gardner. Taking advantage of mutinous members in Ogden's outfit and the presence of Provost, Gardner invaded the British encampment with flags flying and charged that Ogden had committed a breach against American sovereignty that could not go unavenged. Apparently Ogden believed he was on American soil and hastily left the country, but the site of the confrontation was within Mexico, well south of the 42nd parallel—the boundary which divided Bear Lake as does the Utah–Idaho line today.

But for the moment the boundary, along with other abstractions of national sovereignty, had only indirect effect upon the course of events. Rumors of American activities in the Utah country undoubtedly reached New Mexico. Instead of responding with military patrols or licensing their own nationals to trade and trap, the Mexicans redoubled their efforts to keep Taos trappers out of the northwest frontiers, and for a few years Utah lay largely beyond New Mexican influence. The Hudson's Bay Company continued to trap the Snake River country but, with the notable exception of several Ogden expeditions later in the decade, did not push its business southeast of the Portneuf.

The Americans, on the other hand, stayed on. For five years the Great Salt Lake country was the center of the Rocky Mountain fur trade. Indians were peaceful and inclined to trade. Beaver were available, although in diminishing numbers. In addition, the rendezvous—mountain depot and "season of supply, trade and saturnalia"—operated annually from Henry's Fork of the Green, from Cache Valley, and from Bear Lake for half a decade before the fur trade shifted north.[15]

During this period northern Utah and surrounding regions began to be American. Names were changed from the Spanish or the British and a hundred trips spiced with high adventure created an American lore. While too much may be made of it, there is no question that for some the Great Salt Lake country took on subtle but deeply seated aspects of home. Ashley's experience focused on this area, and in his long association with senators and congressmen he projected strong sentiments of na-

---

15. Bernard DeVoto, *Across the Wide Missouri* (Boston: Houghton Mifflin Co., 1947), p. 47.

tionalism that embraced it. More to the point were the sentiments of home that trappers themselves felt for the country. Rarely has a traveler expressed the homing instinct more poignantly than did Jedediah Smith when, after choking across the blistered salt deserts of Nevada and western Utah, he approached the Great Salt Lake and friends waiting at the Bear Lake Rendezvous in June 1827. But let the gaunt and salt-dusted Jedediah make the point:

> Those who may chance to read this at a distance from the scene may perhaps be surprised that the sight of this lake surrounded by a wilderness of More than 2000 Miles diameter excited in me those feelings known to the traveler who, after long and perilous journeying, comes again in view of his home. But so it was with me for I had traveled so much in the vicinity of the Salt Lake that it had become my home of the wilderness.[16]

Frémont's writings suggest that such sentiments were more than the whimsy of a romantic mind. Returning through southwestern Utah in 1844 from a long tour of the Pacific coast guided by Kit Carson and Joseph Walker—both well informed and matter-of-fact—Frémont wrote with evident relief of their "approach to regions of which our people had been the explorers."[17] For 2,000 miles they had heard only Indian and Spanish place names. From the Sevier River Frémont was again in a country which bore the marks of home in its names and in the attitude of his guides.

Thus the discovery of South Pass opened northern Utah to America in 1824. The first Rocky Mountain fur-trading province centered there during the five succeeding years. An area had become a region, vaguely designated by international considerations from the north and south, by location of trapping grounds, and by the relative friendship of its Indians. With the annual rendezvous at its core, it was also a place of business. By right of customary usage, it had become part of America's destiny.

16. Dale L. Morgan, *Jedediah Smith and the Opening of the West* (Indianapolis: Bobbs-Merrill Co., 1953), p. 214.

17. Frémont, *Exploring Expedition,* p. 397.

But change continued to alter context. By 1829 the fur trade had shifted far enough north to necessitate moving the annual rendezvous. Now the Utah country became a peripheral region, still tied to the northern Rockies but increasingly drawn to the Southwest. After 1830 the connection was strengthened by the Old Spanish Trail, which looped through the southern half of Utah and extended its influences to the Uinta Basin and other localities. A new regionalism was taking shape. Trapping continued as an essential. Trade became more and more important, and transportation—a through business—began for the first time to play a role in shaping Utah's traditions.

Events heralding these new relationships had begun to take form in 1826 with the southwest expedition of Jedediah Smith. He and two partners had purchased Ashley's interests and now looked to the unknown country beyond the Salt Lake in hopes of finding the legendary San Buenaventura or other furbearing streams. Of streams and beavers Smith found few; of geography's secrets plenty. It was in loosing the secrets of the Great Basin and intelligent examination of the Pacific Coast that Smith made his great contributions. In threading southern Utah's seared valleys, he approximated the route taken by Escalante a half-century before. In crossing the Mojave Desert to the Mission of San Gabriel, he laid the groundwork for the west end of the Old Spanish Trail. His course north through California and his return via the salt desert showed the San Buenaventura to be an impossibility.

Smith anticipated other explorers by only a few months. On his second trip south from the Salt Lake he saw their tracks and gained a hint as to their identity when Mojaves living on the Colorado told him that whites from the south had divided at their villages. This was evidently the Ewing–Young party, which, according to the marvelous account of James Ohio Pattie, had departed the Rio Grande River early in 1826, trapped down the Gila, and followed the Colorado River north to the Mojave villages. There the party split, one contingent heading east for New Mexico and the other north. The latter group crossed southern Utah to the drainages of the San Juan River, hurried through the parks of Colorado, and penetrated to Clark's

Fork on the distant Columbia drainage before turning south to
New Mexico. The account of this trek, supposedly accomplished in a single season, has inspired skepticism; but
modern scholars agree that Pattie did traverse southern Utah,
contributing to the country's identity not only among southwestern trappers but among the reading public as well, when his personal narrative was published in 1831.

Even earlier, New Mexicans had made occasional trips to the
Utah country. In 1805 Manual Mestas traveled to Utah Lake to
recover stolen horses. In 1813 the Arze–Garcia party penetrated
to central Utah. That even this early venture was not a "first" is
obvious. No more than seven men made the trip; they traveled
known paths and found a guide unnecessary except for one short
section of the trail. Furthermore they traded 109 pelts, considered to "be but a few"; Indians expected them to buy slaves,
and one chieftain waited at the Colorado River crossing "as was
his custom." [18]

As information became more plentiful, interest increased.
The first official trade caravan left Santa Fe for California in the
fall of 1829. Antonio Armijo led it past what would be the Four
Corners of Utah, Colorado, Arizona, and New Mexico to cross
the Colorado River from the south at the Crossing of the
Fathers. From here Armijo's route approximated the present
Utah–Arizona border to the Virgin River and then bore south-
west to California.

Other pack trains followed. They ignored more direct routes,
and the great northern loop of the Old Spanish Trail became the
effective link between New Mexico and California. Passing
northwest through the affluents of the San Juan River, the trail
entered Utah near present Monticello, bore north to cross the
Green River at the modern town of Green River, turned west to
the Sevier Basin, then passed southwest out of Utah and on to
Los Angeles. It is difficult to believe that natural advantages
attracted caravans to the slow miles of this long detour. If the
more southerly routes lacked water, feed, and wood, so did the

18. Joseph J. Hill, "Spanish and Mexican Exploration and Trade Northwest from
New Mexico into the Great Basin," *Utah Historical Quarterly* 3 (January, 1930): 18.

Old Spanish Trail. It seems likely that the trail took its great northern twist in response to trade along its interior.

Not surprisingly, the Old Spanish Trail developed connections with other parts of the West. A key to the regionalism thus emerging was the Uinta Basin, which, because of its central location and its potential for Indian trade and trapping, became something of a meeting ground between the Northern Rockies and the Southwest. From the north came such mountain men as Warren Angus Ferris, Osborne Russell, and John Robertson, who is said to have located on Black's Fork of the Green as early as 1832. In 1836 Phillip Thompson and others established Fort Davy Crockett in Brown's Hole, drawing trade from both the north and the Spanish Trail. Important figures with strong ties to New Mexico included Kit Carson, who wintered in the Uinta Basin in 1833–1834 and reappeared frequently thereafter as trader and trapper. An otherwise unexplained ruin at the confluence of the Duchesne and Green rivers is thought to be the remains of a trading fort established by Carson. Even before Carson, the mysterious Denis Julien had carved his name at a half-dozen sites in the Basin and in the canyons of the Green River.

However, the name which links eastern Utah most closely to the Old Spanish Trail is Robidoux. Antoine Robidoux had been among the first Taos trappers to enter the country in 1824. After trading from temporary sites for several years, he established a permanent post on the Uinta River in 1837 which carried on a profitable trade with trappers frequenting the Green and Colorado rivers. He also did business with Ute and Snake Indians. For a few years after 1839, Robidoux's Uinta Basin location was particularly strategic when the passing of the mountain rendezvous made remaining fur trappers almost completely dependent upon goods coming over the Old Spanish Trail.

But such prominence was fleeting. Emigration via the Oregon Trail was replacing the fur trade as the chief economic force in the intermountain plateau. In response to this development, Jim Bridger opened a short-lived business on the Green River in 1841 and two years later established Fort Bridger in the high meadows of Black's Fork. Too far from the Oregon Trail to catch anything but overspill, Fort Robidoux suffered additionally from the general decline in the fur trade. Deteriorating relations between New Mexico and the Utes also complicated Robidoux's affairs, and in 1844 Indians destroyed his outpost on the Uinta.

Meantime traffic over the Old Spanish Trail had expanded. Horses and cattle, many of them stolen, trailed east along it. Settlers passed west by pack train as early as 1831. By 1837 wagons of the Pope–Slover party are said to have entered Utah by way of the Colorado River en route to California. The collapse of the fur trade and increasing tensions between Americans and Mexicans at Santa Fe led to a modest increment in emigrant traffic after 1840, as the California myth began to exert its pull upon Americans.

Thus the Old Spanish Trail gave the Utah country important ties to the Southwest. New Mexico and California represented markets, outfitting points, and destinations, and Utah lay between them. Simultaneously events altered the vague lines delimiting the country north and west of the Great Salt Lake. Enraptured with visions of a great national passageway to the Orient and with the increasing prospect of a continental nation, Americans looked to Oregon as a place to go. The effective control held for England by the Hudson's Bay Company grew progressively weaker as first fur traders, then missionaries, and finally, in the 1840s, emigrants by the thousand passed along the Oregon Trail.

Initially, this traffic had little effect on the Great Salt Lake country. It lay south of the Mexican border and beyond the main course of the trail to Oregon. On the other hand, it was on a direct line to California and was subject to further definition as the California Trail was worked out. Both Jedediah Smith and Peter Skene Ogden had contributed to this process—Smith insignificantly when he crossed the Great Basin in 1827 by an impossible and forgotten route, and Odgen significantly when he discovered the Humboldt River in 1828. Named the Unknown River by Ogden and called variously the Mary's, the Ogden's, and the Barren River before Frémont renamed it for the great German geographer, the Humboldt flowed almost as if by providential design west across the greatest desert in America, a highroad to California.

First to point up the imperatives of the country through which it ran was Joseph C. Walker, in 1833–1834. Walker was employed by Benjamin Bonneville, army officer on leave, to explore the Great Salt Lake. Leading a large party, Walker worked his way around the north end of the lake and through the deserts beyond the present Utah–Nevada border. Then, supposedly having gone too far to make a safe return, he continued southwest to strike the Humboldt. He followed its diminishing flow to the point where it sinks entirely, then proceeded on to find a practicable passage over the Sierra Nevada range. This feat assumed national importance when Washington Irving served it up to the reading public in the *Adventures of Captain Bonneville*, published in 1837.

Having taken the country's measure, mountain men rarely ventured into the deserts west of the Great Salt Lake. Indeed the next important episode in the exploration of the salt desert occurred only in 1841 and was then the effort of emigrants. The Bartleson–Bidwell party traveled with Thomas Fitzpatrick to Soda Springs and doubtlessly drew heavily from this famed mountain man's fund of information. Yet they learned little about the direct line between the Bear River and California. Taking first a crude pack trail and then a trackless waste, they traced a tedious road north of the lake to Pilot Peak near the Nevada border. Shortly before reaching the haven of its springs, Benjamin Kelsey and his nineteen-year-old wife, Nancy, who was the first white woman to cross Utah, abandoned their wagon. Two days beyond Pilot Peak the rest yielded to necessity, parked their wagons, and packed on to California's promised land.

In the years that followed, various parties worked out the course of the California Trail via Fort Hall. As traffic increased, considerable interaction took place between it and the Old Spanish Trail. Round-trip traffic sometimes passed to California by one road and returned by the other. Occasionally bold and experienced groups cut crosslots over the salt deserts, as in the case of Miles Goodyear, who drove a herd of horses eastward early in 1847 to trade with Oregon migrants. Others like Marcus Whitman, renowned Oregon missionary, and Joseph Williams, a preacher of noisy conscience, found it convenient to make connections between the California Trail and the Old Spanish Trail by way of Fort Robidoux.

The explorations of John C. Frémont also had their place in the development of Utah. An officer in the Topographical Corps of the United States Army, Frémont was a strange mix of past and present. A gentleman adventurer, strangely out of time and place, he was also scientist, observer, and popularizer, the very epitome of American Manifest Destiny. During 1843–1844 and again in 1845 he made major expeditions to the Far West, passing through Utah on three separate occasions. In September 1843 he entered the Utah country by way of the Bear River, headed straight for the Salt Lake, calculated location and altitude, exuberantly tested the waters of the lake in a rubber boat, and visited the island that bears his name today.

After a winter's exploration of the Pacific coast he re-entered Utah in May 1844 via the Old Spanish Trail. At Utah Lake he marveled that it affiliated with the Great Salt Lake and, without understanding the nature of this relationship, proceeded to Washington, D.C. In 1845 Frémont returned to Utah, arriving in the magnificence of early October. Ascertaining that Utah Lake was not a limb of the Salt Lake, he continued his examination of the larger lake, circling its southern limits, and struck eighty miles northwest across barren salt flats to Pilot Peak. He then hurried on to a rendezvous with destiny in California.

Few places provided a happier hunting ground for Frémont than Utah. To him the Great Salt Lake was a wilderness exclamation point, the salt deserts beyond a brooding question. Thus excited, he was almost boyish. Superlatives came easily. His men were the best. Routine was magic—a boat trip on the mountain sea became a national epic, friction with Indians along the Virgin a test worthy of Homeric veterans, and a sweaty climb up the tangled course of the Santa Clara or a crossing of the Sevier in handmade boats of bulrushes fully sufficient to transport Frémont from the reality of foreign soil to visions of an expanded homeland.

For Frémont and for America it was high adventure. But it was more. It was measurement, description, and reporting. And it was synthesis. Myth and mystery coupled with intelligent travel and scientific method produced understanding and regional distinctions. In the vast loop of his 1843–1844 tour from the Salt Lake, Frémont understood once and for all the secret of the Great Interior Basin. Mountain men had been aware of the inward flux of its streams and lakes but, little understanding evaporation, they invented fables of whirlpools and subterranean waterways as the "only imaginable way of carrying off" waters with no visible means of discharge.[19] In Frémont's explorations such vexations of the mind were laid to rest along with lingering suspicions that the San Buenaventura yet rolled. The Enigma of the Great Basin, the last great question of American geography, was solved. Romantic, boyish, scientific, but most of all consistent with the national spirit, Frémont made Utah "neighbor to the nation's mind."[20]

Frémont's salt desert crossing of 1845 precipitated events that would lend tragic emphasis to Utah's character as barrier. With sure sense of what nature would tolerate, mountain men had avoided the salt deserts. But in 1846 the quickening tempo of America's move to California led to a search for shortcuts. On arriving in California late in 1845, Frémont had reported with more enthusiasm than judgment that the arid path by which he came was at least 800 miles shorter than the traveled road and "decidedly better" for wagons, "not only on account of the less distance, but . . . less mountainous, with good pasturage and well watered."[21] This was the rhetoric of promotion and jibed more closely with Frémont's desires than with what he had actually observed. But his report fell upon the ears of one whose desire to bring a flood of emigrants to California made him even more insensitive than Frémont to the imperatives of the barrier land. This was Lansford W. Hastings, promoter with imperial

19. Frémont, *Exploring Expedition*, p. 402.
20. Dale L. Morgan, *The Great Salt Lake* (New York: Bobbs-Merrill Co., 1947), p. 146.
21. Quoted in Morgan, *The Great Salt Lake*, p. 153.

visions for California, author of an influential emigrants' guide, and, until recent efforts to rehabilitate his memory, villain in every account of the Donner tragedy.

Convinced that Frémont's shortcut was the key to his designs, Hastings headed east in the spring of 1846 with a party of horsemen. Well mounted, they had no trouble following Frémont's tracks from Pilot Peak to the south end of the lake. His enthusiasm for the new cutoff unbounded, Hastings hurried on to Fort Bridger to preach California as "garden of the world" and to advise travelers to take what has since been known as Hastings' Cutoff. About a half-dozen outfits, including the Bryant–Russell party on mules and some eighty wagons, accepted his advice. With Hastings leading, the first outfits broke a new road down Echo Canyon to the Weber without undue trouble. From that point all of the wagon companies suffered grief, some wracking and jolting down the streambed of the Weber, while the lagging Donner party spent three precious weeks hacking its way to the Salt Lake Valley via East Canyon, Big Mountain, and Emigration Canyon. As tough as had been the aproaches to the lake, the line of departure over the burning desolation of the salt desert was worse. The packers made the eighty-mile dry march with little more than inconvenience and apprehension. The sixty wagons led by Hastings himself made it by dint of intense suffering and some loss of stock. The Donners made it by the barest margin. Any question remaining as to the practicality of Hastings' Cutoff was answered with stark and terrible emphasis when nearly forty of the eighty-seven members of the Donner party succumbed to the snows of the Sierra Nevada during the winter of 1846–1847. Travel to California continued, reaching crest-tide after 1849. In time, important routes from Salt Lake City south and north provided good connections west, but the country west of the Great Salt Lake was fixed as a barrier in the minds of frontier Americans.

By 1848 Utah's first traditions had taken form. Regionally it had emerged, along with America, in the years since Escalante. Challenging national questions had included the problem of how to react to an open continent. Oregon, California, and New Mexico had become part of the United States. Within the borders thus defined, the interior West had entered the public consciousness more slowly. In the interior, aridity and ruggedness reached a climax. It was a barrier and a passageway, not a destination. Yet by 1850 Utah was part of the United States, its first identifying traditions established. In these same years the past met the future when the Mormons introduced their own distinctive regionalism. With polygamy and political conflict to highlight the process, Utah's period of regional definition continued well beyond the great national era of sectional conflict that ended with the Civil War.

2

The Mormons

$\mathcal{O}$N July 24, 1847, the pioneer party of Mormons pulled out of Emigration Canyon into the Valley of the Great Salt Lake. With little hesitation they proceeded to a site near present Temple Square in Salt Lake City. There they began the processes of settlement. Some explored. Some plowed and planted. All listened to Brigham Young. It was an episode made unique in the annals of the West. The Mormons had come as if impelled to a chosen spot by a force greater than their own, as indeed they believed they had been.

Since that time, the history of Utah has been inextricably associated with the Mormon people. Earlier traditions had nudged the region onto the pathway of identity; but with the Mormons, a place received an indelible image. A nation founded on the concept of diversity within union had come by one of its most vivid distinguishing marks. Neither old dominion, nor slavery, nor the gold rush marked its region more emphatically in the national consciousness.

Rarely has American unanimity been greater than upon this point. It was a cherished tenet of Mormon belief, as attested by their determined and repeated proclamation, that their valley kingdom was a holy place differing from the world as good differs from evil. With nearly equal fervor, but with vastly different meaning, nineteenth-century Americans generally accepted this distinction. To them Mormon country was variously a curiosity, a matter of ridicule, a throwback to priestcraft, or an object of grudging admiration. But in any case it was a break from the ordinary that locked a people and a part of the country in common identity. The United States government also saw Utah in terms of the unusual, finding relics of barbarism in its customs and symptoms of treason in its conduct. Finally, twentieth-century students have found in the Mormon experience and Utah history an additional dimension to the great national drama by which the West was won.

For the Mormons and the American nation the years before 1847 were a time of becoming. The nation had been formed: the Declaration of Independence had invoked a higher law to justify rebellion; the Ordinance of 1787 had opened the West; the common man had been enthroned; and federalism had been established, although sectionalism testified that its meaning was still in dispute. By the 1840s the search for national meaning had been expressed in the creation of symbols and traditions which rendered venerable and renowned a past that was brief and obscure. An entire mythology had come to be. Replete with its own heroes, it was an answer to Europe's long history and a fitting heritage from which to launch the world's greatest future. Privately, men found purpose in economic opportunity and in the institutional and moral improvement of the country. Blessed with plenty and success, American progress created an atmosphere in which all things seemed within reach.

Mormons were both product of and contributing factor to America's dialogue of becoming. Like their fellow Americans, they responded to the country's invitation to restructure life and give new meanings. From familiar forces and values they made a new synthesis, offered a different destiny for America, and gave themselves over to maximizing its impact.

For the Mormon Church the time of becoming began with Joseph Smith. Born in Vermont in 1805, he was taken by his family to western New York after the War of 1812. For the Smiths, a series of inauspicious beginnings had marked the American experience. But a search for spiritual meaning had outweighed their quest for economic and social opportunity. Finding little reward in contemporary Christianity, they had taken recourse in scripture and "sound reason" and in an unrequited yearning for a return to the "ancient order." [1] They adhered to no pattern of success, nor did they espouse the institutional establishment of the era. On the other hand, their failures did not stifle their faith in God or their confidence in themselves and in the American dream.

To Joseph Smith, as to the new nation, all things seemed possible. When he found no earthly authority to act in God's name, he appealed as a boy of fourteen to its ultimate source, announced the utter bankruptcy of all Christendom, restored the gospel together with authority to act in God's name, and in 1830 organized the Church of Jesus Christ of Latter-day Saints. Once committed, he filled the short years of his life with "experiments in theocracy and communitarianism and temperance and polygamy, with expectations of millennium and Second Coming, with worldwide evangelism and practical programs of emigration and colonization." [2]

Smith undertook to bring order and unity to all things through Mormonism. Toward this end he saw all space—worldly and other-worldly—as being of the same order. All mankind was of one vast tradition. As Adam was created in God's image, so modern man and all who had intervened were in Adam's image. Race difference was the product of divine blessings or curses, not of yawning cultural chasms opened over eons of time. Temporal and spiritual power were undivided, blurring the Mormon recognition that "religion was one thing and politics and economics another." [3] All time—past, present, and future—was also essentially the same. The future would fall in two periods: a brief and imminent pre-millennium that pertained directly and in a most practical way to contemporary man, and a less clearly defined future beyond Christ's second coming, which was nev-

---

1. See William Mulder and A. Russell Mortensen, eds., *Among the Mormons: Historic Accounts by Contemporary Observers* (New York: Alfred A. Knopf, 1958), p. 24; and Preston Nibley, ed., *History of Joseph Smith by his Mother, Lucy Mack Smith* (Salt Lake City: Bookcraft, 1958), p. 46.

2. Mulder and Mortensen, *Among the Mormons,* p. 9.

3. David Brion Davis, "The New England Origins of Mormonism," *New England Quarterly* 26 (June 1953):157.

ertheless intimately related to other periods and very much like the known world. To set things in order for the millennium, Mormons raised the voice of warning and gathered to Zion.

Chief unifying element in all this was active and continuing communication between God and man. Longing for God's word, Joseph Smith added to its sacred store, giving the world the *Book of Mormon* and revelation in profusion. The *Book of Mormon* claimed a fuller history for America. Indeed, it approached the ultimate in creating an immemorial tradition. In it were united the Judeo-Christian past and the unknown history of America. Throughout ran the idea of America as a favored land, preserved in the past and destined to be the cradle from which God's earthly kingdom would arise. Central to the favored-land theology as well as to the North American geography was the concept of Zion, which Joseph Smith revealed first as a gathering place in Missouri and later extended to encompass the American continent, with Missouri retaining a special status as the "center stake of Zion." Mormon teaching added heavenly purpose and the direction of divine communication to the American dream of a land especially associated with mankind's advance.

Thus early Mormonism was a response to the greater American ferment. Although it partook of familiar influences, it nevertheless added up to its own unity and purpose. Unlike the national temper, it tended to stress the communal over the individual, the spiritual over the secular, singular associations over plural loyalties, and to regard the United States as a divinely prompted but passing stage in an eternal progression toward God's earthly kingdom, rather than as an end in itself.

Most Americans judged Mormons first "unique, then foreign, then alien, then the enemy of American life." [4] Mormonism seemed a counterculture that rejected America's progress, harked back to intolerance, mixed church and state, and threatened property. Some thought "the very materials of which the society" was composed would at "length produce an explo-

4. Robert B. Flanders, "To Transform History: Early Mormon Culture and the Concept of Time and Space," *Church History* 40 (1971): 109.

sion.'' [5] To a few, the Mormons seemed the "common enemies of mankind," who deserved destruction.[6]

In the hotbed of opposition the seeds of union and separatism matured together. Opposition, or persecution, as Mormons are wont to call it, began in New York with the boy prophet; spread to the entire society in Ohio; erupted in the Mormon wars of Missouri, where old settlers justified expulsion by a "higher law"; terrorized Nauvoo, Illinois, with assassinations and "wolf hunts"; and finally followed the Saints to Utah's isolation. In opposition the church grew—from a handful in New York to hundreds at Kirtland, Ohio, to 10,000 and more in Missouri, to a city of 12,000 at Nauvoo, with a world membership of nearly 50,000 by the time of the great exodus, and to hundreds of thousands in Utah. Opposition was also the refiner's fire, a flux which carried off the dross of summer friends and made the Saints one people.

Driven by their sense of destiny and the reality of opposition, Mormons became increasingly isolated in both self-concept and place of dwelling and came ultimately to be a people apart— what sociologist Thomas O'Dea has called a "near nation." [7] But the demands of bringing unity to a divided world remained. To fulfill them, Mormons performed prodigies of travel.

In the most obvious sense Mormon travel was the product of flight. The Saints were rejected, the open continent beckoned, and precedent—both scriptural and contemporary—was abundant. But Mormon travel came full turn only in the church's effort to harmonize discordant influences implicit in its mission to warn the world and its withdrawal from the world. Carried to extremes, the two influences were incompatible. On the one hand was total isolation, as among *Book of Mormon* peoples. On the other was continuing contact, as Mormon harvesters cried repentance in fields ripe with iniquity. Warning and withdrawal—each was imperative. To yield on either would be to

5. Quoted in Mulder and Mortensen, *Among the Mormons,* pp. 72–75.
6. Quoted in Mulder and Mortensen, *Among the Mormons,* p. 76.
7. Thomas F. O'Dea, *The Mormons* (Chicago: University of Chicago Press, 1957), p. 115.

disrupt purpose and unity. By travel as modern as tomorrow in its negation of distance and as ancient as Father Abraham in its purpose and conduct, Mormons undertook to resolve the dilemma.

As in so much else, Joseph Smith set the pattern. For fourteen years his path was Mormonism's main-traveled way. Along its course he perfected the church, built cities and temples, saw visions of Mormon roads running to the Rocky Mountains, and announced himself a candidate for the presidency. But for Joseph the road ran to neither the White House nor the West but to Carthage jail in Illinois, where he was assassinated on June 27, 1844.

For Smith's followers, the exodus to Utah and the times of Brigham Young lay ahead. Converted in 1832, Young was among the first called as apostles, logged untold miles as a missionary, and matured as a leader when he led the Saints from Missouri to Illinois in the terrible winter of 1838–1839. Judged an "angel of light" by his followers and a "goblin damned" by his foes, he possessed a faculty for migration and colonization unparalleled in American history.[8] If Joseph's appeal came from his unifying vision, Brigham's power was forged on the anvil of migration by the blows of hard miles.

Preparation for the great exodus began when the martyred prophet's body was brought back to Nauvoo. Leaders studied reports of the West, and as persecution increased in the fall of 1845, the Saints agreed to move "as soon as grass grows and water runs."[9] The decision made, they entered into a "temple convenant" by which each committed his all to the removal of the entire church to a wider "field of action" where "God Himself be the sole proprietor."[10] Thereafter every man became a peddler and every home a workshop as outfits were prepared and efforts made to salvage some value from belongings.

8. Richard F. Burton, *The City of the Saints, and Across the Rocky Mountains to California* (New York: Harper & Brothers, 1862), p. 240.

9. Quoted in Mulder and Mortensen, *Among the Mormons,* p. 165.

10. Joseph Smith, *History of the Church of Jesus Christ of Latter-day Saints,* 2nd ed., rev., 7 vols. (Salt Lake City: Deseret News Press, 1952), 7:464–467.

The first wagons crossed the Mississippi River on February 2, 1846. The thousands who poured across Iowa's mud in the weeks that followed encountered one of the most trying experiences in Mormon history. For them there was new meaning in the 137th Psalm: "By the rivers of Babylon we sat down and wept. We wept when we remembered Zion." Loyalty to the United States was at low ebb. Regret and anger replaced patriotism. Doggerel lines current among the exiles lamented:

> This Gentile race the Priesthood hates
> We have no home within the states.[11]

In an explosion of activity, Brigham Young and other leaders comforted and encouraged and, more important, whipped together the tens, fifties, and hundreds by which the Camp of Israel was organized. Roads were opened, streams bridged, and waystations established at Garden Grove, Mt. Pisgah, and Winter Quarters—tabernacle camps, Thomas L. Kane, friend of the Mormons, called them. In addition, over 500 men enlisted in the Mormon Battalion and set out for California and the Mexican War. The Battalion's march involved the Mormons in another of the nation's great travel episodes, but it also destroyed plans to reach the mountains in 1846. The Saints stayed on at Winter Quarters and elsewhere near the Missouri River. Afflicted by malaria in summer weather so hot that "cattle strove to lap wind like hard fagged hunting dogs," and experiencing hunger and exposure in winter, they suffered and died; but preparations went on for the exodus.[12]

In April 1847, 143 men, 3 women, and 2 children headed west. This pioneer party was carefully chosen, well outfitted, and subject to the full brunt of Brigham Young's discipline.

11. George F. Partridge, ed., "Death of a Mormon Dictator: Letters of Massachusetts Mormons, 1843–1848," *New England Quarterly* 6 (December 1836): 610–611.

12. Thomas L. Kane, "The Mormons, a Discourse Delivered Before the Historical Society of Pennsylvania, March 20, 1850," in Daniel Tyler, *A Concise History of the Mormon Battalion in the Mexican War, 1846–1847,* 2nd printing (Glorieta, New Mexico: Rio Grande Press, 1969), p. 87.

Traveling along the north side of the Platte River, the pioneers cut the original track of the Mormon Trail, established its first ferries, and improved its way. At Fort Laramie southern Saints who had wintered at Pueblo, Colorado, joined them. Along the trail they garnered additional information, finding old mountain man Jim Bridger a prime source. As they approached Utah, the pioneers strung out along the trail. Orson Pratt and Erastus Snow led the way, following the trace that the Donner party had prepared the year before at such tragic cost, and entered the Valley of the Great Salt Lake on July 22. The rest followed during the next two days, with Brigham Young arriving on the 24th.

Symbolically 1847 was and has remained the year of the exodus. But only a tithe of scattered Israel had found refuge. Kanesville, on the east side of the Missouri River, became the main outfitting point as Winter Quarters emptied in 1847 and 1848. Those most able and willing to make the trek formed the migration of these two years. It remained to bring those who lacked means or whose faith lagged. The Utah leaders focused the full battery of their persuasive ordnance upon the laggards, and to bring the poor they established the Perpetual Emigrating Fund, a revolving scheme which outlived the exodus to gather the Saints from abroad. By 1852, the exodus from Nauvoo was completed. In execution it had resembled Israel's flight. In spirit it had much in common with *Book of Mormon* migrations. But ironically its timing coincided with a great national thrust into the West.

Once the exodus was completed, the gathering and the warning which impelled it became one of Utah's greatest enterprises. A latecoming and rejected minority in the Midwest, Mormons became Utah's original settlers. To the spiritual goals of salvation and world reform they added the temporal objectives of growth and survival. By proselyting and immigration the Mormons tried to maintain their domination in the region.

With growth a necessity, the warning was always urgent. Before the dust of the exodus settled, missions extended to the world. The British Mission, counting twice as many Mormons in 1850 as Utah, was a firm beachhead on Europe's shores. Scandinavia proved a fertile field, yielding 46,497 converts by 1905. Europe elsewhere was opened, but missionaries there were "gleaners not harvesters of stout sheaves." [13] Proselyting was renewed throughout the United States and missionaries probed tentatively at the isles of the Pacific, at the Orient and South America. Mission work always meant travel going to and coming from the field. Proselyting itself was travel punctuated by meetings and baptisms, threats and disappointments. Jesse N. Smith, a typical missionary, made it from his home at Parowan in southern Utah to Liverpool in two months, used eight separate means of conveyance in a winter trip from England to Copenhagen, and during the years that followed spent most of his time walking. But Smith's travels were local compared to those of Levi Savage, who made a tour around the world that took four years. Bound for Siam, he left Utah via San Francisco in 1852; survived a long voyage and a bout with smallpox to arrive in Calcutta the next summer; shipped to Rangoon on a wallowing coastal steamer with a babel of humanity and a Noah's menagerie of livestock; found apathy among the natives and hostility in the British community; and begged for subsistence and passage home for many months before the American Consul finally arranged passage to Boston late in 1855. On his "native shores again," he returned West with the ill-fated Willie's Handcart Company in the fall of 1856.[14] Doubtless the road-weary Savage would have agreed with Sir Richard Burton's 1860 observation that "almost every Mormon is a missionary and every missionary is a voyager." [15]

Converts too were voyagers. For most American Mormons, the gathering had much in common with the westering experience in general—uprooting, wagons, teams, great western trails, and place of arrival. For Europeans the gathering was a

13. William L. Mulder, *Homeward to Zion: The Mormon Migration from Scandinavia* (Minneapolis: University of Minnesota Press, 1957), p. 58.

14. "Levi Savage Jr. Journal," ed. Lynn M. Hilton, multilithed (Salt Lake City: Savage Family Organization, 1969), p. 53.

15. Burton, *City of the Saints,* p. 424.

"double fracture." Not only did they leave home and fatherland, but in embracing their new religion they crossed the
"sprung longitudes of the mind and the blood's latitudes." [16]
The trip from Liverpool to Great Salt Lake City consisted of
three segments: the ocean voyage; a journey by river, canal, and
railroad through the states; and finally the Mormon Trail to
Zion. The church planned thoroughly, organized minutely, provided the Perpetual Emigrating Fund, and, lacking *Book of
Mormon* wonders, mixed faith and realism in relentless adaptation. As Brigham Young put it, they could not expect the Lord
to "build balloons or come down with his chariots and pick up
the poor." [17]

Costs were considerable. Some Saints fell away in transit. On
ocean crossings death sometimes converted efficiency to horror,
as in the 1864 passage of the *Monarch of the Sea* in which
"about 60 children died which included nearly all the little ones
among us." [18] Cholera and malaria thinned thousands of all
ages from the ranks. For many, debt to the Perpetual Emigrating
Fund hung like a millstone, hampering efforts to get started in
Utah. But in the annals of Mormon migration costs climaxed in
the Willie and Martin handcart companies of 1856. In a momen-
tary lapse from their wonted practicality, Mormon leaders listened too well to the rhetoric of their own promotion—"the
Lord can rain manna on the plains of America"—and turned a
deaf ear to words of caution like those of hardheaded Levi Savage, who, nearly home from his earth-girdling voyage, voted
alone to postpone a late start until another year.[19] Electing at
last to "go with you . . . suffer with you, and if necessary
. . . die with you," Savage made it through, but not before

16. Mulder, *Homeward to Zion*, p. xi.

17. Sermon of November 30, 1870, *Journal of Discourses by Brigham Young, His
Two Counselors, and the Twelve Apostles*, 26 vols. (Liverpool and London: Latter-day
Saints Book Depot, 1855–1886), 13:300.

18. H. N. Hanse, "An Account of a Mormon Family's Conversion to the Religion of
the Latter Day Saints and of Their Trip from Denmark to Utah," *Annals of Iowa* 41
(Summer 1971): 717.

19. *Millenial Star* 18 (1856): 138.

more than 200 less fortunate succumbed in the snows of the Wyoming plains.[20]

Yet the gathering was a "transplanting," not a "tragic uprooting."[21] Saints marched smiling from Liverpool's docks, checked through the authorities in good order, and sang the songs of Zion with dry eyes as the fatherland faded from view. They bore waiting and illness with patience, learned the rudiments of pioneering, and beheld Zion with hope. Between 1850 and 1900 more than 90,000 came from abroad to strengthen Zion's union and redeem its wastelands.

By the roads of the gathering the Mormons came to Utah. By colonization they distributed themselves and became a force in the West. By colonization they made a hostile land habitable and brought its discordant elements into a harmonious relationship with God's kingdom. Initiated in 1847, colonizing was repeated on successive frontiers during the next four decades. Responding in part to the Great Basin environment and in part to the teachings and experiences that made them a chosen people, Mormons developed their most distinctive institutions and practices in the process of colonizing. In other words, the climax of withdrawal from the larger society occurred not in arrival in Salt Lake City nor in the conflict that came to center there, but in the colonizing process—the call, the move, group control over land and water, and the farm village life. Developed to bring a raw environment into harmony with God's will on the one hand, and to protect the independence that its rawness permitted on the other, the practices of colonization proved impossible to perpetuate indefinitely, but until 1890 they distinguished Mormon culture and served as the vehicle of the church's geographic expansion.

Innovation was most dramatic at the beginning. Before the last wagons had entered Salt Lake Valley, the pioneers of 1847 began to experiment with irrigation and oasis life. By mid-

---

20. "Mr. [John] Chislett's Narrative," in T. B. H. Stenhouse, *Rocky Mountain Saints* (New York: D. Appleton and Co., 1873), p. 317.

21. Mulder, *Homeward to Zion*, p. xi.

August Salt Lake City existed in blueprint. Following the City of Zion plat developed in the Midwest, the new city was laid out in a four-square grid, with wide streets and nineteen wards, each consisting of nine ten-acre blocks, which were subdivided in turn into eight building lots. The heart of the city, indeed of the Mormon system, was the temple block that Brigham Young designed a few days after arrival. Some 8,000 acres of land were surveyed in the "big field" south and east of the city and subdivided in five-, ten-, and twenty-acre pieces, with small units close to town for city workers and larger units on the outer limit. Home sites and land were distributed by lot and church assignment on the basis of utilization rather than monopoly or speculation. Land was worked individually but fenced and put under irrigation co-operatively. Water and other resources were allocated for maximum use and co-operative development.

In colonizing, Mormons looked far, talked big, and sometimes acted boldly. During the exodus they had been comforted by convictions that God intended them to "extend their borders . . . to a wider field." [22] As they entered Salt Lake Valley, Brigham Young expressed his determination "to know every hole and corner from the Bay of San Francisco to the Hudson Bay." [23] During the ensuing years Young and his followers showed interest in virtually every quarter of the West. The provisional State of Deseret encompassed almost a sixth of the United States, stretching 1,000 miles from the Columbia's watershed on the north to the Gila on the south and 800 miles east and west. Less ambitious expressions of Mormon empire were also numerous. Brigham Young worked to extend the kingdom to California, Arizona, and the Northwest. Seaports were contemplated in southern California, at the mouth of the Colorado River, and at faraway Guaymas in Mexico. Subsidiary gathering places were designated in such diverse places as the Hawaiian Islands, Vancouver Island, San Bernardino, and Mexico. But new centers of gathering, seaports, and geopolitical schemes

22. Smith, *History of the Church,* 7:463–464.
23. Journal History, July 28, 1847.

never really developed. The effective expansion of Mormondom was by means of colonization that passed through Salt Lake City to areas in its hinterland.

Geographically, colonization proceeded through Utah's scattered but interconnected valleys. In the most general sense, it moved from the close-at-hand to the remote. Yet a variety of influences acted upon the process. During the 1850s, in an effort to substitute a sphere of influence for the political bounds of the State of Deseret, an "outer cordon" of colonies was established at San Bernardino, Carson Valley in Nevada, Fort Lemhi on the Salmon River, and Grand Valley at present Moab. This effort was interrupted by the Utah War in 1857 and 1858, and colonization of successive valleys was resumed within the territory during the 1860s. Notable in the colonizing achievements of this period was "Utah's Dixie" in the Virgin River Basin, which was established to produce cotton, molasses, wine, and other warm-climate crops. During the 1870s and 1880s the Saints ferreted out the last bits of watered land in Utah and extended beyond, colonizing first in neighboring states and finally in Canada and Mexico.

The farm village was perhaps the fullest expression of this procedure. During the four decades of colonization some 450 hamlets and towns were established. Almost all were laid out in the four-square pattern and were located at canyon openings according to the dictates of water and following the cardinal directions. They were promoted as the ideal form of settlement by the church, which believed "a spirit to spread far and wide" would detract from the "influence" it hoped to gain as it grew.[24] With arable land scarce and "water the price of blood," the village and small farms associated with it were the effective means of expanding the area of the church's influence.[25]

This had several important ramifications. Long delay in open-

24. John Taylor to William F. Preston, December 26, 1882, as quoted in Milton R. Hunter, *Brigham Young the Colonizer*, 4th ed., rev. (Salt Lake City: Peregrine Smith, 1973), p. 159.

25. Mulder, *Homeward to Zion*, p. 191.

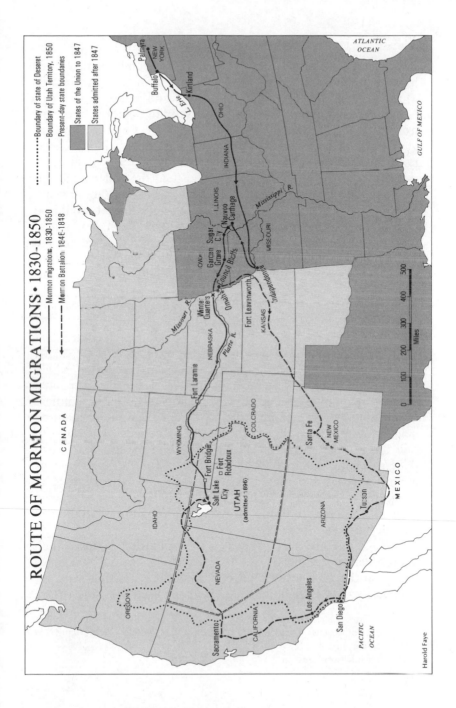

ROUTE OF MORMON MIGRATIONS · 1830–1850

············· Boundary of state of Deseret
– – – – Boundary of Utah Territory, 1850
——— Present-day state boundaries
⟶ Mormon migrations, 1830–1850
⟶ – – Mormon Battalion 1846–1848

States of the Union to 1847
States admitted after 1847

Harold Faye

ing federal land offices gave the church effective control over land distribution in almost all new colonies. As a consequence, Mormons long looked to church custom and authority for such individual land claims as they possessed. In addition, the control of land and water established through village occupation gave the church a claim to Utah that was largely independent of political authority and national sovereignty. As a federal commission reported in 1888, "those who hold the valleys and appropriate and own the water . . . own and hold Utah, and nature has fortified their position more strongly than it would be done by any Chinese wall or artificial defense." [26] Working to unify all things and to forward the interest of the kingdom, the church had manipulated the public lands and natural conditions to its own interests, effectively bringing a region under its control.

Salt Lake City and its surrounding valley quickly became a "gathered place." In the shadow of the rising temple the Saints were secure. Salt Lake City was the place of church control and in many ways the very epitome of Mormonness. However, it quickly passed through the period of colonizing during which Mormon institutions were most distinctive. Thereafter its people became increasingly occupied with matters of business, politics, transportation, and mining, which by their very nature required conduct more consistent with frontier practices generally. In Salt Lake Valley Mormon farmers began to modify the village pattern, taking out individual farms or settling in line villages along the roads and canals. As Apostle E. T. Benson, long in charge of colonizing in Cache Valley, dourly put it, here were "found . . . people living in a scattered condition building in Gentile fashion." [27]

Change in Salt Lake City was a slow invasion against which church leaders frequently warned. The long conflict which focused on the Mormon capital contributed to a lasting sense of peculiarity. But in fighting fire, Mormons used fire, finding the

26. *Report of the Utah Commission to the Secretary of the Interior,* September 24, 1888 (Washington, D.C., 1888), p. 16.
27. Journal History, November 22, 1854.

instruments of their peculiarity to be less useful. Thus Mormons of Salt Lake City and its environs may be said to have turned from many of the distinctive practices that had characterized their own pioneer years, and the Mormon capital may well have become the least Mormon of all Mormon places. Conversely, the hinterland, where the process of the call, the trek, and the establishment of the village repeated itself, became the bulwark of Mormonism in its most distinctive form.

Mormon relations with native Americans were at once an expression of faith and a conquest. The *Book of Mormon* taught that Indians were a fallen people with whom God's spirit had ceased to contend but who were nevertheless united by blood and heritage to ancient Israel. In God's due time, the dark skin and "loathsome" ways of the curse would be lifted and an inherited claim to the American continent be made valid. In the meantime the Saints watched closely for signs indicating that the curse was lifting and experimented with the means of redemption.

The move to Salt Lake Valley displaced few Indians. According to some reports the valley had been a no-man's land avoided by both Utes and Shoshonis, though there is evidence of early bands camping near the Warm Springs. To the south serious friction developed when settlement penetrated Utah Valley. Tensions flared in 1849–1850 and, after discussions with Captain Howard Stansbury of the Corps of Topographical Engineers, Mormon militiamen chastised the Lake Utes. Thereafter Mormon expansion moved relentlessly, occupying the richest valleys, reducing game, and pre-empting forage and water holes. External influences complicated matters, and conflict erupted in the Walker War of 1853–1854. A move to relocate Indians on the Uintah Reservation in the 1860s led to the Black Hawk War. To the far south, Navajos, displaced by Indian wars in Arizona and New Mexico, entered Utah after 1864, taking refuge in Monument Valley on the east and raiding villages and livestock in southwestern Utah. In the north the Battle of Bear River brutally quelled Indian hostility in 1863, when an army detachment under Patrick E. Connor slaughtered more than 300 men, women, and children.

In the main, however, the Mormon occupation of Utah was peaceful. This was due in no small part to the policy of "feeding rather than fighting" Indians. One leader stated in a striking yet melancholy analogy that Mormon policy was to "shoot Indians with tobacco and bread and biscuits rather than with powder and lead." [28] The result was reduced bloodshed and an extended period during which settlers shouldered a primary burden for Indian support. Inevitably Mormons looked upon Indians as their inferiors and in many ways applied a dual standard of morality. Yet they were inclined to attribute hostility to adverse white influence, ascribing Indian wars to their own shortcomings and failure to "fort up" or to the machinations of non-Mormons. Indians were by turn submissive and haughty, begging one day and threatening the next. Elizabeth Wood Kane, who traveled through southern Utah in 1872, described Indians as having

> the appetites of poor relations, and the touchiness of rich ones with money to leave. They come in a swarm; their ponies eat down the golden grain-stacks to their very centers; the Mormon women are tired out baking for the masters, while the squaws hang about the kitchens watching for scraps like unpenned chickens. [29]

As Mrs. Kane suggested, influencing the Indians was a religious duty—the obligation and privilege of every Saint. Practically, however, both obligation and privilege fell upon those who were opening new frontiers. During the first years there was little emphasis upon conversion. Brigham Young laid out the initial policy in 1848, when he declared he had no inclination to "take them in his arms until the curse is removed." In the meantime, teaching was necessary to prepare the way for later regeneration. Likening the process to irrigation, Young said: "[We must] cut channels" for water to run in "and gradually lead it where we want it to go. . . . Just so we must do

28. Franklin D. Richards, as quoted in Leland Creer, *Utah and the Nation* (Seattle: University of Washington Press, 1929), p. 166.

29. Elizabeth Wood Kane, *Twelve Mormon Homes Visited in Succession on a Journey through Utah to Arizona*, new ed., introduction and notes by Everett L. Cooley (Salt Lake City: University of Utah Library, 1974), p. 33.

with this people. . . . by degrees we will control them." [30] All
who encountered Indians were under a general charge to bring
them under Mormon influence. Many traded with Indians, and
tens of thousands settled near them. Brigham Young was appointed Superintendent of Indian Affairs when the territory was
organized and became "the big captain," a symbol of white
power as potent as any emanating from Washington, D.C.

However, the outbreak of the Walker War in 1853 made obvious the need for more forceful Indian policy. In addition to
directing settlers to "fort up," church authorities dispatched
five Indian missions between 1854 and 1856. All were located
on important trails; all were part of what has been termed the
"outer cordon" colonies; three were at points of gentile influence. Mormons lived with Indians, baptized them, gave them
the priesthood and Mormon names, and in a few cases married
them in generally futile attempts at conversion. By the end of
1858 four of the five missions had failed. The Southern Indian
Mission survived in southwestern Utah, where it served as a
forerunner to colonization and remained a base for Indian control and exploration.

Among the mission objectives was insulation of the Indians
from non-Mormon influences. Mormons suspected mountain
men and traders of stirring unrest. Consequently missionaries
focused much attention upon trading bands, particularly those
under the Shoshoni chieftain Washaki and the Utes who followed Walker, "king of the . . . mountains." [31] Made powerful by their wealth, such mobile leaders had wide influence over
less nomadic Indians. Widespread belief among the Mormons
that Jim Bridger had triggered the Walker War led eventually to
efforts to expel him from the country and to neutralize other
mountain traders in what is now southwestern Wyoming.

Efforts to exclude outside influences likewise had serious
repercussions along the Old Spanish Trail and added an episode

30. Robert Glass Cleland and Juanita Brooks, eds., *A Mormon Chronicle: The
Diaries of John D. Lee, 1848–1876,* 2 vols. (San Marino: The Huntington Library
Press, 1955), 1:108.

31. Sermon by Brigham Young, May 8, 1853, *Journal of Discourses,* 1:106.

in slave history to Utah's annals. Calling New Mexican traders
"a horde of outlandish men" whose purpose was to stir "up the
Indians to make aggressions," Brigham Young dispatched men
to keep "every strolling Mexican party" under "close cus-
tody." [32] A few Mexicans were seized and the territory effectively closed to the rest. In ridding themselves of Mexican
traders, Utahns had interfered with an allowable traffic in slaves,
and Walker and other trading chieftains demanded that
local buyers assume the function previously held by New Mexicans. Persuaded by sales techniques that included killing cap-
tive children and general Indian restlessness, the Mormons overcame their scruples and began buying captives "into freedom,"
a custom soon legitimized by an indenture law. Hundreds and
possibly thousands of Paiute and Gosiute children were bound
over to "some useful avocation" in Mormon families. A rhetoric of benevolence accompanied the practice. Brigham Young
expressed the accepted point of view when he declared that the
"Lord could not have devised a better plan" for Indian redemption.[33] Nevertheless, the church assimilated few of the unfortu-
nate Indians, while disease or despair brought untimely deaths
to many of them.

Efforts to keep Indians away from outside influences extended to the United States Army. In contrast to other territories, Utah rarely called upon federal troops to subdue Indian
hostilities. Reservations and Indian agencies also represented an
outside authority and were at times countered by Mormon attempts to gather Indians under their own influence. During the
1870s and 1880s a resurgence of the mission impulse resulted in
the establishment of at least four nonreservation Indian communities. These gathered several hundred Indians, enough of
whom were baptized to excite Mormon hopes that the time of
redemption was near. But this too passed, and with it went the
last vestiges of pioneer Indian policy.

32. *Deseret News*, April 30, 1853.
33. Leland H. Creer, *The Founding of an Empire: The Exploration and Colonization
of Utah, 1776–1856* (Salt Lake City: Bookcraft, 1947), p. 38; and "History of Brigham
Young" (1851), Church Historical Department, p. 846.

The Mormon frontier produced its quota of men with the knack of Indian relations. Brigham Young himself had the gift of influence; George Washington Bean romped with young Indians as a boy at Old Fort Utah near Provo and interrupted the affairs of a busy life to serve as a peacemaker; Christian Lingo Christensen grew up on the Sanpete Valley frontier during Utah's Black Hawk War, preached to the Indians in Arizona, and cherished the reputation of one gifted in tongues; and of course there was Jacob Hamblin, apostle to the Lamanites, Mormon leatherstocking, pathfinder, and peacemaker without peer.

Although Hamblin and his associates continued to expect the Indians to throw off the curse and worked hopefully to teach them the gospel, the chief success of Indian missionaries was as managers of a peaceful conquest. As the pioneer period approached its end in 1882, Apostle Erastus Snow summarized the achievement of Mormon Indian policy with the claim that the United States was "endebted for the spirit of Mormonism that has been diffused through this mountainous country in the maintenance of peace, and the saving to the nation of millions of treasure as well as thousands of lives." [34] Many Indians had been baptized but few had experienced better lives. In terms of civilizing influence, the record was somewhat less bleak but was still disappointing. Peacemaking was thus the capstone of Mormon–Indian relations. In the final analysis, Mormons, like other frontiersmen, met the Indians more as conquerors than as benefactors.

A story often repeated in Utah depicts St. Peter showing a new arrival around Paradise, introducing him to various denominational groups. Upon coming to the Mormons, Peter walks quietly past them, restraining the newcomer with the quiet comment that "the Mormons think they are the only ones here." [35] The story catches a basic attitude of nineteenth-century Mormons nicely. They simply withdrew to themselves and acted as if outsiders were not there. This tendency expressed itself not

---

34. Sermon of February 5, 1882, *Journal of Discourses,* 23:8–10.

35. A variation of this story appears in Nels Anderson, *Desert Saints: The Mormon Frontier in Utah* (Chicago: University of Chicago Press, 1942), p. 420.

only in their determination to avoid gentiles but in the customs and institutions of Mormon life as well. In the years prior to 1869 the small gentile population assured nonfraternization. Sir Richard Burton reported that no more than 300 gentiles lived in a total population of 9,000 at Salt Lake City in 1860. In the hinterland villages gentile population was even more limited. Transients were treated civilly enough, but friendly exchange between Mormon and resident gentile was rare. People who might have been acceptable business contacts in the East or even pursued eagerly as potential converts outside Utah occupied a different position in the territory. George Q. Cannon, member of the first presidency and congressional delegate, put it squarely: "It is because they are in Salt Lake City that I am opposed to them." Acknowledging the unfriendly character of his statement, he continued that he wanted no "power to be brought into our midst as the wooden horse was in to Troy." [36] Similarly, Brigham Young thought association with non-Mormons could only "create a kind of young Babylon . . . in our midst." [37]

Fear of a "young Babylon" was not idle. Indeed, waywardness among Mormon youth was a problem from the beginning. Born on the frontier, the young had absorbed its general wildness as well as their parents' disdain for federal law and the officially appointed representatives of the United States. Whiskey Street, as Main Street in Salt Lake City was sometimes known, was a special hangout for toughs. Similar groups were found elsewhere, and the tranquility of many a village was marred by conduct becoming to Dodge City or one of the "Hell on Wheels" camps of transcontinental railroading notoriety. Sir Richard Burton described one party of young men as having

rowdyish appearance . . . mounted in all the tawdriness of Western trappings—Rocky Mountain hats, tall and broad, or steeple-crowned felts, covering their scalplocks, embroidered buckskin garments, huge leggins, with caterpillar or milleped fringes, red or rainbow colored flannel shirts, gigantic spurs, bright-hilted pistols,

36. Sermon of October 7, 1863, *Journal of Discourses*, 12:296.
37. Sermon of October 6, 1863, *Journal of Discourses*, 12:306.

and queer-sheathed knives stuck in red sashes with gracefully depending ends.[38]

Less colorful but effecting a similar image was a crowd of Mormon youths observed in Nephi during the July 24th commemoration in 1873. Some sat at the door of the meeting house "making disrespectful remarks" as ladies picked their way "through this ill mannerly group." Others staggered along the streets of Nephi "passing a *bottle*" and "as each youth turned the contents down his throat he would pull a wry face, shake his head sneeze and etc., then stammer out some maudlin expression neither elegant nor sensible." [39]

Among the most notorious products of Mormon waywardness were Butch Cassidy and Matt Warner. Raised in the central Utah towns of Circleville and Levan, both young men sprang from a raw environment rendered monotonous and dreary by routine but not yet enlightened by good educational opportunity nor enlivened with extensive recreational activities. Warner rode to Arizona with his father in 1881, expecting to work on a grading contract for John W. Young, son of Brigham. When contracts failed to materialize, he robbed a store that doubled as a bank, rode hell-for-leather across the Painted Desert, and escaped into Utah's canyonlands. By a similar turn of events, Robert LeRoy Parker turned to the Wild Bunch, where as Butch Cassidy he robbed and charmed his way to a sure spot in the folklore of western badmen.

But more to the point here is the effort the Mormon community made to avoid this sort of individual—whether Mormon or gentile. In most activities the two elements had little enough in common. However, the dances and parties for which Mormon communities were justly famed were a meeting ground and a point of continuing friction. The rough element resented any efforts at rejection and attempted to crash Mormon parties. Church-appointed dance managers carefully dealt out tickets and

38. Burton, *City of the Saints*, p. 226.

39. Charles S. Peterson, ed., " 'Book A—Levi Mathers Savage': The Look of Utah in 1873," *Utah Historical Quarterly* 41 (Winter 1973): 12.

otherwise acted to maintain proper decorum and sobriety. Their efforts were sufficient in some isolated hamlets; but where a gentile community bolstered backsliding Mormons, sharp encounters sometimes occurred. Pioneer historian Joseph Fish describes such an event at Parowan on July 4, 1872:

> Some of the rougher element, as it was termed, had been barred out and our dance in the evening was broken up. . . . The rough and rowdy class in the place had increased very much of late and this spirit is encouraged and fostered by apostates of whom we had several in the place. This class, with the government officials, would sustain any measure which had a tendency to break down good order. . . . They would readily sustain . . . thieves and rowdies in opposition to the people. This made it almost impossible to punish lawbreakers, and this state of affairs led them to be very bold in their acts.[40]

In a similar incident at Beaver the next year, the "barred" element patrolled town with "Henry rifles," undertook to force themselves into a party, beat citizens, and when pressed, "fortified themselves in an old saloon." [41]

In its efforts to maintain "good order," the church placed special stress on matters of sexual morality. During the exodus from Nauvoo a police force had backed Brigham Young's authority. Headed by gimlet-eyed Hosea Stout, it worked early and late to subdue evil, destroying private whiskey caches, organizing the distribution of liquors, and whipping young men for "carnal communication," giving "them to understand" that under the "Laws and ordinances of this kingdom" the "legal punishment" for their offense "was death." [42] Similar disciplinary pressure was applied in the Valley. The Old Fort where the first pioneers had housed themselves was quickly dismantled when churchmen learned it had become a trysting place for persons of loose morals. Veterans of the Mormon Battalion were

40. John H. Krenkel, ed., *The Life and Times of Joseph Fish, Mormon Pioneer* (Danville, Ill.: Interstate Printers & Publishers, 1970), p. 136.

41. Autobiography of Joseph Fish, December 23, 1873, Church Historical Department, p. 122.

42. Juanita Brooks, ed., *On the Mormon Frontier: The Diary of Hosea Stout,* 2 vols. (Salt Lake City: Utah State Historical Society, 1964), 1:190–192.

roundly censured for becoming "Idle, Lazy and indolent, in-
dulging in vice, corrupting the Morals of the Young Fe-
males." [43] The Battalion issue came to a head when a half-dozen
"soldier boys cut a Spanish Rusty by riding into the fort with a
young lady sitting in the saddle before," while one of their
number sawed gaily away on his violin. Appalled at this "savage Spanish" custom, the elders ousted the offenders from the
church and fined each $25. [44]

A half-decade later, similar questions contributed to the so-
called "Reformation." Stressing the essential oneness of all
things, church leaders called on members to renew their spiritual covenants and to "consecrate" their worldly possessions to
the upbuilding of the kingdom. The Reformation quickly ran its
course, but the church always proclaimed the oneness of the
kingdom and maintained a general stress against worldly invasion, with special attention to morality, dance custom, dating
practices, and, with increasing emphasis, abstinence from tobacco and alcohol.

Resistance notwithstanding, changing customs penetrated
Zion—sometimes through its youth and sometimes through its
leadership. Even Brigham Young appears to have contributed
by his custom of taking one of his wives—often the attractive
Amelia Folsom—on his numerous tours. The story is told that
women along the route to St. George would vie with one another to clean and press Amelia's dresses, from which they
could take patterns for stylish clothing. That customs of the
young were also changing was suggested in 1882 when Philip
Robinson, an English journalist who traveled through Utah with
an apostle, saw young men and women riding horses double,
cutting "a Spanish Rusty" as it were, without embarrassment
that an apostle observed them or apparent restraint from local elders. As Robinson related, "couple after couple passed us, the
girls riding pillion behind their sweethearts, and very well con-
tented they all seemed to be, with their arms round the object of

43. Cleland and Brooks, *A Mormon Chronicle*, 1:92–93.
44. Cleland and Brooks, *A Mormon Chronicle*, 1:92–96; and Brooks, *On the Mormon Frontier*, 2:343.

their affection." [45] Thus conduct that led to excommunication in 1849 had apparently come into acceptance by 1882.

Families dominated the Mormon experience in frontier Utah. Under ideal circumstances Mormons were converted by families, migrated as families, colonized as families. In short, building the kingdom was a family affair. Large families were essential theologically to bring waiting spirits out of the "pre-existence," making progress possible by uniting body and spirit. Large families were also essential in redeeming Zion's wastes. Birth was hailed as a joy. The mark of a man or a woman's true worth was in the number of righteous children reared. Children were everywhere. Visitors marveled at their numbers, at their tow heads and healthy appearances. At the communal town of Orderville, one traveler found a veritable, and still growing, brigade of children. The town claimed, he reported, to be "independent of outside help, and certainly in the matter of babies there seemed no necessity for supplementing home manufacturers by foreign imports. The average of births is . . . five in each family during the six years of the existence of the Order." [46]

Young and old, men and women, boys and girls, all Mormons worked. They worked in building the kingdom, and they worked to stay alive. They built many of the Mountain West's railroads. They freighted and supplied mines and, as the church's anti-mining emphasis relaxed, they worked mines. Without capital other than sinew and dependability, they became a "service cadre," trusted lieutenants for the captains of industry who made the West.

In work, sex created a clear cleavage. Men went out; women stayed in. Men traveled for church purposes, entered business, worked railroads, and mined, coming in contact with the gentile world at many points. Women kept the home base to which the men returned. In the lives of the young, family-oriented labor

---

45. Philip Robinson, *Sinners and Saints: A Tour Across the States, and Round Them, With Three Months Among the Mormons* (Boston: Roberts Brothers, 1883), pp. 183–184.

46. Robinson, *Sinners and Saints*, p. 234.

eclipsed both education and recreation, and Mormon youth reclaimed the desert, often laboring like Jacob of old for seven years plus seven, and then escaped from a domineering father or family only by subterfuge.

Raising up a righteous generation and keeping what God had given them were cardinal points in Mormon belief, and polygamy contributed to these ends. The West was full of unattached men. Utah's female population, which nearly equaled the masculine, provided a welcome and challenging variation. Mormons believed that good women deserved better men than ordinary frontier drifters. Polygamy provided good husbands and enabled the church to hold its own. It also extended the role of women as keepers of the homehre, placing additional family responsibility upon them in the absence of part-time husbands. Often the women became keen managers, and they always played a prominent role in transmitting the faith to the next generation. Polygamy rendered more complete the withdrawal of Mormon women from the world, creating what one author described as an "almost monastic gloom" throughout the entire society.[47] On a visit in 1859, Horace Greeley met no Mormon women and indeed failed to see evidence "whereby a woman proposes to do anything whatever" other than bear children.[48] Mormon women extended the realm of their activity during the years that followed Greeley's visit, but generally they continued to function within their own society, shielded from the bruising threat of the gentile world.

In other ways polygamy was an adhesive. Although most Mormons were not polygamists, those who were submitted to discipline of the most demanding kind. Courtships were silent, short, and undemonstrative. Marriage itself depended upon the "counsel" of church authorities and permission of previous wives. To some participants and at least one observer, the effective bonding agent of polygamy seemed "a calm and unimpas-

---

47. Burton, *City of the Saints*, p. 215.

48. Horace Greeley, *An Overland Journey from New York to San Francisco in the Summer of 1859*, Comstock edition, with introduction and notes by Charles T. Duncan (New York: Ballantine Books, 1963), p. 139.

sioned domestic attachment,'' while ''romance and reverence'' were ''transferred with the true Mormon concentration, from love and liberty to religion and the church.'' [49] Women were assured husbands, the opportunity of childbirth, and a crucial responsibility on the homefront. Polygamous men entered a fraternity from which there were few exits. If they ''fell out'' with the church or their Mormon peers, they had little recourse unless they emulated Horace Greeley's storied polygamist, who took three wives to California, introduced two of tender years as his daughters, and in due course married them off.[50]

But polygamy made for a loose marital system in a number of ways. It divided and in some cases blunted affections. Women learned independence in practical affairs. Marriage conditions often led to friction. In the prayer setting Jesse N. Smith apart to preside over the Danish Mission, Brigham Young directed him to marry a Danish girl. Knowing the extreme penury and the attitudes of his earlier wives, Smith wanted to demur, but after Young had thrice repeated the injunction, he faithfully followed instructions. On his return to Utah, the opposition of his family and townspeople submitted the marriage to special pressures, but it survived to be a fruitful and long relationship.

Some polygamous marriages did not survive, and a large business was done in unmarrying as well as marrying. Inevitably some bizarre situations developed. John D. Lee of Mountain Meadows Massacre notoriety, upon learning that his sixteenth wife was in love with his oldest son, concluded that ''she should have her liberty,'' gave her a divorce, and performed the wedding ceremony himself, complete with ''a sumptious Supper and Social Party.'' [51]

That polygamy contributed to the rapid growth of Mormon society is without question, although there is evidence that polygamist mothers bore fewer children on the average than their monogamous counterparts. Undeniably, polygamy had great potential for offspring. Pursuing its possibilities, a Mormon peri-

49. Burton, *City of the Saints*, p. 431.
50. Greeley, *An Overland Journey*, p. 153.
51. Cleland and Brooks, *A Mormon Chronicle*, 1:176, 190–191.

odical in England pointed out that a devout Mormon—appropriately called Mr. Fruitful—with 40 wives could have 400 children and add at least 3½ million Saints to God's kingdom by the time he was seventy-eight. Conversely, a gentile with one wife and 5 sons would add no more than 153 descendants in the same time.[52] Actual results were somewhat less startling. With 5 wives of childbearing age, Lorin Farr, stalwart at Ogden, was reported to have 40 children and a total of 258 descendants by the time he was eighty-three. Nahum Curtiss was himself a monogamist, but two of his sons and two of his grandsons had two wives each. By the turn of the century his living descendants numbered 466. Brigham Young had fifty-six children, Joseph F. Smith, sixth president of the church, had forty-two, and Jesse N. Smith, forty-three.[53] By 1900 many Mormons not only were united by the common experience of polygamy but were actually bound by blood and marriage in its proliferating relationships. Mormonism was a polity of matrimony as surely as any practiced by the royal dynasties of Europe.

Together with shared ideals, past experiences, and travel, polygamy was a bond that held the Mormons. They had risen as a church in the East, withdrawn by stages to the West, and established a commonwealth. To a surprising degree, every man knew his neighbor. To bless one was to bless all. To injure one was to disturb the whole. The Mormons approached unity of vision and, more than most of their contemporaries, pursued one course and shared one lot. Theirs was a togetherness that dominated the entire experience of early Utah, including its economic development.

52. *Millennial Star* 19 (1857): 384, 432.
53. Statistics are from N. L. Nelson, "What Constitutes a Mormon Family?" *The Mormon Point of View* 1 (1940): 335–351.

3

Economic Development

$\mathcal{T}$HE Utah from which the first Mormons undertook to wrest a living was a constant challenge. By any previous standard of the American experience it lacked water, good soil, and timber. By standards that would prevail after California's great gold strike, it also lacked mineral wealth. Yet the problem for Utah's economic development was not that it was without resources but that they were widely scattered and in forms that required radical change in the patterns of living and exploitation used east of the Mississippi River. Aborning in 1847 were new exploitive methods by which rampant individualism would seize the West. But Utah's resources proved to be beyond the means of even bonanza exploitation until railroads were built and capital and technology were brought to bear on low-grade ores. In the meantime Mormons attempted to utilize Great Basin resources by what was in many ways a closed economy. Simultaneously merchants built on the tradition of the Santa Fe trade to lay the groundwork for change and prepare the way for the economic invasion that railroading and mining would bring.

The Mormons undertook to control Utah by claiming its water and arable land. But their program to subdue the Great Basin aimed beyond colonizing and village life to the establishment of a self-sufficient economy. To this end church leaders planned, organized, and initiated various enterprises. They also experimented with their own currency and instituted their own manufacturing system. Yet they responded to outside stimuli, regarding economic windfalls as blessings of God. Supported by a willing and co-operative people, the system they established dominated Utah's economy until 1869.

Problems of trade confronted the Mormons as soon as they arrived. It has been said that the pioneer party's entire supply of money consisted of $50 Brigham Young had in his possession. Then and later, money was limited and subject to quick removal from the territory. To meet such a threat to self-sufficiency, the church undertook to provide money substitutes. The process began in 1848, when gold dust brought to Utah by returning veterans of the Mormon Battalion was collected, weighed out, and distributed in circulating packages of from one to twenty dollars. In the years that followed, the church minted its own gold pieces on two occasions and twice offered paper money, based once on gold reserves and once upon cattle. But various economic influences affected these measures, and they failed to provide a satisfactory circulating medium. Church leaders still hoped to turn the shortage of money to the advantage of a self-sufficient economy and to minimize the natural limitations of a barter system.

The tithing office of the church became the major means of organizing and regulating this noncash system. Tithing houses were established throughout the territory, with a general office at Salt Lake City. Although property, labor, and occasionally cash served as tithes, payment in kind predominated. Donations were voluntary, but church leaders stressed full payment in "firstlings of the flock." Culls nevertheless found their way into the tithing yards, as suggested when Brigham Young inveighed against the practice of paying in cows "that would kick a person's hat off" or horses that were "broken-winded." [1] A report that payment in kind resulted in the collection of a "tenth of everything . . . even to the tenth of every egg that is laid" was an exaggeration, but the system did collect an extraordinary array.

1. Sermon of June 3, 1855, *Journal of Discourses*, 2:306–307.

One eastern visitor found tithing warehouses bulging with everything "conceivable that mankind should sell and buy." [2] Not surprisingly, "exchanges" created much business. Produce and labor were traded for other items, thus making the tithing office an active clearing house. "Tithing orders" negotiable throughout the Mormon community were also issued, allowing the establishment and transfer of credits and debits. Humorist Bill Nye told a story that characterized the situation. Failing one day to trade a turkey for tithing scrip, he had no choice but to carry the bird to the box office to pay admission when he took his girl to the Salt Lake Theater. Receiving two pullets in change, he suffered through "the performance with a chicken under each arm." [3]

At root, the church's effort for economic independence rested upon the skills of its people. As an epistle from the church presidency stated, the "gospel's net gathers all sorts of fish." [4] From America and from Europe's shores converts from every industrial background produced a diversified society capable of supporting a "balanced well-ordered economic life." As early as 1850, the census listed eighty-five different occupations ranging from "architects to woolen manufacturers." Included were "butchers, bakers, and candlestick makers; colliers, jewelers, and machinists; cabinet-makers, gunsmiths, and tanners." [5]

Building on these skills, the church involved itself in manufacturing and construction for nearly forty years. The larger manufacturing enterprises were generally unsuccessful. The church sponsored iron and sugar industries in the 1850s and a

2. Robinson, *Sinners and Saints*, p. 166; and F. H. Ludlow, *The Heart of the Continent: A Record of Travel Across the Plains and in Oregon With an Examination of the Mormons* (New York: Hurd and Houghton, 1870), pp. 540–541.

3. Alexander Toponce, *Reminiscences of Alexander Toponce* (Ogden: Mrs. Katie Toponce, 1923), pp. 186–187.

4. James R. Clark, comp., *Messages of the First Presidency*, 5 vols. (Salt Lake City: Bookcraft, 1965–1971), 2:112.

5. Leonard J. Arrington, *From Wilderness to Empire: The Role of Utah in Western Economic History*, Institute of American Studies Monograph No. 1 (Salt Lake City: University of Utah, 1961), p. 11.

cotton mission in the 1860s, backing them by mission calls and the best leadership and skills available. Yet all three failed. Limitations of technology and finance, lack of markets, and natural conditions hampered growth of each. Smaller enterprises did much better. Home industry began with a few mills for flour and lumber in 1848 but had grown by the 1880s to include 75 flour and grist mills, 100 sawmills, 18 furniture factories, 20 shoe factories, a clothing factory which "successfully competes with Chinese labor in the San Francisco market," and 10 iron foundries.[6] Uncounted mountain dairies also converted milk to butter and cheese for home use and export. In addition the church's "Public Works" employed thousands of incoming converts, constructing hundreds of homes, businesses, and church buildings that included the famed Salt Lake City Tabernacle and Temple.

Industrial wages were paid "in chips and whetstones," leaving to the worker the challenging task of collecting his pay and converting useless items to consumer goods. This practice apparently contributed to a preference for the security of farming. A letter to Utah's first farm periodical in 1863 asked, why "must every man turn" to farming when society would be benefited much more if they followed "their life-learned pursuits?" Providing his own answer, the writer blamed "men of opulence" who paid nothing but "flour," forcing skilled workers to "turn farmers to get as good things as the farmers do." [7] A year or two later, Charles L. Walker of southern Utah wrote about the dilemma in his diary:

> Spent the day in collecting debts. It seems rather a curious mode of getting along, to gather a few things together, for instance travel a mile to get 50 weight of flour, the same distance to get a bushel of potatoes, a half a mile in another direction for a few pounds of meat, then in a case of emergency pack a bushel of corn to mill to get it ground to make a little dodger. And so it goes, no money to be had for work. The circulating medium is cotton, corn, molasses

6. *Utah Industrialist* 1 (1888): 79, 155.
7. *Farmer's Oracle*, June 16, 1863.

or other produce, and often takes as long to collect the pay as it
does to work for it. Thus a poor man works to a disadvantage all the
time.[8]

Inequities of the system and failure of heavy industry notwithstanding, Utah's farm villages and home industry made for
a stable and productive economy. However, a third element
turned the economy outward and led ultimately to a meeting
ground for the church-directed self-sufficiency and the individualistic free enterprise that won the West. Mormon economic
historian Leonard Arrington has called this element windfall opportunities. The first such windfall was the gold rush. Beginning
within two years of the Mormon arrival, it had an electric effect
on Mormondom. For three years some 15,000 Argonauts passed
through Utah annually. Midway between Missouri and California, the territory became a vast service point, trading produce,
fresh livestock, and services for manufactured items and cash.
With Brigham Young tacitly admonishing that it was "no sin to
gull" a gentile, Mormons set the standards of trade, selling high
and buying low. For many Mormons it meant enterprise and a
new way of life. The narrow practices of pioneer subsistence
gave way to world-dependent economic activities. An economy
that had operated without currency was suddenly rolling in cash,
and prices for commodities competed with those of outfitting
towns in the Midwest. A struggling valley economy had become
a confident and aggressive commonwealth.

Then, almost as suddenly as it had begun, the gold rush ran
its course. Hard times came again. But in various guises the
world continued to come, providing new windfalls. In 1857 and
1858 the crisis known as the Utah War brought markets for
Utah products and services, as Mormons fed General Albert
Sidney Johnston's army. Thereafter came transcontinental stage-
coaching, the pony express and the telegraph, Civil War prosperity, and finally the transcontinental railroad and large-scale
mining. Each was a windfall, each an expeditionary element

8. Quoted in Andrew Karl Larson, *"I Was Called to Dixie," The Virgin River Basin:
Unique Experiences in Mormon Pioneering* (Salt Lake City: Deseret News Press, 1961),
p. 251.

supported and supplied by a Mormon economy made stable and strong by the very presence of outside influences.

To meet the challenge of the railroad and large-scale mining, the church continued to colonize and added several new activities. Among them were the School of the Prophets, Zion's Board of Trade, and the United Order. The School of the Prophets attempted to create a common front at the policy-making level, bringing priesthood groups together throughout the church to consider the entire question of worldly influence. The Board of Trade consisted of a central agency as well as regional and local boards. It undertook to regulate the various facets of Mormon economic activity so as to acquire the advantages of common pricing, buying, and labor arrangements.

The United Order was a renewal of Mormon communitarianism. In the wake of the Panic of 1873, Brigham Young and other church leaders threw themselves energetically into a program of spiritual and communal economic revival. Mormons everywhere were encouraged to associate in "orders." Individuals deeded property to the order, worked for the benefit of the group, and shared in the product. In established communities this meant little more than co-operative projects. A classic example was Brigham City in northern Great Salt Lake Valley, where a wide program of co-operative enterprises previously initiated by Apostle Lorenzo Snow weathered the Panic of 1873 unscathed. Encouraged by this success, the church carried the experiment further in southern Utah. The outstanding example was Orderville, where Saints long inured to poverty and honed to a fine edge of zealousness by a period of extreme adversity on Nevada's Muddy River joined in an order that during the late 1870s and early 1880s saw them eat at a common table, live in fortlike intimacy, and develop a far-reaching system of enterprises that included livestock and timbering, farming, wool and cotton manufacture, and numerous other activities. People at Orderville and elsewhere in united orders fondly anticipated that a perfect human order would emerge and that in due time the church, and indeed the world, would be the grateful beneficiaries of their efforts.

But such was not to be. Church membership never wholly

supported the United Order, and Brigham Young's death in 1877 removed its most influential advocate. Orders worked best when man stood in the starkest, most elemental relationship to the environment. When nature was benign and when prosperity prevailed, the United Order proved to be more than the Saints could carry. Consequently communities that began under adverse social and physical circumstances were further weakened by factionalism between order and nonorder groups. By the mid-1880s the movement had run its course, leaving an occasional sore spot in the tissue of Mormon society but generally passing into the church's honored tradition.

All in all, Mormon economic activity represented a different way for early Utah. Its method was co-operative and its object was self-sufficiency, but instead of rejecting windfalls it embraced them. Rather than an economy of total withdrawal, it was what may be termed a "neomercantilistic policy," in which the inner strength and growing influence of the Mormon community were prime objectives. Gentiles were to be avoided when their enterprises threatened Zion, but they could be approached—even embraced—if Mormons could choose the terms.

At no point was this more apparent than in merchandising, which began in November of 1848 when Richard Grant, Fort Hall agent for Hudson's Bay Company, opened his packs south of the Old Fort in Salt Lake City. Earlier, Mormons had contacted the company suggesting that the church might well look to the Northwest for its business connections. But the sands of time ran against Hudson's Bay. Even as Grant traded his wares there by the fort, the forces of the gold rush were propelling America westward. Among the first to respond were the Pomeroy brothers of Weston, Missouri. With thirty-four wagons of goods and groceries, they had set out for California but stopped short to sell in Salt Lake City. Livingston and Kinkead followed almost immediately, with goods worth $20,000. The same year Benjamin Holladay, of stagecoaching fame, appeared with a cargo worth $70,000. Finding ready sales, he was back the next summer with a stock valued at $150,000. Others followed. Patterns established in the Santa Fe trade predominated.

Wagon trains left Missouri in the spring, arrived in the early fall, made a quick sell-off, and returned home to outfit for another year. The first years were boom times. According to eyewitness accounts, buyers literally stormed the stores, nearly "crazing the twenty five or thirty clerks," crowding from outside "fearful the goods" would be gone before they had laid in a supply.[9] In the main it was an itinerant business carried on by men who came and went.

A few merchants, however, belonged to the Mormon community. The Reese brothers, John and Enoch, are said to have been the fourth firm to establish in Salt Lake City. William Nixon, "father of Utah merchandising," his protégés the four Walker brothers, and Thomas Williams came shortly thereafter.[10] Such men as William Godbe and H. W. Lawrence began mercantile careers working for Nixon or Williams, while Horace S. Eldredge and Hiram Clawson got their start working for the church purchasing department and Brigham Young. A surprising number had Missouri connections. Nixon had employed the Walker boys in St. Louis, and William Jennings spent several years there on his way West. William H. Hooper and others served as agents for Holladay and other Missouri-based firms.

However, early Mormon merchants traded more in California and Nevada than did their gentile peers. As early as 1851 John Reese established a store at Mormon Station in western Nevada. William Nixon, William Jennings, and the Walkers also traded there during the 1850s. By 1854 Mormon merchants were plying the "Mormon corridor" to and from California, making brief stands in goods-hungry southern Utah towns along the way, and tapping the Salt Lake City market several weeks before the Missouri trains arrived.

As the 1850s progressed, cattle became a primary medium of exchange. Mormons had driven some 30,000 head of stock from Nauvoo. Herds supplemented by additional foundation

9. Santiago [James H. Martineau], "Pioneer Sketches: A Journey in 1854," *The Contributor* 11 (1890): 183.

10. Hubert Howe Bancroft, *History of Utah 1540–1886* (San Francisco: The History Company, 1889), p. 763.

stock from California and Santa Fe grew rapidly. The gold rush, too, contributed to the increment in cattle, and by 1860 the census listed no fewer than one seventh of the nation's graziers as living in Utah. Merchants took cattle in exchange for goods and trailed them to the West Coast and other mining regions, where they were sold for cash.

The Utah War attracted a large business community and made for prosperity. Salt Lake City flourished as the major western depot. Near Camp Floyd west of Utah Lake was Fairfield or Frogtown, as it was less euphoniously known. In it could be found the full spectrum of military supply activities. Fort Bridger was changed from the eastern outpost of Mormondom to a military post. To it came William A. Carter, merchant, judge, and as it turned out, long-time resident. At Fort Bridger, too, was a retail outlet of Russell, Majors and Waddell. Appointing A. B. Miller as Utah representative, the great freighting firm also had a livestock depot at Millersville east of Fort Bridger, its main store at Salt Lake City, and a sutlery at Camp Floyd.

For a time Russell, Majors and Waddell did a booming business. Their Salt Lake City store occupied "the very best stand on Main Street," averaged "$3,000 a day in gold," and employed thirteen men during the winter of 1858–1859. One can hardly imagine a more unlikely set of clerks than that portrayed by Richard Ackley, one of the employees. Three were Mormons—one a bishop "employed to give the place cast," one a native of Texas with "but one wife," and the third a son-in-law to William Hickman of avenging-angel notoriety and "bad in every way." The gentile clerks were also impressive. Miller had commanded a hardshooting company of proslavery riders in the "Kansas War" and employed several of them in the store. George Hewitt wore a huge "pair of horse pistols," slept "in the snow to make him hardy," and worked out with his fists on a sack of flour (until one of his coworkers slipped a stone into the sack). John Lainhart accepted a poke containing $5,000 in gold from a gambler for deposit and carelessly lost it under a counter for several weeks. "Big Dick from Buffalo" banished all doubt that he was as hard as he talked when he gunned down a hapless Mexican who "jumped over our fence." Before winter was over Ackley was transferred to the Camp Floyd store, which did a credit business with some 1,200 soldiers, collecting directly from the paymaster. At Russell's direction, Ackley toured central Utah, buying wheat "payable in merchandise" at $4.50 per hundred which they had ground into flour and sold to the military for $30 per hundred in cash.[11] During the autumn of 1859 Ackley ended his Utah mercantile career when he went to Fort Bridger to collect a sight draft for $33,000 from William Carter and closed both Millersville and the Bridger store.

After 1860 business entered a period of growing complexity. Utah's population grew and spread. Merchandising became increasingly an urban affair and less a mountain rendezvous. The general upsweep of business that accompanied the Civil War contributed to good times. Johnston's army was gone and Camp Floyd was little more than a memory, but in their place came Colonel Patrick E. Connor's California Volunteers, bringing with them a continuing need for supplies and material. Colorado and Nevada came into their own as mining communities. Idaho and Montana mines were also opened, and trade that had run only east and west moved increasingly northward. It all made for prosperity yet failed to produce an ample supply of money. In money's place a three-cornered trade developed in which states' goods, Utah produce, and the cash markets of the mining West were the essential anchor posts.

Among the traders who operated in this three-cornered trade was Alexander Toponce. Restless and hard-working, Toponce passed from Utah to Montana to Idaho and California, dealing with Salt Lake City merchants, Brigham Young, Wells Fargo, bishops by the dozen, and hundreds of Mormon settlers. His purchases included states' goods, pork, trotting horses, game-cocks, railroad ties, land, butter, eggs, leather goods, wagons, and draft animals. He paid in gold, in "Lincolnskins" or greenbacks, in "jawbone" or credit, and frequently in merchandise.

---

11. Richard Thomas Ackley, "Across the Plains in 1858," *Utah Historical Quarterly* 9 (July–October 1941): 190–228.

Unable to move goods in a Salt Lake store, he took to the road in southern Utah, trading his merchandise for cattle. Farmers brought in 1,500 cattle at Provo, and with the bishop advising "with cattle owners" Toponce made the rounds. "We would walk along to where some farmer, perhaps a danishman, was holding his little herd . . . and he would jerk off his cap and say, 'Dees haar bees my cattle, Beeshup.' " The bishop would counsel the Dane to sell so tithing accounts could be settled and children clothed to "make a decent appearance at meeting," and with the Dane saying "Aw! Aw! Das is all right," the transaction was consummated. Continuing on to Fillmore, Toponce accumulated 6,000 cattle which he trailed to Nevada and sold for $46.50 per head—or nearly $100,000 each for himself and two partners.[12]

Toponce's success was more than routine. But of all merchants Williams Jennings was most sensitive to the nuances of the Utah trade and most completely its master. He emigrated from England in 1847, ran a butcher business in St. Louis, married a Mormon girl, and, loading three wagons with goods, sought his fortunes in Zion. Soon converted to Mormonism, he parlayed his goods into a prospering business. Like no one else, Jennings played the full market: freighting and contracting; trading in cattle, Utah produce, and manufactured items; butchering cattle and manufacturing leather goods; and selling wholesale and retail. In 1865 he built the Eagle Emporium, which reputedly did an annual business of $2,000,000. Thereafter he made his wealth and talents available to the church as it moved into co-operative merchandising.

Merchants made church leaders uneasy from the first. The aggravation of the Missouri connection of many merchants combined with a latent distrust of mammon and merchandising's challenge to Mormon hegemony to create friction very early. Leaders suspected the Pomeroy brothers, who brought the first train to Utah, of having participated in the Missouri persecutions and ordered them to move on. Only after proving that they had supported the Saints were they permitted to market their

12. Toponce, *Reminiscences*, pp. 153–159.

goods. Similarly, a letter from General Alexander Doniphan, who had befriended the Saints in Missouri, secured the blessings of Brigham Young for Ben Holladay. Church leaders also resented the money that merchants carried away and often fulminated against them as profiteers. Nevertheless, the two factions coexisted in relative peace until the mid-1860s. Indeed, relations were often intimate and cordial. Holladay began business in a building provided by Brigham Young, and William H. Hooper, a devout and influential Latter-day Saint, was his Utah representative. Lesser gentiles, too, got on well with church leaders, as Alexander Toponce illustrated in his bantering relationship with John Taylor and his admiration for Young, in whom he saw "nothing of the cheese-paring skinflint." [13]

Forces making for friction were greater than common interests, however, particularly after 1864. In spite of the church's various programs, the merchants were gaining capital and influence. Famine conditions caused by drought and new colonies in southern Utah in the mid-1860s tragically emphasized the widening gulf between church and commerce. Shaken, the church renewed its emphasis upon self sufficiency and broke openly with the merchant community, which included some of its own people.

The tension of the period showed up sharply among Mormon merchants. Living in effect in two different worlds, they responded variously. William Jennings, Horace S. Eldredge, and William H. Hooper cast their lot with the church. For others, including the Walker brothers and William Godbe, business became the more consuming force. In the case of the Walkers the problem came to a head in 1864, ostensibly over tithing, but also as result of church demands that prices be set in the public interest rather than for profit.

The church experimented with several expedients to reduce the merchants' control. Among these were a pricing convention aimed at letting producers share in the general prosperity, cooperative buying and selling, and commission buying of consumer goods. The immediate effect of these efforts appeared in

13. Toponce, *Reminiscences*, pp. 86–87.

an improved exchange rate after 1865 and in extensive commission buying.

The church's campaign against profiteering merchants reached fullest expression in the co-operative mercantile movement initiated in 1869. Calling for all members to cease trading with unfriendly merchants, the church established Zion's Cooperative Mercantile Institution (ZCMI), taking the stock and assets of subscribing Mormon merchants as well as many smaller investments. Retail co-operatives were then established in each ward or village, and profits were diverted to local shops and factories to produce the needs of the people. Each authorized institution displayed over its door a sign bearing the legend "Holiness to the Lord" inscribed above the pictured "All-seeing eye of Jehovah." Trade with the co-ops became a matter of much social and church pressure. Even before the co-operative movement began, twenty-two gentile firms had offered to sell to the church, a proposal that Brigham Young flatly rejected. With the new drive, many suffered serious losses. Walker Brothers's sales dropped from $60,000 to $5,000 per month, and stores less firmly established went out of business.

In the ensuing years ZCMI flourished. The best commercial talent in the church supported it, and for many years it enjoyed both direct and indirect church patronage. It encouraged home industry and quite likely reduced costs to consumers, although soon it was widely believed it as well as local co-ops were profiteering. Walker Brothers's trade rebounded by 1871, enjoying special briskness at Mormon conference time. Mormons found themselves increasingly subject to the forces of supply and demand, as an 1871 incident at Weston in Cache Valley illustrates. Crickets had been bad that year, but several Weston farmers had raised a wagonload each of oats for sale. They hauled these to Corinne, Utah's gentile capital after the railroad came, and sold them to "outside" merchants. Under no stigma for selling to gentiles, the farmers went too far when they purchased kitchen ranges for $37.50 that were priced at $50.00 at ZCMI. The next Sunday their bishop called them "all up to ask forgiveness." Some recanted, even offering to get rid of the stoves, but not expecting to have to. Others used the scriptures to parry the bishop's criticism, while one allowed he could not say "I feel sorry, because I feel pretty good; my wife don't have to sit on her knees and cook." Finally, as tension continued to mount, mechanic William Gill wryly likened the gospel to pure spring water that had run through the sagebrush, heat, and filth until when it "gets as far as Weston, it gets so you can hardly use it." [14] The resulting laugh broke the tension. The bishop had done his duty, Weston's women had escaped cooking on their knees, and the Corinne merchants had the business.

After 1869 the era when merchants and the church monopolized enterprise passed rapidly. Livestock followed the national trend to become a business in its own right, rather than a mere adjunct of merchandising. With the public domain open to private entry after 1868, land assumed increasing speculative and commercial functions, and real estate became an active business for the first time. As land transactions and mining promotions increased, banks played roles of increasing importance, and by 1873 seven banks were found in the territory. But the appearance of railroads and mining altered the character of economic activity in the territory more than any other development.

Transportation had always been crucial. Very early Mormons had experimented unsuccessfully with the Great Salt Lake Valley Carrying Company and the B. Y. Express. Later, church wagon trains conveyed each year's emigrant quota and loads of equipment and states' goods. After an initial period when anyone who happened to be making a trip took the mail, regular postal service was established to the east in 1850 and to the west in 1851. Although snows closed the territory "from four to six months in the year as if barred by a gate," weekly passenger service existed between April and December by 1857.[15] Russell, Majors and Waddell catapulted to national prominence and lasting fame as chief freight contractors for the Utah War.

14. Lars Fredrickson, *History of Weston, Idaho*, ed. A. J. Simmonds (Logan: Utah State University Press, 1972), pp. 21–22.

15. Lieutenant Sylvester Mowry, as quoted in Andrew Love Neff, *History of Utah 1847 to 1869*, ed. Leland H. Creer (Salt Lake City: Deseret News Press, 1940), p. 722.

Thereafter the company went on to run a mail and passenger service via the central overland route and to establish the Pony Express. When it failed in 1862, Benjamin Holladay took over its stage property and mail contracts; in 1864 he contracted in his own name for the Missouri River–Salt Lake City run and operated westward to California jointly with William Dinsmore. Sensing the winds of the time, Holladay sold out in 1866 to Wells Fargo, whose operations virtually encompassed the West. In addition to its importance to merchants, freighting was a way of life for many farmers and townspeople who utilized draft animals and off-season time to carry goods from the states and to surrounding territories. With the advent of railroads and mines, freighting became even more important as ore and goods were moved to and from the railheads. Born and bred to river country where water transportation was a great convenience, early Utahns looked to the Colorado River and the Missouri in hope of developing water connections with the world. But despite a brief period in the 1860s when traffic on the Colorado seemed promising, water transit simply was not to be.

The coming of the railroad unlocked Utah, changing a desert fastness to a national highway and a burgeoning economic region. Utah's rail age was initiated by the transcontinental railroad, which came in 1869 with an outburst of national pride and publicity. For the Union Pacific, built from the east, and the Central Pacific, which ran its line from the west, Utah was both a prospect of trade and an oasis of labor on a population-short frontier.

Upwards of 300 miles of grading was done by Utah labor, and ties were cut for a like distance. All told some 4,000 Utahns worked on the great undertaking. Important local contractors for the Union Pacific were gentile Joseph F. Nounnan of Salt Lake City, Brigham Young, and his sons Brigham, Jr., Joseph A., and John W. A firm headed by Apostle Ezra T. Benson took contracts with the Central Pacific. Much to the distress of Salt Lake residents, the railroad bypassed the capital city, taking instead a route north of the Great Salt Lake where the rails were joined on May 10, 1869. Although one reason Mormons took grading contracts was to forestall the need to bring in a large outside labor force, a full quota of "Hell-on-Wheels" camps came into the territory. Railroad interests established a more permanent community at Corinne, which sought boisterously to make itself Utah's foremost railroading town before land gifts at Ogden persuaded railroad officials to establish junctions there.

Mormon separatism notwithstanding, the church embraced the railroad with enthusiasm and during the years after 1869 effected what was in some ways a unique chapter in western railroading history. The first effort in this development was the construction during the fall of 1869 of the Utah Central line connecting Salt Lake City with the transcontinental road at Ogden. Launched in a ceremony where the first ground was broken with a farmer's shovel in contrast to a miner's pick, the entire undertaking was handled as a Mormon project. Brigham Young planned the road with help from bishops along its line. Jesse W. Fox, church surveyor, served as chief engineer; Joseph Young was general superintendent; John W. Young directed the track-laying crew; and Mormon volunteers from the wards along the way did the grading. In addition, rails and rolling stock for the Utah Central were acquired from the Union Pacific in lieu of cash payment for grading done on the transcontinental line, thus making the entire Utah Central road the product of local effort. By early January 1870 the Utah Central Railroad was complete, and on the 10th some 15,000 spectators watched as Apostle Wilford Woodruff drove home a last spike of Utah iron to dedicate the line.

Once committed, the Mormons proved to be determined railroad-builders. William Jennings, William H. Hooper, and John Sharp, a canny Scot whose standpat tactics did much to turn the power of the Union Pacific to Utah's advantage, made great contributions. Brigham Young and his three sons were instrumental in building the Utah Southern and the Utah Northern. These lines, together with the Utah Central and several lesser roads, spanned three quarters of the territory by 1873. One son, John W., remained active during the rest of the century, promoting roads in Utah and neighboring states and taking grading and tie contracts in Colorado, New Mexico, and Arizona. In their railroading activities the Youngs appear to have been fully aware of money's potential for influence. John W. Young was especially responsive. Holding that railroading would "really do more good in giving us influence with the World than anything we have ever done," he was a prized lieutenant to his father, whose own vision included enough shadings of capitalism that he could understand him.[16] John Young was, however, a thorn in the side of his brethren, who believed that the kingdom's influence was less a matter of capitalistic power and more one of traditional Mormon separatism.

But the determination of the Youngs and the volunteer labor of the rank and file proved insufficient to control a railroad system in this freebooting era. The Union Pacific was a factor to be reckoned with from the first. This was partly a result of its slowness in paying Brigham Young more than a million dollars for grading on the original Union Pacific line. With thousands of unpaid workers and numerous subcontractors, the U.P.'s unpaid obligations caused near panic among the Mormons and led to a resourceful effort to collect on the part of Young and his agent Bishop John Sharp. Sharp's shrewd and "home-grown financial maneuvers" produced first applause, then respect, among Union Pacific leaders who contributed indirectly to Utah railroading when they paid off grading debts in rails and rolling stock for the Utah Central and directly when they made loans and took over stalled construction on other Mormon lines.[17]

In addition, Utah shipping was a significant item to the Union Pacific. Claiming five sixths of the business moving into Salt Lake City and nine tenths of the ores carried out by 1871, the Union Pacific employed most of the competitive tactics of the era to maintain its advantage. This was particularly apparent in the case of coal, which fuel-short Utahns hoped the railroad would make both abundant and cheap. However, freight rates were raised to the limit, bringing the cost of coal worth $2 at the railroad's Wyoming mines to $10 in Salt Lake City and underselling coal freighted by wagon from Coalville fifty miles to the

16. Robert G. Athearn, *Union Pacific Country* (Chicago: Rand McNally, 1971), p. 266.

17. Athearn, *Union Pacific Country*, p. 112.

east by only the barest margin. When Mormons undertook to build their own line from Coalville, the U.P. built competing trackage, manipulated the Park City market, and otherwise crushed competition. By the 1880s the company had acquired control of the Mormon railroads. Resentment was widespread, but local efforts had hastened the day of a statewide railroad system and by the standards of the era the Union Pacific had often been co-operative and helpful.

Another important chapter in Utah's railroad story was the penetration of the Denver and Rio Grande Railway westward and northward after 1880 to bring Salt Lake City into its operating region. The brainchild of William Jackson Palmer, the Rio Grande system was planned to provide north-and-south service for the Rocky Mountains mining country. However, as his line approached New Mexico, Palmer ran into stiff competition from the Atchison, Topeka and Santa Fe Railroad, which had claimed the only two passes allowing access south. After two years of fighting, the Rio Grande finally abandoned its plans to enter New Mexico and turned west into Utah along the Colorado River.

The Rio Grande promised much to Utahns. As earlier roads had done, it provided work for farmers and ranchers. Coal-mining towns blossomed in the eastern part of the territory and provided Salt Lake City with a new supply of coal. Developing a link between the Central Pacific line and the railroads east of the Rockies, the Rio Grande entered into a brisk competition with the Union Pacific, which naturally delighted Utahns. But the honeymoon ended quickly. The construction boom passed, as did hopes that competition would reduce coal prices. As Robert Athearn, historian of western railroading, has noted, the "Mormons discovered, that so far as railroads were concerned, there was no chosen people." [18] Frustrating though this discovery may have been, few denied that the railroads represented progress. Utah was now served by the transcontinental road and the Rio Grande line, and an extensive system of local roads

---

18. Robert G. Athearn, "Utah and the Coming of the Denver and Rio Grande Railroad," *Utah Historical Quarterly* 27 (April 1959): 141.

made internal distances manageable. Together these developments made possible a new era in mining.

Although mining activity in Utah before 1869 was negligible, three important chapters in mining history—Mormon opposition to mining, the mining activities of Patrick E. Connor, and the emergence of Mormon dissent to Brigham Young's policy of self-sufficiency—had already been written.

The church had opposed mining from the first, calling it the most adverse of lotteries. Mormon leaders rejected it as a system that would scatter the Saints and contribute little to the growth of the kingdom. Further, they regarded it as a specialized industry that would distort the balanced economy they were trying to establish. The here-today, gone-tomorrow character of mining was held in special odium, and church members were discouraged in numerous ways from following mining crazes about the West. Indeed, no single aspect of secular life was denounced more regularly and emphatically. So successful was the church campaign that in 1860, when men occupied in mining approached 80 percent in neighboring Colorado, the Utah census listed no more than four miners.

Yet two years later, mining had invaded the territory. The principal figure behind this development was Patrick E. Connor, who commanded a detachment of California Volunteers assigned to Utah as an outgrowth of the Civil War. A super-patriot much decorated in the Mexican War, Connor had enough California experience to be fully caught up in the enthusiasms of the mining frontier. Convinced the Mormons were rebels, he led his troops with fixed bayonets directly into the "City of the Saints" and established Camp Douglas some two miles east of town. He found little justification for the violent solutions to the Mormon question some of his battle-thirsty troops might have desired, so he sought a more subtle kind of conquest. Reasoning that a mining rush would engulf the disloyal Saints with loyal miners, he sent his troops out to prospect. Within a short time they had located deposits, staked claims, set up districts, and made unsuccessful attempts to smelt Utah's low-grade ores. With a promoter's touch, Connor established his own newspaper, *The Union Vedette,* and tried to sweep away early reverses by redoubling efforts to find placer minerals. But his effort was premature. Mining proved to be prohibitively expensive and yields low. Consequently, Connor and the California Volunteers moved on. But the general's outspoken efforts to bring about a metamorphosis in Utah's society, together with his open use of the military for what was essentially private enterprise, had deepened Mormon antagonism toward mining.

However, Connor left a legacy of interest in mining and contributed to a growing climate of change. We have seen that the Walker brothers withdrew from the church in 1864 rather than pay tithes or fix prices. A few other Mormons also saw need for change, and in 1868 a small but influential group of merchants called the New Movement, or Godbeites, openly opposed Brigham Young's policy of economic nonintercourse. Led by William S. Godbe, the group denounced the active role of church leaders in economic policy and urged Mormons to embrace the national economy and unite with non-Mormons in an effort to develop Utah's economy. Loyal to many of the church's teachings, the Godbeites nevertheless struck at an extremely sensitive spot when they argued that development of a specialty product was the basis of prosperity and that for Utah that specialty was mining. In an effort to become a second voice that would in time alter popular opinion and church thinking, they established a number of periodicals including the *Utah Magazine* and the *Salt Lake Tribune*. The Godbeites quickly learned that advocating economic change was tantamount to heresy and were excommunicated. Once out of the church, the businessmen of the group were subjected to the commercial sanctions attendant to the co-operative movement. These fell especially upon Godbe and Eli Kelsey, who turned to mining.

After 1869 mining developed quickly. Mining districts flourished along the Wasatch Front, on the Oquirrh Mountains west and south of Salt Lake City, at Rush Valley west of Tooele, and at numerous central and southern Utah sites. At the Little Cottonwood District east of Salt Lake City, miners staked no fewer than 3,500 claims on an area 2.5 miles square in the 1870s. Three decades later Albert Potter, chief grazier for the Forest Service, reported that mining operations had denuded the area of timber so completely that he could find no club large enough to kill a snake. Perhaps the most important mining district in territorial times was the Park City District, where claims were first located in 1869 but failed to attract much attention until two years later. Thereafter Park City's riches laid the foundations of numerous mining fortunes, including those of the Hearst family. The Ontario Mine owned by George Hearst and others had yielded more than 37 million ounces of silver and paid $14 million in dividends by 1904. The Silver Horn Mine of Beaver County in southern Utah, sold to Jay Cooke of Northern Pacific Railroad fame for $5 million in 1879, and Silver Reef in the sandrock formations north of St. George were also important. These two highly productive mines attracted miners and set swarms of prospectors scouring southern Utah. They flourished briefly with all the color and brave optimism of mining booms elsewhere, breaking the sleepy rhythms of southern Utah and bringing new prosperity to freighters, peddlers, and producers of Dixie wine as well as to those more directly connected with the mines.

All told, the decade of the 70s was a time of production and excitement—the heyday of Utah's age of silver. Where the territory's limited production of precious metals had run 97 percent to gold between 1864 and 1869, silver accounted for more than half of a vastly increased yield in the 1870s, while gold dropped to a poor fourth behind lead and copper. Silver rose from a mere "450 ounces . . . in 1865 . . . to 470,000 in 1870, 1.7 million ounces in 1871" and averaged approximately 4 million ounces throughout the 1870s, to provide nearly 15 percent of the nation's total.[19] The territory also produced between 20 and 50 percent of the nation's lead during the 1870s and 1880s. After a booming expansion in the early 1870s, surface deposits played out, and ores mined at lower levels were more costly to extract and even more resistant to reduction. Until the end of the century mining continued a moderate growth but required improved metallurgical techniques and great sums of capital.

19. Leonard J. Arrington, "Abundance From the Earth: The Beginnings of Commercial Mining in Utah," *Utah Historical Quarterly* 31 (Summer 1963): 215.

Attracting capital in the later decades was complicated by a period of unscrupulous promotion and frenzied investment in Utah mines during the early 1870s, which did lasting injury to the reputation of Utah mining properties as investment prospects. A number of factors contributed to the early enthusiasm. First, the transcontinental railroad unlocked the territory's treasure trove and thrust it into the eyes of the world with dramatic emphasis. Efforts of certain Utahns, including the Walker brothers, William Godbe, and Warren Hussey, president of the National Bank of Utah, may also have over-promoted certain properties in the years after the railroad's advent. More important, the first years of the 1870s were a time of soaring investment in the United States and abroad, and a substantial amount of money found its way to Utah. Foreign investment was of special importance, with Dutch, French, and English companies all operating in the territory.

The British proved to be particularly vulnerable to Utah promotions, investing more than $15 million in twenty mines between 1871 and 1873. Although all of these mines are said to have lost heavily, the most notorious was the "Emma, of Evil Fame." [20] Involving a swindle of spectacular proportions, the Emma scandals rocked the entire investment world, precipitated a congressional investigation which produced nearly a thousand pages of testimony, and left a reputation that to this day marks it as a classic example of unscrupulous mining promotion.

Located in Little Cottonwood Canyon, the Emma Mine produced spectacularly during 1870–1871. Its ores were shipped for processing to Swansea, Wales, where they attracted considerable attention in British investment circles. As the mine passed peak production, it was sold to Erwin Davis of San Francisco and reorganized in New York. With the backing of William M. Stewart, later senator from Nevada, it was taken to England for promotion and sale. In England its development was undertaken by a London promoter named Albert Grant, whose detractors

20. Bancroft, *History of Utah*, p. 742; and W. Turrentine Jackson, "The Infamous Emma Mine: A British Interest in the Little Cottonwood District, Utah Territory," *Utah Historical Quarterly* 23 (Autumn 1955): 339–362.

said he had donated to Leicester Square "in order that his name
might for once be connected with something 'square.' " [21] The
Emma was duly incorporated, enthusiastically endorsed by big-
name authorities, touted in a prospectus that was the very
"acme of sensationalism," and dignified with a board of directors of unimpeachable reputation, including no less a figure than
Robert Cumming Schenck, United States Minister to Britain.[22]
Thus made bona fide, the Emma sold well in Britain. However,
after initial dividends had been paid from capital stock, the entire package came unriveted. Troubles of every sort beset the
enterprise. Difficulties at the mine included property disputes,
flooding, personnel problems, and ores that defied reduction.
Worst, the Emma inexplicably quit producing. The minister
withdrew in embarrassment. Amidst wild maneuvers and
charges and countercharges that finally caused Schenck to resign
from his diplomatic post, the Emma sank into a sea of lawsuits.
The impact spread to mining properties throughout the West as
British investors lost interest and turned to other prospects. Not
surprisingly, Utah mining was especially hard hit. With the
best-known mine in the territory branded far and near as a loser,
the industry suffered not only the loss of British investments but
a general loss of vigor and movement. The Panic of 1873 hit
hard, and Utah's mining business recovered more slowly than
that in neighboring states.

Nevertheless, mining continued to be a dominant activity during the remaining years of the century. In each decade, the
number of people employed increased at a rate far above the national average. Demand for labor led to a new era in Utah immigration. Cornishmen, Finns, Chinese, Japanese, and later
southeastern Europeans came in increasing numbers. The demand for equipment and supplies that mining created contributed to numerous new enterprises that greatly broadened the
"horizons of local commerce." [23] Even more significantly,

21. Clark C. Spence, *British Investments and the American Mining Frontier
1860–1901* (Ithaca, N.Y.: Cornell University Press, 1958), p. 144.
22. Spence, *British Investments,* p. 145.
23. Arrington, "Abundance from the Earth," p. 219.

mining fed upon itself to usher in Utah's copper industry in the years before 1900.

For two decades, distance and the nature of Utah's resources had reinforced Mormon self-sufficiency. During this period merchants were the most constant outside economic influence. When railroads and mining breached the territory in 1869, they brought the exploitive economy by which the West was subdued. The impact upon the territory was profound. With it came new people, new opportunity, and new influences. Salt Lake City became more than the City of the Saints. Ogden emerged as a major regional shipping center. The Mormon village was no longer the only form upon the land. Added were mining camps, railroad towns, and a variety of smelting and reduction works. Tension was and continued to be an important element, as the closed system of the Mormons and the free enterprise of the era functioned in the same field. Inevitably such tensions came to focus in the processes of politics, providing an interesting and challenging test for America's territorial policies as Utah was prepared for statehood.

4

Near-Nationalism and the American Dream

N the minds of Brigham Young and the solemn men who met with him on January 19, 1863, the times were almost unspeakably rich with promise, yet burdened with the most awesome responsibilities. To the east the Civil War raged, surprising observers and participants alike with its fury. However, few in the Mormon capital were surprised. To the contrary, the war's fierceness was fully expected. Far removed from the battle, the legislature of what has aptly been termed the Ghost State of Deseret waited that January day upon Brigham Young, governor without portfolio. Together with the legislature of Deseret, two senators, and a congressman, Young had been elected the year before on a provisional basis in connection with a bid for statehood that Congress had chosen to ignore.

The congressional rebuff failed to deter the men who made up the government of Deseret. With no official status, they played out a strange pantomime, meeting annually to listen to Brigham Young deliver a governor's message and to rubber-stamp the enactments of the territorial legislature. They were, in effect, a state-in-waiting, product of Mormon faith in the imminence of Christ's second coming and reflection of the Mormon yearning for self-government. In short, Deseret was the incipient Kingdom of God—Christ, its prince in exile. Organized first by

78

Joseph Smith as the political arm of the Mormon movement, the kingdom had been maintained in Utah by Brigham Young, who had struggled to give it meaning in the American context and to graft it onto the American body politic. As a Utah phenomenon the kingdom had appeared first as the Provisional State of Deseret in 1849. During Young's years as territorial governor its identity had been subsumed in that of Utah Territory. With Young out of power in the early 1860s, the kingdom surfaced again as the State of Deseret and until the decade's end was a lingering reflection of Mormon millennialism.

The strange career of Deseret was in no small way the result of a different vision for America. Merging millennial expectation with the American dream of world regeneration, the Mormon community of the 1850s became what Thomas O'Dea has termed a "near nation." [1] While they rejected secession and other forms of rebellion, they saw themselves in nationlike terms and assumed an increasingly deviant approach to the objectives and character of government. They held the U.S. Constitution, with its provisions guaranteeing freedom of conscience, as a sacred shield, yet to them it was imperfect and in urgent need of revision. America's territorial system, with its federal controls and carpetbaggers, was regarded as "a relic of Colonial barbarism" quite as worthy of rejection in the 1850s as the British system had been in 1776. [2] With its doctrines of natural law, the Declaration of Independence was a vexation for Mormons who had seen mobs take recourse in "higher law" to drive the Saints and murder the prophets. The American Revolution was a powerful symbol, the founding fathers inspired, and the nation that emerged the product of God's decree to create an environment where His embryo kingdom could prosper. In Mormon belief distinctions between church and state

---

1. O'Dea, *The Mormons,* p. 115; for studies on Mormon millennialism and the State of Deseret, see Klaus J. Hansen, *Quest for Empire: The Political Kingdom of God and the Council of Fifty in Mormon History* (East Lansing: Michigan State University Press, 1970); and Dale L. Morgan, "The State of Deseret," *Utah Historical Quarterly* 9 (April, July, October 1940).

2. Brigham Young, Governors Messages, December 13, 1857, Utah State Historical Society.

blurred; they themselves were the true heirs of the revolution. Sovereignty was God's, the right to rule divine, government the special province of the Priesthood, and the rights of voters properly limited to consent. As John Taylor, future president of the church, explained, "God appoints, the people sustain." [3] Similarly Brigham Young held that with God at the helm, there was "no such thing . . . as two sides to the question." [4] Opposition came from Satan and was thus destructive of government. Party politics, like frequent elections, provoked discord and brought self-interest and corruption.

A people who read divine will in the dual workings of the revealed word and the signs of the time naturally judged political events by their own standards. Beginning in 1832 when Joseph Smith predicted that the North and the South would divide and wars erupt that would make "a full end of all nations," the Saints expected the collapse of worldly government and viewed America's sectional struggle as the beginning of that collapse.[5] As the Civil War drew on in 1863, Brigham Young told the legislators of Deseret that the government of the United States "is going to pieces, and it will be like water that is spilt upon the ground that cannot be gathered." [6] For the moment it was the duty of Deseret's officials to hold ground gained by the kingdom and keep the machinery of its government intact. In due course the Saints would be called upon to "let the water on to the wheel . . . start the machine in motion . . . and give laws to the nations of the earth." [7] Deseret and the kingdom of which it was part were in this sense expressions of millennial expectation. As Mormons undertook to implant the kingdom into the American system and at the same time maintain its identity as a successor state to the collapsing nations of the world, they followed what may be called the politics of near-nationalism.

The attitudes and conduct of near-nationalism appeared

3. Sermon by John Taylor, April 8, 1853, *Journal of Discourses,* 1:230.
4. Sermon by Brigham Young, April 8, 1871, *Journal of Discourses,* 14:92.
5. *Doctrine and Covenants* 87:6.
6. Journal History, January 19, 1863.
7. Journal History, January 19, 1863.

strongly in the Provisional State of Deseret in 1849. Acting to elaborate the church organization that had been their only government since their arrival in Salt Lake Valley into an American state, Mormon leaders called for a convention. A constitution was drawn, Deseret's vast bounds were set, officers were chosen "by what process . . . I know not," according to one of them, and delegate Almond W. Babbit was dispatched to Washington.[8] There Deseret was whipped and tossed in the upheaval that vexed territorial adjustments after the Mexican War. Had it prospered in Congress, Deseret would have been a major step in the growth of home rule. As it was, Utah emerged a territory in the Compromise of 1850. Brigham Young became its governor. Although the arrangement was distinctly second-best, the Mormons accepted it as consistent with God's will as well as the mandate of their country's government.

In the early 1850s they exploited control of the legislative and executive branches to develop a veritable fortress of home rule. Its cornerstone was legislation giving original jurisdiction in civil and criminal cases to the territorial probate courts. This unusual arrangement placed effective control of the judiciary with the Mormons rather than with the federally established district courts. To extend local control even farther over judicial functions, the lawmakers also created offices of territorial attorney general and marshal. These officers, like the probate judges, were appointed by the assembly, which under Utah practice tended to concentrate both temporal and religious authority in the hands of the same men. Laws making the United States district courts dependent upon the legislature for appropriations further increased local power. Additional legislation placed land distribution and the militia under local control, limited taxation and revenues, prohibited compensation for most public offices, controlled elections, effectively outlawed the common law as an instrument against polygamy, and severely restricted both the practice and profession of law. All told, it was a formidable if homespun defense for self-government and went far toward making Brigham Young autocrat over an independent system.

8. Brooks, *On the Mormon Frontier*, 2:358.

However, it was in the sermons of the time that Mormon near-nationalism was exercised most freely. Brigham Young, his two counselors Heber C. Kimball and Jedediah M. Grant, and to a lesser degree Apostles John Taylor and Parley P. and Orson Pratt used sermons as the vehicle for a vigorous and colorful assault on what America had become. They stirred group loyalty and an urgent sense of mission by recalling persecutions, denouncing opponents as immoral and corrupt, and speaking of violence in vivid language and with strong and earthy humor. In a characteristic diatribe Jedediah M. Grant raged:

> I have a gun and a dirk in good order . . . and am ready and able to make holes through such miserable corrupting rascals. . . . They will threaten us with U.S. troops! Why your impudence and ignorance. . . . We ask no odds of you, you rotten carcasses, and I am not going to bow one hairs breadth. . . . I would rather be cut into inch pieces.[9]

Though the pulpit patriotism was sometimes excessive, what leaders asked of the Mormon people was fundamentally peaceful. "Natural means" rather than rebellion or secession would increase the kingdom and simultaneously "diminish the power and reduce the influence" of the United States.[10]

Federal appointees reacted in two ways. Some were deeply offended, finding conspiracy and treason in the rhetoric and governmental irregularities of near-nationalism. Others were apparently unmoved by either irregularities or bombast. But enough officials were disturbed to propel the Mormon problem into national affairs. Indeed, friction between Mormons and outsiders began when the first slate of appointees raised questions about federal appropriations and Brigham Young's informal exercise of power. Whether by premeditation or the enthusiasms of oratory, one of the appointees, Judge Perry E. Brocchus, found himself responding in kind to Brigham Young's railing condemnations of former President Zachary Taylor, and a confrontation soon sent the outsiders into hurried retreat. Similarly,

9. Sermon by J. M. Grant, March 2, 1856, *Journal of Discourses,* 3:234.
10. *Millennial Star* 24 (1871): 337–338.

questions of district court jurisdiction in 1856 erupted into a wild controversy and the angered departure of Judge W. W. Drummond. As storm clouds spread, land and Indian agents and various other appointees also withdrew. Once in Washington, runaway officials mixed truth and fiction in charges of treason, church domination, holy murder, and polygamy.[11] Inevitably such charges cankered relations and resulted in efforts to resist Mormon self-determination.

In this situation the centripetal force of the great issues that divided the nation can hardly be overestimated. Despite Utah's isolation, Mormons found themselves drawn increasingly into the prevailing sectional strife. The web of sectionalism was especially entangling after the church publicly acknowledged in 1852 that its teaching sanctioned the practice of polygamy, which provided a peculiar institution in which the parallels to slavery were too close to be ignored. Soon fleeing officials, land questions, Indian policy, and bids for statehood were related one way or another to sectionalism. By 1856 a sloganeering Republican dubbed slavery and polygamy "twin relics of barbarism" and John C. Frémont campaigned for president on a platform calling for their abolition.[12] By a similar token Illinois Senator Stephen A. Douglas, champion of popular sovereignty and one-time friend of the Mormons, offered polygamists no hopes for self-determination when he told an Illinois audience that polygamy was a "loathsome, disgusting ulcer" that should be "cut" from the body politic.[13]

But for the moment, the slavery issue protected polygamy. To excise one ulcer was to expose the other. On the other hand, the "twin relics" association increased national attention on Utah and complicated its quest for home rule. The great sec-

11. The Mountain Meadows Massacre and a few incidents of unexplained violence during the 1850s and 1860s, together with Mormon references to sins that could be atoned for by the shedding of blood, resulted in many unsubstantiated reports that Mormon leaders directed their followers to kill enemies of the church.

12. See Richard D. Poll, "The Mormon Question Enters National Politics," *Utah Historical Quarterly* 25 (April 1957): 127.

13. Quoted in Howard R. Lamar, *The Far Southwest 1856–1912: A Territorial History*, Norton Library Edition (New York: W. W. Norton Co., 1970), p. 340.

tional struggle had a nationalizing influence upon Utah and the Mormons that was even more paradoxical. Their attention was drawn to it as by a magnet, and their ideas about the Kingdom of God were focused by it. Their words regarding it were various, but the reckless spirit of near-nationalism it provoked is clear. By it, the ungodly were "preparing for their own utter overthrow, and the nation in which we live is doing so as fast as the wheels of time can roll." [14] Or "the South will secede from the North, and the North will secede from us, and God will make this people free." [15] And again: "We are going to possess the earth. Why? Because it belongs to Jesus Christ, and he belongs to us, and we to him; we are all one, and will take the kingdom and possess it under the whole heavens, and reign over it. . . . Now, ye kings and emperors, help yourselves, if you can." [16] Such sentiments were expressed in Mormon meetings far from the political halls of worldly accounting. They reflected ardent faith that worldly times were yielding to an eternal order and an almost overwhelming confidence that the Saints stood at the epicenter of change.

Ironically, even subjugation by a federal army and Brigham Young's forcible removal from the governor's chair served more to fix the destiny of transition in Mormon minds than to establish federal authority. President James Buchanan, stigmatized as soft on polygamy, used indictments in which W. W. Drummond and other Utah appointees charged the Mormons with treason as an excuse to appoint Alfred Cumming of Georgia governor in the spring of 1857, and dispatched the Utah Army to install him. Making its way west in various detachments, the Army lacked effective leadership until Colonel Albert Sidney Johnston, later to die a Confederate general at Shiloh, assumed command late in the fall. Brigham Young learned of the approaching Army in July and moved immediately to mobilize the Nauvoo Legion, a territorial militia that was in effect a church army. The Legion fortified passes, and guerilla

14. Sermon by Brigham Young, April 6, 1861, *Journal of Discourses,* 9:3.
15. Sermon by Heber C. Kimball, April 6, 1861, *Journal of Discourses,* 9:7.
16. Sermon by John Taylor, April 8, 1853, *Journal of Discourses,* 1:230.

forces were dispatched to harass government livestock and burn supply trains in a successful delaying tactic. During the fall, Cumming, Chief Justice Delano Eckels, and other federal officials took up their quarters with the Army, which wintered in anger and discomfort at Camp Scott near Fort Bridger.

As the Army approached, Mormon leaders fanned flames of resistance with even more reckless speech. Heber C. Kimball cried: "Good God! I have wives enough to whip out the United States for they shall whip up themselves." [17] Somewhat more restrained, Brigham Young reckoned "that the thred was cut between us and the U.S." He also told the Saints that if they would assert their independence they "should be a free people but if not . . . the kingdom should be rent from" them, and he later wrote Thomas L. Kane that Utah would soon "assume her rights and place among the family of nations." [18]

In the main, the flame of Mormon resistance was nonviolent. In southern Utah, however, the situation had fanned a spirit "in the breasts of some to wish their enemies might come and give them a chance to fight and take vengeance." [19] At Mountain Meadows on September 11, 1857, this tinder of hate and fear ignited with tragic consequences. After encouraging an unsuccessful Indian attack upon a train of Missouri and Arkansas emigrants, Mormon militiamen slaughtered upwards of 100 men, women, and older children. Seventeen children too young to tell the story were spared. Indian Farmer John D. Lee has been most intimately associated with the Mountain Meadows Massacre, but the tragedy involved many individuals, became a blight to the entire region, and created one of the heaviest burdens territorial Utah had to bear.

By the spring of 1858, however, the Utah War generally had cooled down. Mormons reckoned the costs of resistance and assumed a more conciliatory stance. At the same time they ap-

17. Quoted in Mulder and Mortensen, *Among the Mormons,* p. 297.

18. See Brooks, *On the Mormon Frontier,* 2:636; Juanita Brooks, *The Mountain Meadows Massacre,* new ed., 4th printing (Norman: University of Oklahoma Press, 1970), p. 25; and Hansen, *Quest for Empire,* p. 165.

19. Sermon by George A. Smith, September 13, 1857, *Journal of Discourses,* 5:223.

pealed for public sympathy by the "move south," temporarily abandoning all settlements north of Utah Valley. In Washington President Buchanan studied the charges against them, tabulated costs, and concluded that he had acted in haste. More important, he found that a national consensus on which to base his action was wanting. Consequently, a peace commission carried the President's pardon to the Mormon people and ratified negotiations that Cumming and Young had already substantially worked out.

As Yale historian Howard Lamar has observed, however, a clenched fist bore the president's pardon, for the Army continued into Utah. But the strategy of delay nevertheless had its day. The Mormon aversion for quartering troops was acknowledged when Johnston established Camp Floyd west of Utah Lake some fifty miles from Salt Lake City, and Brigham Young was able to work upon divisions between military and civil and between executive and judiciary to frustrate effective exercise of federal power. Once again the Mormon problem was caught in the arms of sectional division, this time on a very personal basis. Both Alfred Cumming and Albert Sidney Johnston were southerners who ultimately returned from Utah to the Confederacy. That each was soft in his own way on the Mormons seems related to their ultimate loyalty to states' rights and the peculiar institution of their own section.

Thus in time the judges left, the governor left, and the Army departed. The War between the States had taken each in turn. But the Saints remained. Utah had been occupied, but to what avail? To Mormons the lesson was not one of subordination to federal authority but a deepening conviction of God's governing hand and their special destiny as the keepers of a state-in-waiting against a national doom that was already unfolding. As the war surpassed all precedent for savagery, the Saints continued to wait, expecting the North and the South to destroy each other. While war-tense visitors of the era may have exaggerated, there is no doubt that the "perished Union" was a favorite theme. As Fitz Hugh Ludlow, a "young literary bohemian from New York," vividly recounted, "all the saints were inoculated with a prodigious craze, to the effect that the United States was

UTAH
A photographer's essay by Joe Munroe

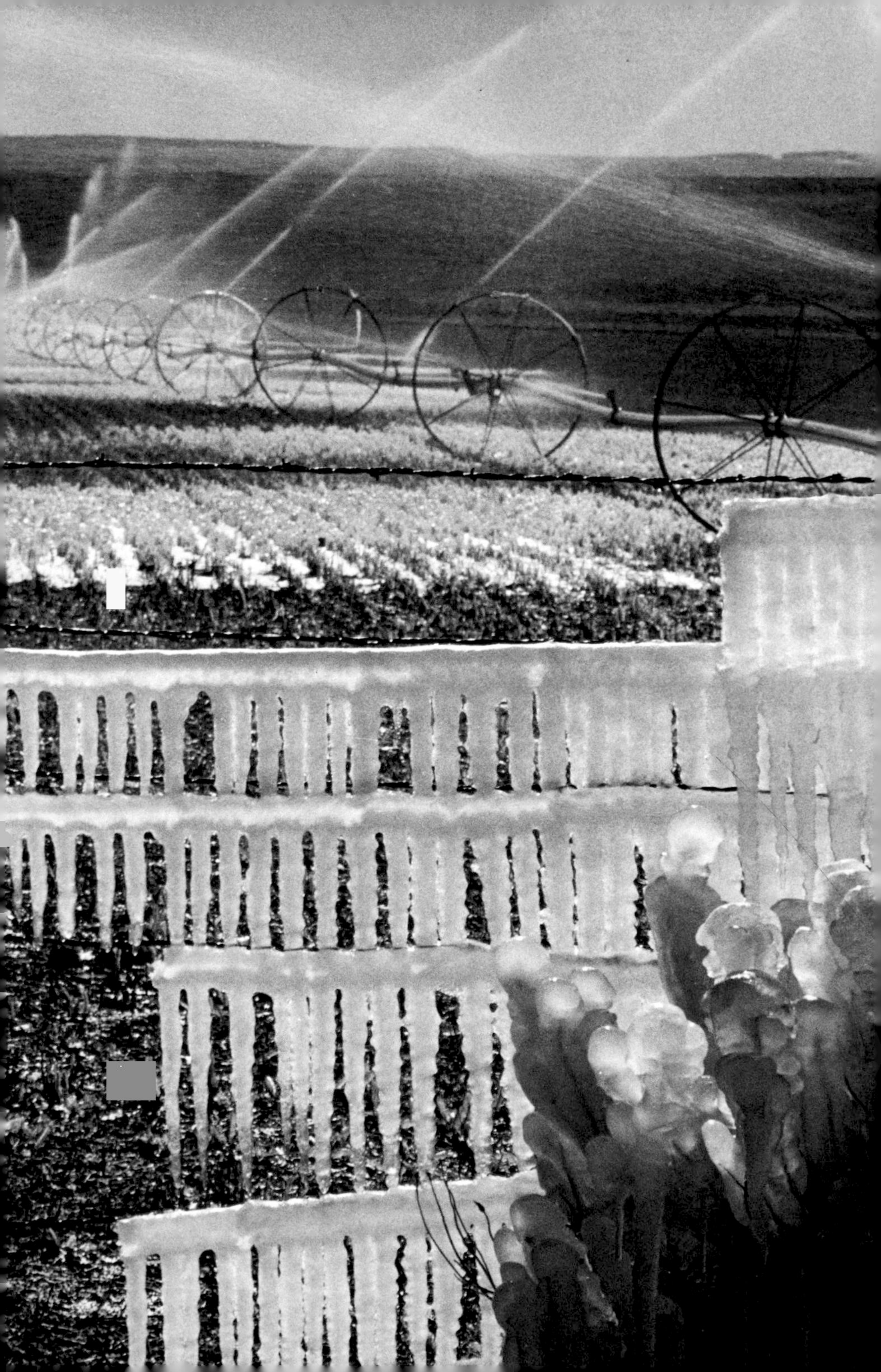

Photographs in Sequence

Farmer near Hurricane.
Farmer plowing field with peaks of Zion National Park in the background.
Sugar beet harvest near Lehi.
Irrigation on a freezing morning near Loa.
Outskirts of Logan.
Cattle roundup near Moab.
Sheepherding near Nephi.
Mormon Tabernacle Choir, Salt Lake City.
World's largest copper mine, Bingham Canyon.
Natural Bridge, Capitol Reef National Park.
Desert salt flats near Wendover.
Motorcyclist on shores of Great Salt Lake.
State capitol, Salt Lake City.
United States Department of Agriculture experimental station, Logan.
Causeway over Great Salt Lake.

to become a blighted chaos, and its inhabitants Mormon prose-
lytes and citizens of Utah within the next two years." [20] Stephen Harding, an Indiana abolitionist appointed governor by
Abraham Lincoln in March 1862, found Utah quite as much
"an enemy country as . . . Richmond or Charleston." [21]

Yet Utah was loyal. The Union was its recognized and functioning government. With the Army gone, Brigham Young led
the way for a new statehood movement in 1861 and 1862.
When it failed, as we have seen, Young kept Mormon near-nationalism alive by refurbishing the State of Deseret as the
earthly form of God's government. Thus convictions of the
"perished Union" and a different version of the American
dream led the heaven-on-earth nationalism of the Mormons to
its highest pitch. For fifteen years they had worked with dual
purpose to function within the American nation and to lay the
foundations of their own emerging role in a new world system.
The product had been first the Provisional State of Deseret, then
the territorial system of Brigham Young's era as governor, and
finally the Ghost State of Deseret in the 1860s.

Inevitably commitments and hostilities survived to make the
fifteen years following the Civil War a time of impasse in Utah
politics. During this period the federal government often worked
against itself and public opinion was irresolute; but by a ponder-
ous and sometimes agonizing process, public consensus and
consistent policy began to evolve. For Mormons it was a time of
adjustment and defensive maneuvering. The end of the war had
jolted Utah only less than the South. With peace, isolation
ended. The expected collapse of the United States had not occurred, and millennial immediacy had to yield to more conventional views of the future. The politics of near-nationalism were
supplanted by what Howard Lamar has termed a policy of "superior virtue," a shrewdly conceived and ably conducted public

20. Mulder and Mortensen, *Among the Mormons*, p. 347; and Fitz Hugh Ludlow,
"Among the Mormons," *Atlantic Monthly* 13 (April 1864): 489.
21. Quoted in Robert Joseph Dwyer, *The Gentile Comes to Utah: A Study in Religious and Social Conflict 1862–1890*, 2nd ed., rev. (Salt Lake City: Western Epics,
1971), p. 17.

relations program that undertook to reverse the church's negative image and achieve the objective of home rule.[22]

The impulse to show themselves in the best possible light on which the politics of superior virtue rested had always been strong among Latter-day Saints—particularly in missionary activities. In the realm of politics the prophets of the new order were the Mormon delegates to Congress. During the period of near-nationalism when leaders in Utah often seemed bent on giving offense, the delegates functioned in Congress with poise and persuasive polish. During the 1850s Territorial Delegate William H. Hooper and his predecessor John M. Bernhisel repeatedly reclaimed success from disaster and fully merited the grudging admiration expressed by Senator Shelby M. Cullom, an ardent anti-Mormon from Illinois, when he called Hooper the "Mormon Richelieu." [23] Utah leaders applauded and supported their delegates in every way short of concessions in mood and conduct that would have defused the explosive Mormon question.

However, evidence of developing moderation in Mormon leadership may be seen as early as 1857 when Daniel H. Wells succeeded to the first presidency on the death of Jedediah M. Grant. Although Wells commanded the Nauvoo Legion and was devoted to the church, he was moderate in temper and broad in background and replaced the belligerence of Grant's last years with a voice of restraint. In time even Brigham Young's posture changed from the sagebrush jingoism of the near-national period to one of passive resistance. Equally an indication that the public front of Mormonism was penetrating Utah was the prominence after 1872 of George Q. Cannon, an urbane and gifted English convert who for decades served as territorial delegate, apostle, and counselor in the first presidency. John Taylor, who headed the church after Brigham Young's death in 1877, and Wilford Woodruff, a veteran of the church who succeeded to

22. Howard R. Lamar, "Statehood for Utah: A Different Path," *Utah Historical Quarterly* 39 (Fall 1971): 316.

23. Stanford Orson Cazier, "The Life of William Henry Hooper, Merchant-Statesman," unpublished master's thesis, University of Utah, 1956, p. 101.

the presidency in 1887, assumed positions of restraint and patriarchal wisdom. The emergence of the policy of superior virtue was also apparent in the growing importance of younger Mormons with a professional bent. As part of this movement Mormons gave up what had been a strong aversion for the law. They turned increasingly to courts to defend their rights, employed the best attorneys, and sent favorably disposed lawyers such as John F. Kinney and Thomas Fitch to Congress as delegates and lobbyists. A number of young Mormons also went to the best law schools in the nation and entered the legal profession.

Although the mood of Mormon leadership shifted, self-determination remained the keystone to Mormon policy, with the rights of the church as a minority religion at its crux. With isolation ended, they sought to protect these rights by a monopoly of military, judicial, educational, and electoral functions, as well as by the politics of polygamy. Encompassed within their efforts were various arrangements that seemed to most Americans to breach the principle of separation between church and state.

At the national level a number of ambiguities complicated relations. The interplay of opposing national purposes precluded concentration on an issue regarded by most Americans as irritating but unimportant. Lingering sectionalism, party lines, separation of powers, and an incoherent territorial policy retarded effective action. Not only did the interplay of factions and a lagging consensus provide the Mormons with an extraordinary field of action, but the kind of minority they were also contributed. However outlandishly regarded they may have been, Mormons nevertheless enjoyed most of the benefits of citizenship. At no time were they excluded from the pale of the law as were native Americans and blacks. Thus the Mormon controversy took on the nature of a family squabble, bitter and noisy, but settled essentially within the parameters of American rights.

During the Civil War and the years that followed, the federal government's Utah policy had little consistent line beyond the feeling that polygamy, like slavery, was conspiratorial. In Congress a number of early polygamy measures culminated in

Justin Morrill's Anti-Bigamy Act of 1862. The Morrill Act established penalties against polygamy and placed severe property
limits upon the church but was made ineffective by the territorial court system and the transfer of church property to Brigham
Young.

The Morrill Act coincided with Abraham Lincoln's Utah
measures, which have been referred to as a hands-off policy but
which were in reality a mix of the stern and the soft which adversely affected the territory. Not only did Lincoln preside over
Utah's dismemberment when Nevada and Colorado territories
came into being, but he appointed spoilsmen who sometimes
had little beyond their personal interests to commend them. The
inconsistency of Lincoln's Utah administration was undoubtedly
related to the pressures of the Civil War, but two events early in
his administration also suggested that the Mormon problem still
existed. In Utah his first territorial governor, John W. Dawson,
was quickly branded a corrupt and immoral man and was chased
from the territory with a beating. A few months later attempts of
civil authorities to arrest the leaders of a community of religious
dissenters resulted in the killing of several people in the so-
called Morrisite War. Lincoln's second governor, Stephen S.
Harding, was embroiled in the aftermath of the Morrisite affair
and became an implacable foe of the church. James Duane
Doty, the last Lincoln governor, adroitly managed things to
"prevent collisions" between the "three powers governing this
country; the Mormon Church; the military and the Civil," but
did it with an eye to becoming senator rather than as a consistent element in federal policy.[24] President Andrew Johnson
sought to postpone an upheaval, directing Governor Charles
Durkee "to do nothing," a policy that historian H. H. Bancroft
noted was "faithfully executed." [25]

Further evidence of the hard line in Lincoln's policy appears
in the establishment of a military district in the territory. In
command was Patrick E. Connor, who occupied Salt Lake City
with sabres rattling in October of 1862. He brutally chastised

24. Quoted in Lamar, *The Far Southwest,* p. 364.
25. Bancroft, *History of Utah,* p. 622.

Shoshoni and Bannock Indians who had harassed overland migration along the Oregon Trail in the Battle of Bear River and then turned his troops to mining activities. In so doing Connor limited the influence of his troops as an occupying force by doing little to quell Indian hostilities throughout the territory. In addition to sharpening the Mormon sense of self-help, this failure contributed to the continued strength of the Nauvoo Legion, which maintained a full complement of 13,000 men until the end of the Black Hawk War in the late 1860s. Supported locally, the Legion was largely under church control and represented an imposing countervailing force to the Army's presence.

By the late 1860s anti-Mormon forces were on the rise. Armed intervention seemed possible with General William Tecumseh Sherman, the Utah gentiles, and various newspapers threatening or calling for a military showdown. A "gentile ring" emerged, and an opposition slate appeared for the first time in the election of 1868 when William McGroarty, a "bold if obscure" candidate, ran for delegate, receiving a paltry 105 votes against Hooper's 15,068.[26] The town of Corinne grew up as a gentile center, and the newly founded *Salt Lake Tribune* soon became a violent voice of opposition. In 1870 the Liberal Party was created to challenge the Mormons at the polls and keep Utah before the eyes of Congress and the nation. Ulysses S. Grant succeeded Johnson as president in 1869, dispatched Vice President Schuyler Colfax and General Phil Sheridan to Utah to assess affairs, and in his messages to Congress called for removal of the stain of Mormon disloyalty.

Meanwhile Radical Republicans in Congress worked to find a majority on the Mormon question, offering legislation to dismember the territory, grant Mormon women the vote, substitute commission government for home rule, reduce the strength of the Mormon-controlled probate courts, and strengthen the antipolygamy measures of the Morrill Act. Their efforts failed to produce a majority, but the features of the Cullom Bill, vigorously debated in 1860, pointed the way. Drafted by a humorless Utah Liberal named R. N. Baskin and Senator

26. Lamar, *The Far Southwest*, p. 380.

Shelby M. Cullom, the bill would have drastically extended federal authority in Utah and disqualified polygamists from jury duty and public office, but it fell short of passage.

In 1870 President Grant undertook to mold the various anti-Mormon forces into a coordinated campaign. Key figures in his assault were Governor J. Wilson Shaffer, whose battle cry was "never after me shall it be said that Brigham Young is governor," and Chief Justice James B. McKean, for whom the Utah bench was a divine calling quite as "much above the duties of other courts and judges as the heavens are above the earth." [27] Shaffer arrived in March 1870 to find everything wrong. Brigham Young was "lawgiver and autocrat," territorial legislators his "subservient instruments," the governor's chair a "mere sinecure," and holy murder still rampant. Determined to cleanse this "Augean Stable," Shaffer called for sterner federal laws, intervened in territorial politics, and undertook to assert control over the Nauvoo Legion.[28] To reduce the Legion's role, federal troops were dispatched to establish Camp Rawlins near Provo in the early summer. A few weeks later Shaffer struck directly at the church when he countermanded orders from Daniel H. Wells, commanding general of the Legion and member of the first presidency. Adding insult to injury, he placed Patrick E. Connor in charge.

The controversy that ensued rolled like a thunderstorm through the valleys of the Wasatch, but the courts carried the most effective thrust of Grant's campaign. The first challenge grew from Shaffer's call for strengthened federal measures. The federal court ignored probate court jurisdiction and, with jurors chosen in breach of territorial law, ruled in favor of Paul Engelbrecht, whose liquor store had been destroyed as a nuisance by Salt Lake City officials when he refused to pay a heavy license fee. Encouraged, court authorities initiated several cases that focused on polygamy. Thus court action was already gathering

27. See Dwyer, *The Gentile Comes to Utah,* p. 66; and Gustive O. Larson, *The "Americanization" of Utah for Statehood* (San Marino, Calif.: The Huntington Library, 1971), p. 73.

28. Dwyer, *The Gentile Comes to Utah,* pp. 67–68.

momentum in the summer of 1870 when McKean arrived, openly announcing his intention to "trample" any "Local or Federal laws obstructing" his mission to subjugate the Mormons.[29]

Virtually unhampered by due process, McKean quickly procured a number of important indictments, including one against Brigham Young. While the formal charge against Young was lascivious cohabitation, it was in McKean's eyes a test of "Federal Authority against Polygamic Theocracy" and involved a situation in which the "government of the United States . . . finds within its jurisdiction another government claiming to come from God . . . whose policies and practices are in grave particulars, at variance with its own." [30]

With all its apparent force, the Grant administration's campaign was in many ways ineffective. The Mormon majority still prevailed and through the newly organized People's Party—in itself a concession to conventional politics—continued to smother the Liberal Party at the polls. The politics of superior virtue concentrated on showing the amiability of Mormons, even under persecution. The aging "Lion of the Lord" set the pattern. Hauled into court, Brigham Young not only refused to roar but also hired the best gentile attorneys and turned away wrath by mild and co-operative demeanor. Working through contacts opened by their railroading enterprises and through that tried and true "friend to the east" Thomas L. Kane, Mormon lobbyists pleaded their case to a national audience. Simultaneously the territorial assembly gave women the vote, thus joining Wyoming to lead the nation in this reform measure.

In quest of a platform proclaiming this spirit of conciliation, Utah made another bid for statehood in 1872. The annual meetings of the Ghost State of Deseret had been quietly dropped two years before and the old Constitution of Deseret retired by popular vote. Although Congress made no move to favor it and Gov-

29. Edward W. Tullidge, *Life of Brigham Young; or, Utah and Her Founders* (New York, 1876), pp. 420–421.

30. For the entire ruling see Orson F. Whitney, *History of Utah,* 4 vols. (Salt Lake City: George Q. Cannon & Sons Co., 1893), 2:598–600.

ernor George I. Woods openly opposed it, a constitutional convention was duly convoked. A "safe though not ungenerous" gentile representation gave notice that the convention intended to diassociate itself from Mormon monopoly.[31] Its compromising temper appeared most emphatically in a prefatory ordinance inviting Congress to prescribe "some prohibitory clause concerning polygamy" and in the selection of gentiles Frank Fuller and Tom Fitch to carry the document to Congress, which did not reciprocate the mood for compromise.[32]

Ironically, Utah's polite rebels, the Godbeites, materially softened Grant's hard line. Confident that forces within the church would soon make polygamy and church rule obsolete, they convinced General Sheridan that a show of military force would only redouble Mormon resistance and influenced Grant to think that time, not force, was needed. Furthermore, the Godbeites found themselves strange bedfellows for Utah's fire-eating gentiles; what had been regarded as a promising alliance failed to materialize, weakening the forces of change.

Faction within government also worked against Shaffer and McKean. Division resulted in a complete breakdown between the Army and civil authorities in September 1870, while Shaffer's move to assert his authority over the Nauvoo Legion was still at full tilt. Troops at Camp Rawlins rioted in Provo, jeopardizing his plan to supplant the Legion with federal troops. Shaffer angrily condemned General P. T. DeTrobriand, commander at Camp Douglas, indicating publicly that the Army ought to be ordered from the territory. DeTrobriand hotly retorted that, lacking the instincts of spoilsmen, the Army's interest would indeed be served if it were placed beyond the reach of Shaffer and his likes. Although Shaffer died suddenly at this point, DeTrobriand showed not only that he was a reluctant scapegoat but that he was loath to allow civil authorities to maneuver him into bloodshed. In the "wooden gun rebellion" of the following year, he sidestepped a call to shoot Legionnaires to prevent their parading on the fourth of July, announcing that troops would be

31. Dwyer, *The Gentile Comes to Utah,* p. 126.
32. Morgan, "State of Deseret," p. 151.

on hand but that civil officers would have to give the order to fire.

But it was from Judge McKean's court actions that the clearest evidence of factionalism emerged. The severity and questionable legality of his case against Brigham Young attracted a number of important gentile lawyers to the aging prophet's aid. Even long-time opponent Patrick E. Connor dropped his hostility, at least momentarily, and many gentiles supported statehood in 1872. A still more fundamental show of internal division appeared when the Supreme Court in 1872 reversed a district court ruling on the Englebrecht case, thus supporting the judiciary arrangements of the territory and rendering most of McKean's work unconstitutional. Naturally, Mormons were jubilant, Congress had stopped short of effective anti-polygamy legislation, and a Supreme Court decision protected home rule. Effective agreement within the federal government did not exist. As in the case of the Utah War, a major offensive had apparently fallen of its own weight.

However, much had changed. A time of increasing control had been introduced, and this time there was no Civil War or other major crisis to divert attention. The moral outcry against polygamy gathered force, as Protestants in Utah and across the land inveighed against it and crusading feminists zeroed in on it. Cries of priestcraft, lawlessness, and disloyalty heightened to a frenzy. In addition, opponents had taken careful measure of other Mormon irregularities and worked out an increasingly cogent case against them. The Nauvoo Legion, with its mix of church and state, was under attack. So too were tax systems that supported the church's Perpetual Emigrating Fund and Mormon schools. Gentiles charged that the Saints were overwhelmingly foreign in birth, hence a special threat to American ways. By a similar token, critics said that the Mormon custom of permitting one man to hold several offices breached the division of powers. Equally un-American because they contributed to the Mormon monopoly of public office were laws limiting compensation for public service. Finally, Mormon opposition to free public schools also seemed un-American and threatening.

During the late 1870s, however, anti-Mormon sentiment in

Congress diminished somewhat. Southern Democrats again began to assert themselves, diverting attention to a new set of problems and opposing anti-Mormon legislation on partisan and philosophical grounds. For related reasons Rutherford Hayes's administration made occasional position statements on the Mormon problem but was otherwise inert. Lacking a firm policy, federal appointees to Utah continued to vary in style and capacity, as the three governors of the 1870s demonstrate. George I. Woods shared the bitterness of Wilson Shaffer but lacked his direction and force. Samuel B. Axtell took Mormons at face value and as a result gentiles dubbed him "Bishop Axtell." The gentiles lamented his perfidy, and he was soon transferred to Arizona. George W. Emery reflected the do-nothing stance of Grant's last years and the Hayes administration but showed outstanding political acumen by keeping both gentiles and Mormons relatively happy.

After a brief summer of good feeling following the Shaffer–McKean offensive, the Liberal Party regrouped and remained a vociferous and unwavering voice of opposition, angling increasingly for a settlement of the Utah problem that favored their views. They continued unsuccessfully to oppose church candidates at the polls but, with the aid of sympathetic governors, managed to keep the Mormons off balance and on edge.

The passage of the Poland Law in 1874 demonstrated the growing federal control of the era. An outgrowth of the struggle to control the territorial judicial system, the act transferred jurisdiction over criminal and civil cases from the territory's probate courts to the federal courts, abolished the offices of territorial attorney general and marshal, and provided a formula placing an equal number of gentiles and Mormons on juries. By the end of 1874 the Supreme Court had upheld the Poland Act. With the probate courts finally out of the way, the district courts took initiative throughout the middle and late 1870s. Picking up the loose ends left by the Shaffer–DeTrobriand explosion, Judge Cyrus Hawley worked toward the establishment of a military outpost at Beaver to support his Second District Court. By 1873 Fort Cameron was established, and at long last the court initiated proceedings on the Mountain Meadows Massacre in 1874.

Several men were indicted, but John D. Lee was the only one brought to trial. Although the first trial revolved around Lee, it also involved an effort to implicate the church and its leaders. The trial ended in a hung jury. In a second trial, Lee personally was the object of the prosecution. An all-Mormon jury found him guilty and sentenced him to death—a sentence carried out at the site of the massacre on March 23, 1877.

A trial of a different sort was that of George B. Reynolds. Arrested for bigamy in 1874, Reynolds became the defendant in a celebrated test case that ran on until 1878, when the Supreme Court handed down a ruling of great long-range significance. The Court distinguished between religious belief and practice, holding that Mormon polygamy made "religious belief superior to the law of the land." [33] Previously Mormons had used the First Amendment's guarantee of religious freedom to justify polygamy. Now they had recourse only to God's law and, judging it superior to secular law, continued to resist. But the gathering forces of reform and government were uniting to turn a time of impasse into one of crusade and retreat that finally resulted in Mormon surrender after 1890.

The Reynolds decision mobilized anti-Mormon forces throughout the nation. The *New York Sun* took the lead, as newspapers stepped up their attack on polygamy. Denunciation of the practice was stock in trade for publicists and lecturers. Kate Field, for example, reported that it was common in Utah to "see a man sitting on the fence with his whip in his hand, while his wives toiled in the field," and John H. Beadle placed an indelible stamp of retrogression on the Saints when he vowed that the "face and head" of Daniel H. Wells bore "involuntary witness to the truth of Darwinism." [34] John P. Newman, Methodist chaplain of the Senate, made his pulpit an arena of anti-

33. From the opinion of Chief Justice Morrison R. Waite, quoted in Dwyer, *The Gentile Comes to Utah*, pp. 115–116.

34. *Salt Lake Herald*, May 14, 1887; and John H. Beadle, *The Undeveloped West: Or, Five Years in the Territories; Being a Complete History of that Vast Region Between the Mississippi and the Pacific, Its Resources, Climate, Inhabitants, Natural Curiosities, etc., etc. Life and Adventure on Prairies, Mountains and the Pacific Coast* (Philadelphia: National Publishing Co., 1873), p. 11.

Mormonism and tilted lustily on the field of polygamy with veteran defender Orson Pratt. Protestants generally launched a "Sectarian crusade," establishing missions and schools in Utah that enrolled some 7,000 children by 1889.

Governor Eli H. Murray, a determined and colorful young Unionist from Kentucky appointed at the end of the Hayes administration, accelerated the anti-Mormon movement. He sparred relentlessly with the assembly, called attention to the mix of church and state in the Perpetual Emigrating Fund, and noisily supported the Liberal Party. Within months of his arrival he carried the Liberal effort to unseat Delegate George Q. Cannon to Congress when he issued a certificate of election to Allen G. Campbell, who had garnered fewer than 1,500 votes out of 20,000 cast. Murray argued that Cannon was an unnaturalized alien. Cannon successfully defended his seat, but the issue quickened congressional interest and during its next session twenty-three bills and hundreds of petitions dealing with polygamy were introduced.

The single measure that emerged was the Edmunds Bill. Senator George F. Edmunds had been instrumental in imposing Radical Reconstruction on the South and regarded the Republican Party's original "twin relics" slogan as an unfulfilled mandate. He was so cold in personal qualities that he merited the nickname "Iceberg of the Senate," and he held that "no one of the provisions of the Constitution has any application as it respects what we may do in the Territories." [35] With questions of rights and sovereignty thus dismissed, he introduced a bill calculated to outlaw polygamy and break the church politically. Becoming law in 1882, the Edmunds Act imposed heavy fines on polygamy, gave lesser penalties for cohabitation, and declared children of polygamist unions to be illegitimate. A five-man "Utah Commission" was established to register voters and manage elections.

35. See Lamar, *The Far Southwest,* p. 390; and Richard D. Poll, "The Political Reconstruction of Utah Territory, 1866–1890," *Pacific Historical Review* 27 (May 1958): 118.

The Utah Commission arrived in September and immediately began a registration process that ultimately disfranchised 12,000 polygamists. Because no elections could be held until the Commission had duly registered voters, the August election of 1882 came and went, leaving offices unfilled. In the scramble for power that ensued, Murray appointed scores of officers to previously elective positions. Mormon incumbents, however, refused to be unseated, basing their resistance on an obscure territorial law that required them to remain in office in the absence of an election.

However, the real impact of the Edmunds Act was felt through the courts. Applied with remorseless zeal by Judges Charles S. Zane, Jacob S. Boreman, and Orlando Powers, the act finally provided an effective means of prosecuting polygamists. The judges, supported by a phalanx of lawyers and deputy marshals, launched what was widely called "the raid" in the 1884 case of Rudger Clawson. The Clawson case established precedent for empaneling grand juries from open venire, seating all-gentile trial juries, imprisoning wives who refused to testify, and imposing severe penalties. Now able, as one U.S. Marshal later recalled, to empanel juries that "could convict Jesus Christ," the courts nevertheless moved slowly into action, grinding out only three convictions in 1884 and twenty-three the following year but accelerating thereafter to ultimately send some 1,300 polygamists to prison.[36]

With many constitutional rights in abeyance for Mormons, Salt Lake City residents on July 4, 1885, awoke to find American flags at half-mast over Mormon buildings throughout the city. After they received negative replies to queries whether the flags were lowered because John Taylor, aging church president, or President U. S. Grant had died, anti-Mormon forces in the city exploded. Wild with fury at the "insult," gentiles stormed to and fro, and Governor Murray called desperately for troops to redress the slur on America's honor. The *Salt Lake Tribune* released a series of editorial attacks, scornfully adding that it

36. Fred T. Dubois, as quoted in Larson, *"Americanization,"* p. 112.

would "hear no more of Mormon love for the Stars and Stripes." [37]

Mormons, some of whom had evidently lowered the flags in reaction to the recent trials, were equally militant. Editorials fumed that the Saints were the "most loyal community within the pale of the Republic," and one orator lamented that nothing remained for Utah but "fragments of local government," like crumbs falling "to Lazarus from the rich man's table." [38] During the days that followed the incident reverberated across the country in the anti-Mormon press. Just as the casual response to the beating of hapless John Dawson—Lincoln's first governor—had signaled the might of the priesthood and the preoccupation of the nation in 1861, so the flag incident heralded the national attention, federal control, and church retreat that dominated Utah in the 1880s.

Mormons, however, entertained little thought of capitulation during the early and middle 1880s. Rudger Clawson's statement as he was sentenced to four years' imprisonment expressed their determination: "Whenever . . . the laws of my country should come in conflict with the laws of God . . . I shall invariably choose the latter." [39] As the raid intensified in 1885 John Taylor told his followers in an emotional farewell sermon that he could "die for the truth" but would "Never! No. Never! . . . disobey my God [or] forsake my wives and children." [40] Asked what the Saints should do, he quietly told them to avoid their adversaries. Taking his own advice the aged patriarch went into hiding. Two years later he died "on the underground."

For polygamists, "hell appeared on every corner." [41] The alternatives were simple but heartrending—yield an essential point of faith and abandon loved ones, or take the consequences. Families were broken and women and children were moved like pawns in a game. Groups collected defense funds

37. *Salt Lake Tribune*, July 5, 1885.
38. *Deseret News*, July 7, 1885.
39. *Salt Lake Tribune*, November 4, 1884.
40. Sermon by John Taylor, February 1, 1885, *Journal of Discourses*, 26:152, 155.
41. Joseph Fish, "History of the Eastern Arizona Stake of Zion and of the Establishment of the Snowflake Stake, 1879–1893," Church Historical Department, p. 36.

and hired lawyers, as a people who had despised the law sought its recourse. But most often, polygamists followed John Taylor's example and ran. Some went underground locally; some fled beyond territorial boundaries; others accepted missions to Europe or added escape colonies to the pattern of Mormon settlement. Monogamists stayed on to run the church and fight its battles. Women and children managed farms and businesses. But many polygamists were caught and tried. Most of them went to prison unrepentant, becoming a unique "penitentiary society" that maintained dignity through restraint, bedbugs, and filth. From the experience emerged a folklore replete with enemy-of-the-people deputies, houses with polygamy pits, and a great stock of escape stories.

The 1885 inauguration of Grover Cleveland, the first Democratic President since the Civil War, resulted in something of a thaw but failed to break the grip of the anti-Mormons. Caleb W. West replaced Mormon-baiting Governor Murray. Democrat West not only preferred "to substitute persuasion for force" but for party reasons often opposed the Utah Liberals, who were affiliated with the Republicans.[42] Cleveland made himself available to John A. Young, Frank Cannon (son of George Q. Cannon), and other Mormon agents who explored just and humane means of getting at the "community evil" but sought "assurance that the object of the administration" would be to "secure obedience to the law . . . not to exterminate the Mormon Church or to persecute its 'prophets.' "[43] In the spirit of these conversations Cleveland appointed eminent New York jurist Elliott F. Sanford chief justice of the Utah bench. Purging the Third District Court of its crusading spirit, Sanford encouraged "cohabs," as polygamists were locally called, to surrender. A great many, anticipating leniency, gave themselves up. The mounting number of convictions that resulted enabled Democrats to argue that they, not the Republicans, had done the most to eradicate plural marriage.

The Cleveland thaw also had important partisan overtones.

42. Larson, *"Americanization,"* p. 130.
43. Quoted in Larson, *"Americanization,"* p. 231.

Since the mid-1870s the Republicans had held a narrow margin
of power nationally, and both Democrats and Republicans saw
eight or ten western territories as the key to the future congressional balance. With Cleveland's election, territorial politics entered a new phase that culminated in the admission of six states
in 1890. In this climate Utah was a prize worthy of careful attention from both parties, as well as a national problem. Mormons made numerous overtures to the Cleveland administration,
including the formation of Democratic clubs and several attempts to secure the President's support for statehood. His response was almost plaintive: "I wish you out there would be
like the rest of us." [44] But Mormons *were* different, and, the
balance of political power notwithstanding, Cleveland and the
Democrats took no effective step toward Utah statehood. Sensing that the church was finally coming to bay, anti-Mormon
forces clamored for complete surrender. Polygamy and the temporal powers of the church had drawn the main fire until the late
1880s, but now there was talk of disfranchising all those who
believed in polygamy and of destroying the church. Under the
leadership of Fred T. Dubois in Idaho and E. S. Stover in
Arizona, "test oath bills" were passed to take the vote from all
Latter-day Saints in those territories. In 1887 Congress passed
the Edmunds–Tucker Act, which enlarged the power of the federal courts and strengthened the Utah Commission. More significantly, the Edmunds–Tucker Act dissolved the church as a corporate entity, placing its assets in the hands of receivers. The
election of Republican Benjamin Harrison as president in 1888
led to another round of anti-Mormon activity in Congress. One
result was the Cullom–Struble Bill, which, if passed, would
have totally stripped Mormons of their franchise.

Harassed in court and battered by partisan politics, even Mormons began to realize that this storm would not blow itself out
against the ramparts of the Wasatch or disappear in the wind
tunnels of national politics. Then, as if adding to the fury of the

44. Quoted in Brigham H. Roberts, *A Comprehensive History of the Church,* 6 vols.
(Salt Lake City: Deseret News Press, 1930), 6:152.

nation, came the devastation of 1887—the worst winter ever sustained in the Rocky Mountains and the blow of John Taylor's death in exile. Looking for a way out, young Utahns revitalized Democratic clubs. Others defected from the People's Party, voting with the Liberals first in Summit County, where the Park City mines gave outsiders extraordinary strength, and then in Ogden and Salt Lake City where the Liberals finally tasted victory in 1888 and 1889. In this case as when the politics of superior virtue first supplanted near-nationalism, the agents who met the world were the cutting edge of Mormon change. At the front of this rank were John T. Caine, John W. Young, Frank Cannon, John Henry Smith, and Franklin S. Richards. Keenly attuned to the absolute determination of Congress, they engineered the Scott Amendment to the Edmunds–Tucker Act, which asked for six months to abolish polygamy in Utah. When the amendment failed they became prime movers in the Constitutional Convention of 1887, where they wrote an anti-polygamy clause into Utah's sixth constitution. Also evidence of changing times was the People's Party caucus held before the 1888 session of the territorial assembly in recognition of the four Liberals who now sat in the assembly. In another remarkable display, the People's Party joined moderate Liberals in Salt Lake City to choose a fusion slate of city officers.

But change hinged ultimately upon Wilford Woodruff, who followed Taylor as president of the church. Still moved by visions of a victorious kingdom "independent of all earthly powers and clothed with legal as well as divine authority," Woodruff hestitated, seeking "the mind of the Lord," until October 4, 1890, when he announced the Manifesto.[45] This famed proclamation denied that the church was still solemnizing plural marriages and declared Woodruff's intent to submit to the law and influence all Mormons to do likewise. In keeping with the Manifesto's surrender, the territorial assembly made its sym-

45. Wilford Woodruff, November 24, 1887, as quoted in Lamar, *The Far Southwest,* p. 401; and Frank J. Cannon and Harvey J. O'Higgins, *Under the Prophet in Utah* (Boston: C. M. Clark Company, 1911), p. 98.

bolic peace with the world when it acted to provide free public schools, thus ending a division between Saint and gentile only slightly less bitter than that which polygamy had caused.

Accommodation followed surrender. The People's Party was abolished, and Mormons sought in the politics of pluralism the security that the politics of unity had denied them. The national parties assumed conventional roles in Utah. By a sleight of hand that can only be explained by the church's continuing influence and by a determination to associate with power, many—perhaps most—Mormons joined their former enemy, the Republican Party. Others remained loyal to the Democrats. Before the end of the century the nation would witness the spectacle of monolithic Mormonism flagellating itself over partisan questions.

Meantime Presidents Harrison and Cleveland extended amnesty to polygamists, and Congress at last passed an enabling act inviting Utah to submit a constitution for statehood. The fair climes of accommodation marked the ensuing convention. Apostle John Henry Smith, who more than any other church leader had tempered in the bitter politics of the years just past, presided. The delegates themselves, "a curious lot of former opponents," demonstrated partisan division and professional interests that obscured the retiring lines of the Mormon–gentile cleavage.[46] The constitution they produced was cautious and conservative but included a clause prohibiting polygamy. It was ratified in November 1895 and immediately submitted to Congress, where it was expedited with a rush. On January 4, 1896, Cleveland signed the statehood act, and Utah joined the Union.

A withdrawal from America that had begun a half-century before had ended. Mormons had fled to an area renowned for its alien character, where they had tried to create their own system. Nevertheless, America came to Utah with the Mormons. It came in the Mormon sense of mission that brought the gathering to focus on Utah. It came in the sense of destiny that mixed the American dream and visions of heaven on earth. And it came in the nationalizing influences of America. In time gentiles became its local agents. Sectionalism caught the Mormon dream of

46. Lamar, *The Far Southwest,* p. 407.

heaven on earth and for a few years gave it a specific context in time. Sectionalism also provided the scales upon which Mormon deviation was measured and by which national policy was meted out. Mormons who had undertaken to reform and give new meaning to the American experience were themselves formed by the broader community.

Utah had become a distinct American section, its political experience marking it quite as dramatically in the national consciousness as did the Great Basin geographically. Yet the long conflict had brought Utah's people to look to the nation and had made them truly American.

5

The Economics of Nationalism

AND the Magician said: 'Know that under this stone there is a treasure, which is destined to be yours, and which will make you richer than the greatest monarch in the world.' " [1] In a delightful chapter entitled "He Sold Aladdin's Lamp," Lafayette Hanchett, a mining man with a literary turn, wrote of Samuel Newhouse's fortunes in Utah mining. With a fine eye for irony, Hanchett chose the *Arabian Nights* passage to illustrate how Newhouse had developed worthless properties into fabled wealth in the Highland Boy and Boston Consolidated mines—now the Bingham open-pit copper mine—and by premature sale lost control of undreamed fortunes to the Utah Copper Company (later Kennecott) as technology and high finance swept a resource that produced more than one third of the copper used by the allied forces in World War II from local currents into the mainstream of the national economy. In a way the Newhouse story was Utah's story and his irony the state's irony, for under the stone of its low-grade ores and desert distances lay treasure beyond that of "the greatest monarch." Destined first for Mormon stewardship, Utah's resources had passed during the twenty-five years after 1870 to local developers like Newhouse and in the quarter-century following statehood had be-

---

1. Lafayette Hanchett, "He Sold Aladdin's Lamp," *The Old Sheriff and Other True Tales* (New York: Margent Press, 1937), p. 132.

come increasingly caught in national developments and markets. The Guggenheims and the "Standard Oil Crowd" had entered the field on one front; John L. Lewis, Mother Jones, and Joe Hill on another; and speculative agriculture on yet another. Filled with irony though the takeover was, the new did not obliterate the old but was superimposed upon it, making for an increasingly complex society in which nationalizing waves of technology, finance, and management elaborated the pioneering and local patterns of the Great Basin frontier.

In no phase of human endeavor was the mix of the new and the old more apparent than in mining. Vast companies were formed, fortunes were made, and in some localities the very face of the land was changed, but prospectors and hunch players continued to play an important part. Through the state's canyons and across its plateaus they probed and searched, guided by smatterings of geological knowledge, vague tales of Spanish diggings, legends of the Indian silver of Pish-la-ki, or mysteries like the Monument Valley treasure of James Merrick and Ernest Mitchell, who had been killed by Indians after making a rich strike in 1880.

Now and then booms turned hunches to burning passions. In 1889 Jack Summers, who had accompanied John Wesley Powell through the canyons of the Colorado River, stumbled on gold in Bromide Basin of the Henry Mountains. There Eagle City blossomed, then withered and died as the gold played out, leaving little more than tales of Spanish *arastras* and a local tradition of adventure.

When hunches turned to faith, prophets sometimes emerged, mixing secretiveness and suspicion with publicity and promotion as they attempted to launch booms and at the same time maintain control. Of such stuff was Marion Fowler, whose hunch was fixed upon Miner's Basin on the northwest slopes of the La Sal Mountains. Touting the Basin's virtues but watching all comers with a jaundiced eye, Fowler high-graded a little ore, gathered followers about him, struggled to open connections with the world via the Denver and Rio Grande Western Railroad, and faced down a decade-long Forest Service raid on his claim. At death his mantle passed to a nephew who maintained a lifelong vigil in expectation that his uncle's faith would finally yield dividends.

Somewhat different was A. K. Strouse, whose personal interest in a claim on the south slope of the Abajo Mountains quickly burned out, but whose story that a deceased daughter had shown him a "mine worked 300 years ago by the Spanish" created a magic that was quite as enduring as Marion Fowler's.[2] Strouse's "Dream Mine" attracted Walter Lyman and other Mormons from the little town of Blanding, who worked it for decades and drove a tunnel deep into the side of the Abajos. The mine produced no pay dirt of importance, but it nevertheless took a significant place in local development when the tunnel was adapted to convey water from the north drainage of the Abajos to satisfy Blanding's desperate need for domestic water.

Only less fired by the legendary was Cass Hite. On the trail of Merrick and Mitchell in the early 1880s, he inquired of their doings and the fabled Navajo mines with such persistence that Indians soon dubbed him Hosteen Pish-la-ki (Mr. Silver). Hoskaninni, a Monument Valley Navajo, successfully diverted Hite in 1883 when he called his attention to placer gold in the canyons of the Colorado River. For decades Hite was the region's inveterate promoter, turning everything to his consuming passion. His efforts finally overcame the remoteness of the region to create a modest boom in the 1890s. Sustained by publicity generated when Robert Brewster Stanton made a spectacular but unsuccessful attempt to open a railroad through the canyons of the Colorado, the river boom continued into the twentieth century. Canyonland gold proved to be so finely pulverized that all but the most primitive methods of recovery failed. At no time were more than a thousand men at work in the canyon, and few fortunes were made.

Nevertheless, the country was thoroughly explored and the way opened for a major assault on the river's treasures. Robert Stanton returned in the late 1890s, haunted by evidences of gold. Always one to think big, he planned to make one grand sluiceway of the entire stretch of the canyons from the commu-

2. *Emery County Progress*, December 16, 1900.

nity of Hite to Lee's Ferry in Arizona, and to bring giant barges to dredge its bottoms and sandbars. Backed by eastern capitalists, Stanton formed the Hoskaninni Company. By 1901 the first great dredge had been delivered at the Green River railhead and its parts dragged the dusty distance to the river and assembled a few miles downstream from Hall's Crossing. More than 100 feet long and powered by five gasoline engines, the huge machine made only two runs. The first reclaimed gold that Stanton valued at $30.15; the second, $36.80. Although the company had spent $100,000, the dredge was left to rust, a monument to the plateau environment's resistance to technology. It was ultimately engulfed as Lake Powell rose in the 1960s.

The lure of wealth from the earth attracted many to coal mining as well. Like the precious metals, coal produced a variety of responses, with pioneer wagon mines at one end of the spectrum and great corporate enterprises at the other. Located throughout the state's three major coal areas—Coalville, Carbon County, and Iron County—wagon mines supplied markets too small and too remote to attract large producers. In a 1902 survey of Utah's mountain ranges, Albert Potter, chief grazier for the Forest Service, found scores of the wagon mines, many of which had been worked for twenty years. Some were operated by one man alone, others by local businessmen to provide winter employment for sons and teams. In Iron County the Jones and Bullock Mine met Cedar City's needs and provided one of life's small routines, as teams and wagons pulled out of town at 4:30 each morning, harnesses jingling and iron wheels rattling on frozen ground. To make coal pay, petty entrepreneurs opened yards, worked to develop coking coal, promoted their properties in the local press, and generated electricity. Yet it was a rare wagon mine that did more than meet expenses and pay occasional wages.

At the other end of the spectrum was the Utah Fuel Company, a subsidiary of the Denver and Rio Grande Western Railroad. Accelerating its tracklaying in the early 1880s to claim the coal fields of eastern Utah before the Union Pacific could make them part of its fuel monopoly, the D&RG acquired the Winter Quarters and Pleasant Valley mines near Scofield in

1882 and in the years that followed took control of the Castle Gate and Sunnyside coking properties as well. By 1900 Utah Fuel's production topped a million tons and represented 90 percent of the state's output. Independent operators entered the field after 1906. Led by Charles N. Strevell of Independent Coal and Coke Company, Fred and Arthur Sweet of Standard Coal Company, and Jesse Knight of Spring Canyon Coal Company, they more than tripled Utah's production by 1912. By 1916 Utah Fuel's share of the market had dropped to 40 percent, but it gave ground stubbornly, cutting prices, holding property at gunpoint, and exploiting labor, as well as enjoying shipping rate advantages of "not less than 25 cents a ton." [3] Price and Helper grew as railroad centers, while elsewhere the mining camps of Latuda, Rains, Standardville, Spring Canyon, Wattis, Hiawatha, Kenilworth, and others took on the stone and frame homes, boarding houses, stores, and other vestments of company towns. Carbon County was created from Emery County in 1894 and reflected the new society and its coal mining interests.

As much a field for the hunch-player and prospector as Utah mining was, the trend during these years was to consolidation; at Park City, Mercur, and Bingham, big enterprises came increasingly to dominate the scene. Hunch and chance continued to play a significant role, but they now found better application in the fields of technological development and high finance.

At Park City hope lingered for silver. Prospectors talked confidently of a fabulously rich "Silver Belt" stretching along the peaks of the Wasatch, worked claims, lived frugally, and looked to the development of late-blooming mines like the Silver King. The Silver King was an appropriate vehicle for their hopes. Organized in 1892, it not only gained steadily during a generally disastrous decade for silver, but in the dominating influence of Thomas Kearns gave evidence that the little man could still make it big. Born in Canada, Kearns had early taken to the long roads of western mining. He touched base at Deadwood, Wyatt Earp's Tombstone, Utah's Tintic District,

---

3. Thomas G. Alexander, "From Dearth to Deluge: Utah's Coal Industry," *Utah Historical Quarterly* 31 (Summer 1963): 239.

and Pocatello, Idaho, before he finally put down at Park City in 1883. There he formed a lasting association with David Keith to develop the Mayflower properties and the Silver King Mining Company, which was incorporated at $3,000,000. A millionaire at thirty-eight, Kearns seemed to have unlimited horizons. He became United States Senator in 1901, made the *Salt Lake Tribune* his public voice, built a great mansion on Salt Lake City's South Temple Street, and turned to an increasingly diversified business career.

But as promising as were Kearns's horizons, the best prospects in Utah mining lay with Mercur and Bingham. For Mercur the years after 1890 brought new life. Developed as a silver district in the early 1870s by Lewis Greeley, it had enjoyed a time of excitement. Although the town of Lewiston clung tenatively to the south slopes of the Oquirrhs for a time, the mine played out entirely by 1880. Signs of gold powder in the area's low-grade ores were identified in 1883, but canny operators avoided the property on the assumption that gold so finely pulverized could not be profitably extracted. However, in 1890 the Mercur Gold Mining and Milling Company was organized by a group of Nebraskans led by John Dern and his son George H., later Utah's governor and Franklin D. Roosevelt's first Secretary of War. The "Nebraska Farmers" were saved by the timely introduction of the McArthur–Forrest cyanide process and their construction of America's first cyanide plant at Mercur in 1893. The process enabled them profitably to work ores containing as little as one-half ounce of gold per ton, restored Mercur's fortunes, and transformed the district's desolation. Pipelines were laid, railroads constructed, and a new town—called Utah's Johannesburg by imaginative promoters—was built on Lewiston's long-empty foundations.

Among those attracted by the upsurge was Joseph R. DeLamar. A "plunger" who headquartered in New York City, DeLamar had made his first fortune salvaging a derelict Dutch vessel. Now he operated throughout the Great Basin West in a strike-and-run pattern that picked up questionable properties, reorganized them, applied highly skilled management to put them in paying shape, and moved on while their buoyancy lasted. His freebooting methods led one writer to observe that had he lived in the "times of Great Elizabeth, he would have harried the Spanish Main, chased the heavily laden galleons and taken tribute of the conquistadors." [4] Utilizing the nation's first long-distance transmission of high-voltage power, DeLamar put the original Mercur mill out of business and by 1899 forced a merger with the Dern interests. In the fifteen years that followed, Mercur flourished, yielding a total of $18,000,000 before diminishing gold percentages made even the cyanide process unprofitable.

Meanwhile developments at Bingham Canyon took an even more important turn as lowgrade copper ores became Utah's greatest mining industry. Significant in a number of ways, Bingham's development shows the old merging into the new in most dramatic circumstances. The Bingham playoff revolved around two men and one of the nation's great financial powers—Enos Wall, Daniel Jackling, and the Guggenheim family.

Wall appears to have been the first to anticipate the potential of copper at Bingham. An inveterate hunch-player, he had much in common with the Marion Fowlers and the Cass Hites of Utah's mining frontier. Unlike them, he had done well in mining since he came to the territory in the 1860s with Alexander Toponce. He had acquired properties on both sides of Salt Lake Valley and at Silver Reef in Utah's Dixie, where the body of ore in his Kinner Mine was said to be so abundant that it went "straight down to hell." [5] But even such promising prospects had limits, and in 1880 Wall pulled out for Idaho, leaving behind an unmet payroll. In Idaho he managed mines for a group of Omaha investors, nettled other managers by supporting a strike for $4 wages, and was finally fired because of a crowd of "hangers on" who seemed to his employers "to toil not, neither do they spin." [6] Returning to Utah, he began to pick up

4. A. B. Parsons, *The Porphyry Coppers* (New York: American Institute of Mining and Metallurgical Engineers, 1933), p. 57.

5. From an account by Pat Murphy, foreman at the Kinner mine, in G. W. Barrett, "Mines, Miners and Mormons," *Idaho Yesterdays* 14 (Summer 1970): 6.

6. Barrett, "Mines, Miners and Mormons," p. 5.

abandoned properties at Bingham and Mercur. He sold the Mercur property and a silver-and-gold claim at Bingham at good profits, but he doggedly continued to expand his low-grade copper holdings—Wall rock, men in the know derisively called them.

During the 1890s he approached at least a half-dozen potential buyers. Some "praised the properties with faint damns." [7] More shared the appraisal of the *Engineering and Mining Journal* that the more of this type of ore a company had, the worse off it was. Among Wall's potential buyers was Joseph DeLamar, who had collected a remarkable set of managers and engineers around him, including men with experience all over the United States, Africa, and Mexico. Of particular note in the Bingham story was Daniel Jackling, a young metallurgist who managed DeLamar's cyanide mill at Mercur and now reported favorably on Wall's property. Adverse copper prices and the staggering costs of developing the volume necessary for profit led DeLamar to view Jackling's report of Wall's property with coolness. Although he ultimately exercised an option on one quarter of Wall's holding for $50,000, DeLamar never really lent his support to Bingham's development.

Jackling soon left DeLamar, but Bingham's copper mountain remained in his mind. In 1903 he launched the work of a lifetime in which he pioneered the application of technology, mass production, and big capital to low-grade copper ores. As his first step, Jackling formed the Utah Copper Company with Colorado associates, bought out DeLamar, and paid Wall more than a half-million dollars in stocks and cash. Wall retained a 20-percent interest in the company and sat as a director. Jackling then enlisted financial support from the Guggenheim family and built a mill at Magna and a smelter at Garfield, which on completion represented the world's largest copper-reducing facility. The company initiated open-pit mining, and by 1909 11 mammoth steam shovels, 21 locomotives, 145 dump cars, and 16 miles of railroad track gave the operation the necessary volume to make its low-grade ores profitable.

---

7. Parsons, *Porphyry Coppers,* p. 68.

In 1910, Utah Copper acquired the neighboring Boston Consolidated properties of Samuel Newhouse, thus gaining control of an entire mountain of ore. To exploit this resource, the company enlarged its mills and built the Bingham and Garfield Railroad and a huge steam-generating plant. In time the plant abandoned the noise and dirt of steam power for electricity as it continued to expand. By 1929 it had a milling capacity of 60,000 tons per day and had turned a mountain into a gigantic pit widely heralded as the "biggest thing that men have made." [8] Indeed, it may well have been "the greatest industrial sight on earth," as John D. Rockefeller declared during World War I.[9] By 1930 Utah Copper accounted for 50 percent of Salt Lake City's assessed valuation and 13 percent of the entire state's.

But for Enos Wall it was a dream gone wrong. From the first he had criticized Jackling's management. In opposition, as in development, he was untiring. He was also bitter and resourceful, fighting Jackling from his position on Utah Copper's board and, when expelled from there, in the courts, in the public press, and in a mining journal established specifically to oppose his enemy. Tough and influential though he was, Wall was guided by a dream quite as stubborn and unyielding as the hunches and hopes that had held Marion Fowler on the slopes of the La Sals. Mass production had supplanted the halcyon days of homespun invention and development by instinct, in which Wall had thrived best.

Significantly for Utah, even the practical genius of Jackling paled alongside the wealth of the Guggenheim family. Although they never participated in active management of the Utah Copper Company, the Guggenheims influenced major points of development. Their first invasion came in the financing of Utah Copper's early development after 1903. The assimilation of Boston Consolidated vastly strengthened the Guggenheim inter-

8. Parsons, *Porphyry Coppers*, p. 45.

9. H. J. O'Connors, *The Guggenheims: The Making of an American Dynasty* (New York: Coviei Freide, 1937), p. 290.

ests, as did the adjustments out of which Kennecott Copper emerged in 1915. Finally in 1936 Kennecott acquired all the property and assets of Utah Copper in what might be called a triumph of finance over technology. All told, Kennecott's takeover reflected an economy that had become "peripheral to the core economy of the nation rather than being the core of its own regional" system.[10] As such it was a symbol of change that was given an added dimension by the activities of working men and labor unions.

Utah was never the promised land for labor. Industry was slow to develop and, when it did, opposed organized labor with an extraordinary determination. The church had little in common with labor as a movement and complicated its development in a number of ways. National and regional labor agitation often adversely affected public opinion and stiffened resistance. On the other hand, labor activities elsewhere created hope among Utah workers, provided a fragmented philosophical framework in which they could function, taught them to expect progress, and offered a certain amount of organizational help. Thus prompted, Utah workers stirred themselves sufficiently to provide one of the state's significant themes during the turn-of-the-century decades.

Labor made little mark upon Utah society before 1890. Notwithstanding its interests in the crafts and in skilled workmen, the church was quick to identify unions as a threat. Violence and strife provoked deep fear among Mormon leaders, who denounced early activities of the Knights of Labor in Ogden as the conspiracies of secret combinations. Convinced that unionism was little more than the "selfishness of the poor," church leaders sometimes justified failure to pay workers in the name of building the kingdom and, in something of a paradox, aligned themselves with business and the Republican Party at a time when those very forces were actively opposing the church.[11]

Nevertheless, labor penetrated the territory. Various craft

---

10. Arrington, *From Wilderness to Empire*, p. 17.
11. Clark, *Messages of the First Presidency*, 2:262.

unions had first organized at Salt Lake City and Ogden in the
1850s. By 1889 they had loosely affiliated themselves in the
Utah Federated Trades and Labor Council, and their limited objectives and nonviolent methods had come to represent the main
thrust that labor developments in Utah would take. In Ogden the
railroad brotherhoods participated successfully in an 1884 strike;
the Knights of Labor talked the common cause of all workers,
yet ironically secured themselves by stirring up anti-Chinese
fears. At the mines and smelters, questions of pay and working
hours occasionally resulted in spontaneous organizations and violence. For example, efforts to limit the Saturday workday to
nine hours at Eureka collapsed when a ten-hour faction clashed
with their laboring brethren in 1873. An 1876 move on the part
of management to lengthen the working day from eight to
twelve hours at the Midvale smelters resulted in a situation in
which "the hands rebelled and were discharged." Six years
later two organizers at the Germania smelter "were arrested for
coercing other workers," whereupon their followers meekly
went back to work under the old terms.[12] At Pleasant Valley's
coal fields a visit from Stake President A. E. Smoot nipped a
strike in the bud, which suggests that the strikers may have been
Mormons. And in 1880 and 1881 unpaid miners at Silver Reef
seized Enos Wall at his Kinner mine, and workers at the Stor-
mond Company, confronted by a wage cutback, closed the mine
and ran its manager out of town. Wall escaped, and about forty
strikers were arrested, tried, fined $100, and sentenced to 100
days in jail. These were not auspicious beginnings. Events had
awakened strong anti-labor sentiments and defined a sharp gulf
between the craft unions and miners.

During the 1890s labor assumed more assertive patterns that
dominated it for the next three decades. Craft unions extended
their demands to include collective bargaining and closed shops.
When management responded with collective action and the
church charged that union methods interfered with "the divine
rights of human beings," many of the craft groups affiliated

12. *Salt Lake Tribune,* October 21, 1876; and *Deseret News Weekly,* October 22,
1882.

with the American Federation of Labor.[13] Efforts of the Independent Workingman's Party to make labor a political issue in 1890 foundered on the shoals of polygamy. The movement divided along Mormon–gentile lines but contributed to the passage of far-reaching constitutional provisions and to laws prohibiting the employment of women and children in underground mining and providing for an eight-hour day in mining and public works.

The economic distress and strikes of the mid-nineties also contributed significantly to the growing complexity of the Utah labor scene. The National Guard was used for the first time to deal with working men when an "industrial army" of unemployed men showed up in April 1894, en route from California to Washington to ask for public works programs. Within a few days workers formed an "Industrial Army of Utah" and by the end of the month they set off for the East, four hundred strong, part of a national movement that ended in failure and made 1894 "a year of jubilee" for tramps.[14] Out of this period of social unrest also came radical groups, who found in unionism a life-and-death struggle between labor and capital. Most important in the immediate sense was the Western Federation of Miners, which had its Utah beginnings in 1893 and enjoyed a period of resurgence after 1897, when it was organized in many of the silver and copper mines of the state.

The plight of Utah workers in turn-of-the-century years was not enviable—a fact most tragically apparent among coal miners who worked under the most adverse and dangerous conditions. On May 1, 1900, an explosion ripped through the Pleasant Valley Coal Company's Mine Number Four at Scofield. Highly combustible coal dust flashed through one mine and into another, leaving a terrible toll in its wake. Afterdamp—lethal gas that hung heavy in the poorly ventilated tunnels—struck down many who escaped the explosion, including would-be rescuers.

13. See Sheelwant Bapurao Pawar, "An Environmental Study of the Development of the Utah Labor Movement: 1860–1935," unpublished Ph.D. dissertation, University of Utah, 1968, p. 133.

14. *Salt Lake Tribune,* August 12, 1895.

When the stunned town had finished the count, it was apparent that 200 men and boys had been killed in the most tragic mining disaster the nation had experienced. As a folksong recounted, the Scofield Disaster was a family, as well as a civic, tragedy:

> Oh, mothers and wives of the miners,
> Who perished so suddenly there,
> Did you give them a loving embrace that morn,
> Did you bid them "Goodbye" with a prayer? [15]

Almost as if the Scofield blast had triggered it, Utah's labor relations entered a new time of complexity and conflict. Industry and business expanded dramatically, as did Utah's labor force. A tide of immigrants created social complications. The union movement, fed by national successes, mounting class-consciousness, and ideological developments, assumed new variety and vitality. The United Mine Workers penetrated the Utah coal fields in a meaningful way. The Western Federation of Miners stepped up its campaign in the metal mines, and after 1904 the Industrial Workers of the World agitated in both the coal fields and metals, as well as in construction and the various crafts. Erupting labor conflict in neighboring states—especially Colorado and Idaho—sent shock waves through the ranks of Utah labor, touching off latent tensions. Management's intransigent opposition to unions deepened and its capacity to fight back improved as managers combined in employer associations, manipulated public opinion, controlled courts, and adopted increasingly ruthless practices to control the work force. Continuing to feel that union activity was prompted by "tyranny and compulsion," the church regarded radical "efforts . . . to set labor against capital and make them natural enemies" as especially reprehensible. [16] Nevertheless the church was opposed "to the combination of capital to oppress and grind down labor"; and though its members provided a reservoir of conservatism from which strikebreakers and company guards could be drawn

15. From a folk ballad discovered by LaVerne J. Stallings and published in *Western Folklore* 18 (April 1959): 174–176.
16. *Deseret Evening News*, September 2, 1901.

throughout the entire period, Mormons may have been the largest single element in union rank and file.[17]

Labor was itself divided. On the one hand were the Industrial Workers of the World or Wobblies, who called for class war. At the other extreme were the urban affiliates of the American Federation of Labor, who saw matters in terms of group interests and "unionism pure and simple" and aimed at narrowly defined economic and social goals. Shifting in between were the Western Federation of Miners and the United Mine Workers.

A brief strike in 1900 at Scofield—an aftershock of the mine disaster—preceded a period of conflict in 1903–1904 that encompassed the coal fields throughout Carbon County. At stake were the right to organize and various other protests. Organizers from the United Mine Workers infiltrated company lines and formed unions at most of the camps. For a time the order of the day included parades and rousing speeches that assured workers that the company advocated "Calico . . . for you people and silk for us." [18] Although strikers flew an American flag upside down, "murdered" a company guard's cow, and notified strikebreakers "to be buying" coffins, the miners were restrained in their actions and union organizers took great pains to avoid violence.[19] The company based its public appeal on nativism and local sentiments. It made the most of the fact that many Italians were on strike and that outside organizers—"walking agents," they called them—were involved, and charged that the Utah strike had been called in sympathy for a larger Colorado strike. Union men were discharged and expelled from company towns. Half of them owned homes built on company land and sustained heavy losses for which they were apparently never compensated. Company gunmen and the National Guard patrolled Carbon County. In April 1904 a visit by Mother Jones, a colorful octogenarian called variously the miners' Joan of Arc and a "heartless, vicious creature," reawakened the excitement.[20]

17. *Deseret Evening News*, September 2, 1901.

18. *Salt Lake Herald*, December 11, 1903.

19. Quoted in Allen Kent Powell, "The 'Foreign Element' and the 1903–04 Carbon County Coal Miners' Strike," *Utah Historical Quarterly* 43 (Spring 1975): 130.

20. Powell, " 'Foreign Element,' " p. 146.

About 120 hapless Italians who protected Mother Jones from a comic-opera attempt to quarantine her for smallpox were arrested and railroaded in company-controlled courts until their keep seemed to outweigh the advantages of their prosecution.[21] Finally, as 1904 wore on, the excitement subsided. To the surprise of some of the boys who had toughed out the winter in Carbon County camps, the National Guard survived. In the mines it was business as usual. And tent colonies of displaced strikers dwindled as the Denver and Rio Grande provided penny-a-mile tickets for one-way passage. Labor had gained little, but the strike had established a precedent for union agitation that erupted now and again in the coalfields as short pay, the "padrone system" for contract labor, and national events prompted.

The padrone system led directly to a strike of some 5,000 workers at Bingham in the fall of 1912. Miners there were a polyglot collection of Japanese, Italians, Cornishmen, and newly arrived Greeks. Few Greeks spoke English, and most of them paid tribute to Leonidas Skliris, a labor czar who operated an empire that reached to Montana and Colorado from luxurious quarters in the Hotel Utah. Skliris became the major strike issue to his fellow Greeks, who resented his control over them and felt certain he was in league with the Utah Copper Company. In addition a pay raise and the right to organize were at stake, and Charles Moyer, national president of the Western Federation of Miners, worked desperately to turn the upheaval into a disciplined and lasting union. Utah Copper's Daniel Jackling utterly refused to recognize the union, denied that the padrone system existed, and imported thousands of strikebreakers from Mexico and elsewhere. Governor William Spry sent in the National Guard and otherwise worked to control the strike.

Although armed Cretans occupied canyon barricades and picket lines held for a time, odds against the strikers were overpowering. By December the strike had collapsed. The Federation was still unrecognized, and "alien labor" had suffered another setback in public opinion. The single product was nev-

21. *Deseret Evening News,* April 30, 1904.

ertheless important to labor. Skliris had lost his power, and the padrone system was in the open where labor could combat it more effectively.

The Utah labor scene was enlivened in the years after 1905 by the activities of the Industrial Workers of the World, whose organizers came to the state shortly after the new union was established. In the beginning IWW activities were confined mainly to the mines, where there was strong opposition. By 1913, however, the union had spread to heavy construction; in June about 1,200 men struck with little warning at five camps of the Utah Construction Company, which was pushing to complete a new Denver and Rio Grande track over Soldier's Summit. Strikers made a few demands, but the action folded almost as quickly as it had erupted. Utah Construction improved upon the nonrecognition policy of the Utah Copper and Utah Fuel companies when it not only refused to recognize the Wobblies but blandly announced that no strike existed. Many employees pulled out, unwilling to join the union or to be branded as scabs. Upwards of 150 Wobbly ringleaders were arrested, and Utah Construction hired replacements and continued its push on up the Summit.

Tensions still crackled throughout the radical movement, and organizers launched a series of "free speech" demonstrations in Salt Lake City during August. A "citizens' group" headed by an employee "of the Utah Copper Company in charge of deputy sheriffs at Bingham" disrupted the first of these, injuring the speaker, J. F. Morgan, a Wobbly organizer at the Utah Construction strike.[22] Six more men were injured in the ensuing melee, and the Wobblies were forced to abandon their "free speech" campaign.

But far and away the most notorious Wobbly episode in Utah history was the Joe Hill case. A Swedish immigrant of a radical turn who had a flare for poetry and song, Hill worked his way to San Pedro, California, lived in a Wobbly jungle called Happy Hollow for a time, and in 1912 moved to the Park City mines. He fell ill and during the winter of 1913–1914 recuperated at

22. *Salt Lake Tribune*, August 13, 1913.

Sandy, a suburb of Salt Lake City. In January 1914 grocer John G. Morrison and his son Arling were killed in an exchange of gunfire with two assailants, and Hill, who had a gunshot wound treated, was charged with murder. He was found guilty in a trial remarkable for Hill's refusal to explain his wound and the overwhelming but circumstantial nature of the evidence. During the trial, Hill became a Wobbly martyr and his case perhaps the most celebrated ever tried in Utah. Protest meetings and an avalanche of appeals and threats failed to change the verdict, and authorities prepared for Hill's execution. While Hill waited, both President Woodrow Wilson and the Swedish Consul applied pressure on Governor Spry, in the hope of a pardon. The attempts failed, and Hill, asserting he did not want to be found dead in Utah, was executed on November 19, 1915, and his body immediately shipped to "Big Bill" Haywood—himself a onetime Utahn—at Chicago. The following year Hill's ashes were scattered on every state but Utah in response to the doggerel rhyme of his last will: "My body . . . I would to ashes it reduce, and let the merry breeze blow, my dust to where some flowers grow." [23] The Joe Hill case revived all the old saws, including Mormon conspiracy, class warfare, and corrupt officials. While such charges had little factual basis, the case, as indeed the entire Wobbly experience in Utah, pointed up the state's essential conservatism and the impotence there of radical labor and its methods.

Even as the Hill action unfolded, events were moving Utah labor into a period of progress. The conservative affiliates of the AFL were in good repute, reaping the rewards of their general stability and the support the Federation gave the nation in World War I. In addition Utah went Democratic in 1916, electing Simon Bamberger governor and a full slate of Democratic officers. Following the trend that had enabled Woodrow Wilson to put together an unprecedented body of progressive legislation in 1913, the 12th Utah Legislature passed numerous liberal laws in

23. Joe Hill, "My Last Will," in *Songs of the Workers*, 29th ed. (Chicago: Industrial Workers of the World, 1956), p. 5.

1917, including several that served labor well. A state industrial commission was created, and in what has been termed the "Magna Carta" of Utah labor an "Act Bettering Conditions of Labor" made it "not unlawful for workmen and women to organize." [24] The law also limited the use of labor injunctions, permitted peaceful picketing, and implied legality for strikes. In the prosperity of the war years labor made rapid advances, although strikes did not meet with universal success.

But wartime gains were fragile. Encouraged by progress and insensitive to the whirlwind of opposition that the red scare of the postwar years would unleash, Utah's workingmen pushed for additional increases. Both the public and management reacted adversely. Strikes were repressed. Utah managers improved upon the old industrial alliances, now making them part of the so-called American Plan by which the open shop and company unions completely negated the advances of the war years. Ignoring the national temper, Utah coal miners joined the United Mine Workers in a nationwide strike in 1922. Nativism and class cleavage lent a special bitterness to the strike as "100 percent Americans" lashed out at Greeks and Italians. Several men were killed, the National Guard was mobilized in what was by then a well-rehearsed response, and bitter hatred toward immigrant groups was fanned. In time the strike ran its course, leaving labor prostrate. The postwar shift in sentiment appeared in legislation as early as 1919, when an anti-picketing law was passed, and again in 1923 in a right-to-work act that prohibited the closed shop and greatly weakened the position of organized labor.

Labor activities of the first quarter of the twentieth century ended much as they had begun—with a mining disaster. While the trials growing from the 1922 strike drew on, the Number Two Mine at Castle Gate exploded on March 8, 1924, killing 127 men. Left to shift for themselves were 417 dependents. Fifty of the dead were Greeks. Their widows keened "high-pitched dirges recounting extemporaneously the life and hopes

24. See Pawar, "Utah Labor Movement," pp. 330–332.

of the dead" and wore black "dresses, stockings and black Mother Hubbard caps for the rest of their lives." [25]

Their lament might well have been for labor. After a long, slow period of growth capped by the promise of the war years, events had forced the labor movement into a dormant period from which it would emerge only when New Deal legislation revived it in the 1930s.

In spite of increasing industrialization, the land remained the source of livelihood for most Utahns during the decades after 1890. Rural population exceeded urban until 1930, and agricultural workers led all other categories. Nevertheless, the general movement in Utah, as elsewhere, was away from the farm. A move from the self-sufficiency of Mormon farming to commercial agriculture foretold this trend.

Even in the years before 1890 forces creating change were numerous and insistent. Mining markets continued to expand, enabling farmers to make agriculture more a commercial enterprise and less a response to windfall opportunities. Rail transportation opened even broader markets. Wheat from Cache Valley—"Utah's granary"—sold in markets as remote as Liverpool, while San Francisco newspapers referred to S. W. Sears, manager of the Ogden ZCMI, as "Utah's Wheat King." [26]

Livestock led in the developing commercialism. The scope of livestock enterprises as well as the total number of animals increased dramatically. Mormon villagers pooled their animals in co-ops. Some ran large mountain dairy operations—one in northern Utah milked 700 cows and employed dozens of Danish milkmaids. Others organized sheep co-ops, some of which grew very large and became increasingly commercial. The Deseret Land and Livestock Company ultimately ran 65,000 head of sheep and owned 220,000 acres of land, an area comprising 3.7 percent of all privately owned property in the state in the 1930s.

25. Helen Zeese Papanikolas, *Toil and Rage in a New Land: The Greek Immigrants in Utah*, published as *Utah Historical Quarterly* 38 (Spring 1970): 177.

26. Tullidge's *Quarterly Magazine* 2 (1881): 228; parts of the section on agriculture have been revised from Charles S. Peterson, "The 'Americanization' of Utah's Agriculture," *Utah Historical Quarterly* 42 (Spring 1974): 108–125.

At Heber a cattle pool leased 76,000 acres on the Ute Reservation, and cattlemen at Bluff pooled their stock in the mid-1880s and competed so vigorously for ranges already claimed by gentile stockmen that they became known as the "Bluff Tigers." [27] For years Mormon stockmen continued to prefer village life over ranching. This inclination combined with the easy yield of virgin ranges to create great prosperity in turn-of-the-century "cow towns." Bluff, for example, boasted with some justification that it was the richest town per capita west of the Mississippi. The livestock boom also financed the construction of thousands of substantial brick and stone houses, many of which continue to grace the state's village landscape. After 1900 the co-ops tended to become partnerships or companies, and larger stockmen left the villages to commute between ranches and commercial centers. Ranges adjacent to the settled valleys had become overstocked, and by the late 1870s cattlemen like the Bennions of Salt Lake and Skull valleys drove large herds into the canyons and breaks of the San Rafael and other rough country. Thousands of "Utah cows" were also trailed to Arizona, where they were traded for town sites and became the foundation stock of John W. Young's Arizona Livestock Company, which ran 30,000 head on the San Francisco Mountains by 1885.

Simultaneously, cattle came into Utah from several directions. Texas cattle were trailed through the territory, but Utah rarely was their destination. Exceptions include Frank Whitmore's longhorns, which, crossed with native Devon–Shorthorn mixes in the late 1860s, produced oxen much sought for their walking gaits; and the Elk Company's pinch-hipped Texans, which produced generations of "runnygades" and spawned a colorful forklore of wild cow stories in southeastern Utah.[28] In the latter locality small cattlemen moved onto virgin ranges in the late 1870s and early 1880s; but they sold out by the mid-1880s to the Pittsburg Cattle Company at La Sal and to the

---

27. John Riis, *Ranger Trails* (Richmond: The Dietz Press, 1937), p. 51.

28. Karl Young, "Wild Cows of the San Juan," *Utah Historical Quarterly* 32 (Summer 1964): 250–267.

Carlisles on the Abajo Mountains, who ran large outfits for a decade or so before selling out in turn to Mormon stockmen. Preston Nutter turned quick profits on cattle bought in Great Basin settlements and grazed on the plateaus and canyon country between the Colorado and Green rivers. He picked the best from the entire region as he calved on the Arizona Strip south of St. George, trailed north, and fattened his steers in the Nine Mile and Strawberry country between Price and Vernal. In the northwest, what may have been Utah's largest cattle operation was established during the national ranching boom of the early 1880s by a son of Charles Crocker of Central Pacific railroad fame. Young Crocker was just getting started on the railroad lands north of the Great Salt Lake with upwards of 45,000 head when the bitter winter of 1887 killed half his stock and led him to quit the business. After the turn of the century, outfits like Nutter's and the Ireland Land and Cattle Company dominated vast tracts of government land while younger men like A. J. Scroup and Charlie Redd survived poor grazing conditions, vacillating markets, Forest Service cuts, and hard times between the early 1920s and World War II to become major figures in the ranching business.

While Utah's cattle industry was impressive, it lagged behind that of neighboring states. By contrast, the growth in the sheep industry was remarkable. More than a million head ranged the state in 1889, and ten years later the number had quadrupled. To some degree this was the business of transients like F. B. Saunders, who bought and sold stock but also trailed sheep over vast parts of the state in quest of good grazing. Farmers with land adjacent to mountain ranges also found sheep profitable.

Utahns learned the rudiments of sheep management by hit and miss. Important among their discoveries was the fact that the state's drought-wracked deserts had adequate precipitation to make them ideal winter pastures for sheep, which ate snow for moisture and thrived on desert brush. Driveways extended to deserts southwest of the Salt Lake and in southeastern Utah, and into neighboring states. The economy of entire counties came to rest on sheep, and men and boys of the turn-of-the-century generation found their best opportunities for employment and advancement in the sheep business. State law paid bonuses for upgrading stock, and congressmen listened attentively when sheepmen spoke. Although progress in improving strains was evident from the first, special credit must go to John H. Seeley of Mt. Pleasant, who dominated Utah's purebred sheep business before 1920. Seeley procured breeding stock from Ohio, France, and Russia and provided foundation animals for Rambouillet herds throughout America and in Russia and Japan. As elsewhere, sheep suffered from an adverse image and were blamed for a wide variety of ills. In the first two decades of the twentieth century, poor markets and Forest Service grazing restrictions led to reduction in numbers only less dramatic than growth had been in the 1890s.

After 1890 other sectors of agriculture experienced a similar change from self-sufficiency to commercialism. Underlying the entire process was the shift from a land business based on Mormon stewardship to one of commercialism and speculation. In this new situation farm acreages increased sharply from 1.3 million acres to 4.1 million in the 1890s. Improved farmlands nearly doubled, and irrigated acreage increased by 132 percent. The upward thrust slackened during the next decade but still resulted in an increase of 79 percent in improved land and saw nearly 10 percent of the total area of Utah claimed for farming by 1910, a remarkable statistic in view of the fact that estimates of arable land rarely exceeded 4 or 5 percent. But the land boom continued, with settlers entering an average of 575,000 new acres each year between 1909 and 1918.

Behind this expansion were two land developments that altered the physical as well as the social forms of Utah agriculture. The first, federal land entry, had been a factor since 1869 when the government opened federal lands (all of Utah until that time) for legal entry. Holders of small village farms were finally able to get legal titles, and the physical form of Utah's land pattern underwent a marked change. The new homestead farms were larger and located on highline canals and along section lines away from the farm villages, reducing the near monopoly the older pattern had once held on the landscape. A typically

American system of distribution based on federal land provisions and speculation had been superimposed upon the pioneer pattern.

The second great development was dry farming. In some degree farmers blundered into dry farming, but it was also the product of the more expansive spirit of the 1890s. Folklore suggests that Brigham Young predicted that wheatfields would someday cover the benches of the territory. No one knows whether his prediction rested on the Mormon assumption that God would transform the elements or whether he anticipated new methods, including dry farming. But it is clear that for several decades most Utahns were convinced that irrigation was essential. Indeed, the first successful dry farming experiences were sometimes met with disbelief. It is said David Broadhead of Juab County was jailed for perjury when he took oath he had raised wheat without irrigation on his homestead. Broadhead apparently regained his freedom, as he later proved up on the land and fittingly named it Perjury Farm.

Investigations at the Utah Agricultural College in Logan led to the establishment of the science of arid farming and to the creation of six experimental farms spanning the state by 1905. Under the inspiration of John A. Widtsoe, president of the Agricultural College, the movement worked out the techniques of dry farming, applied capital and technology, and attracted thousands of people to its banner. One of these was Will Brooks. Educated at the Agricultural College in the days of Widtsoe's greatest enthusiasm, Brooks ramrodded a crew for the Utah Arid Farm Company, a commercial enterprise that took up 8,000 acres in Juab County. The following year he moved to San Juan County, an El Dorado of the new life, where he homesteaded and took desert entry on several hundred acres, managed the college's experimental farm, entered the livestock business, opened a store, and taught school.

Pierce Hardman of Cache Valley also made a successful living at dry farming. Looking far and wide on Cache Valley's West Side, Hardman found no farming opportunity and finally followed his brother to Arbon Valley near the Utah-Idaho border in 1914, where he entered a dry-farm homestead. He built a cabin with dirt floor and roof and was well on his way toward proving up when he was drafted into World War I. On his return he purchased an additional 320 acres with a house, a windmill, and a chicken coop. Later he acquired more land, until he had well over a section. Without tree or flower to ease the starkness of his wheat lands, he spent the years working early and late, tending his horses summer and winter, playing baseball on summer Saturdays, entertaining fretful children through snowbound winters, and contemplating with pride that he was making it pay. Finally, when tractors liberated him from winter care of horses and his children required higher education, he bought a home in Logan and commuted. During his lifetime he and his kind had created a landscape of isolation, lived in it, and left it to erode.

At the heart of the new commercialism were great land and water development projects. Many of these began in the late 1880s and came full cycle after 1890, adding a patently speculative element to the land boom. None gave brighter prospects than did the Bear River Canal project. Bear River promoters put together a complex scheme which included eastern capital, modern technology, diversion of the Bear River, and railroad grant lands. The project built two great canal systems, conducted promotional campaigns in Utah and the Midwest, sold the area as a vast orchard region, and offered municipal and irrigation waters as well as electricity to communities as far south as Ogden. Unfortunately many of the commercial developments failed in the face of natural problems too great for their economic resources.

Not surprisingly, debt provided another index of changing times. Under the old order, most farmers worked their small farms without money. One pioneer illustrated the situation when he recorded in his diary, "in these parts . . . prosperity prevails—except in money matters." [29] The limited use of cash and credit is apparent in the extremely low level of mortgaged farms throughout the territorial period. Church president Wil-

29. "Journal of Levi Mathers Savage," ed. Ruth S. Hilton, mimeographed (Brigham Young University, n.d.), p. 46.

ford Woodruff and Heber M. Wells, Utah's first state governor, cited this enviable record to separate irrigation congresses during the 1890s. But even as they spoke, commercialism had begun to alter the mortgage pattern. In 1890 only 5 percent of Utah farms were encumbered. By 1896 the number had doubled. By 1900 it had doubled again, a fourfold increase in mortgages in ten years. Examined against the surge in total farm acres, this may not have been excessive, but once started, the trend continued. In 1910 25 percent of all farms were mortgaged, and by 1920 the figure had risen to 48 percent.

Crop patterns also underwent a marked change. Markets for sugar beets, dairy products, wheat, truck crops, and fruit all were found far beyond the state boundaries. Sugar beets became one of the most viable elements in the agricultural picture and an integral part of rural life. In an attempt to exploit the new commercialism for its members, the church sponsored construction of a sugar plant at Lehi, Utah County, in the early 1890s at a cost of $400,000. After a slow beginning complicated by inadequate funds and crop problems, the Lehi plant began to pay after 1896. By the end of the century it was processing 36,000 tons of beets per season and buying beets from 600 farmers. In 1903 a million-dollar plant was constructed at Garland in Bear River Valley and a number of competing companies erected factories at Ogden, Logan, and Lewiston and in neighboring Idaho. Most of these were consolidated in 1907 under the Utah-Idaho Sugar Company, a $13 million combination. By 1917 Utah was producing sugar worth $11 million—a sum that increased to $28 million in 1920, making sugar second only to metals in Utah manufacturing.

Sugar beets provided farmers with a means of converting family labor to cash, and by 1917 no fewer than 9,000 farms raised them. Beets rounded out slack seasons and provided feed supplements for livestock. Generations of young people grew up in the beet fields, planting, thinning, hoeing, and topping, while parents made Christmas cash during sugar-manufacturing campaigns. The clockwork of beets determined school vacations and local holidays. Towns lived for months in the scorched air of processing and seemed never free of the stench of beet pulp. Thus sugar beets not only provided entree to national markets for Utah but permeated its very air and became inextricably intermixed with the state's culture.

Another industry that showed great promise in the turn-of-the-century years was the orchard business. Interest in horticulture was not new. Early settlers had planted orchards and berries almost immediately. Thousands of family orchards soon graced the territory and fruit was bartered locally and peddled at army installations and mining towns and to immigrants. Nurseries flourished, and areas of suitable climate and soil were located. But pioneer orchards were not kept up. Frost-free belts proved to be few in number. Blight and pests struck, and by 1890 few boasted about Utah fruit. Then with the commercial developments of the 1890s fruit was hailed as a "Cinderella" crop. Great irrigation projects were promoted on its prospects. Small farmers planted orchards, organized orchard associations, and sent delegations to study fruit-bearing regions. Typical was Cache Valley, where orchard products were valued at $3,204 in 1890 and $64,432 in 1910 and reached a peak near $200,000 in 1920. Then as trees came into production it was discovered that Utah fruit competed poorly on national markets. Distance and late seasons interfered. Fruit shipped to the Midwest often arrived late and was dumped, leaving farmers with nothing to show. Sobered, hundreds of orchard men turned elsewhere. Pulling as many as 140,000 trees a year, they reduced orchard acreage drastically between 1912 and 1916.

Farmers were uneasy in this new environment and responded quickly—often too quickly—to any prospect of profit. Indeed an almost frantic quest took place, as many farmers changed from hay to berries, to apples, to peaches, and from wheat to beets, to carrots or peas, to dairy cows and to poultry, and sometimes repeated the process totally or in part. As the search for markets went on, change became the common denominator. Farming was still a rural, slow-paced way of life. Thrift, home gardening, a cow, and a few chickens still remained. But under the new conditions such practices added up to temporary relief, not to an acceptable way of living, and an almost desperate quest for profits dominated farm life. This was especially true after 1920 as agriculture entered a prolonged period of depression.

In farming, as in the state's economy generally, institutions dedicated to preserving an independent Mormon commonwealth had accommodated themselves to national influences. After 1890 economic development came to resemble patterns elsewhere in the West. Competitive capitalism triumphed. Utah's fortunes depended upon markets and control centers far beyond its confines. Absentee ownership was common. The state depended upon the export of metals, wool, and a few other unstable raw materials while it imported most of its consumer goods. Although it felt national labor influences, Utah lacked both the economic vigor and climate of social liberalism in which organized labor could flourish. All told, the economic picture in the early years of this century fell short of the expectations Utahns entertained for it in the years after statehood.

6

Other Utahs

$\mathcal{S}$ TAND at the rim of the Great Basin or in the heart of Salt Lake City or among Utah's northern European majority. Look outward from any of these vantage points and one sees "other Utahs." At Soldier's Summit or elsewhere on the Great Basin's rim one looks out to the broken country of the Colorado Plateau. In Salt Lake City lies the heart of metropolitan Utah; outward is the world of village, mining camp, and ranch. Yankees, British, and Scandinavians account for most of the Mormon–gentile majority; beyond stand the files of latecomers—immigrants from southern Europe, the Orient, Mexico, and elsewhere. Prominent are the Great Basin, Salt Lake City, and Utah's northern European majority. Contrasted are Plateau, rural countryside, and ethnic minority—"other Utahs." In its way each involves its own duality and each constitutes a countervailing element in the Utah experience. The Colorado Plateau stands in juxtaposition to the Great Basin, the city to the countryside, and ethnic minorities to the Mormon–gentile majority. Each has been instrumental in moving the state into the mainstream of national life.

It is easy to understand why the "other Utahs" have often been obscured by the shadow of urban development along the Wasatch. Salt Lake City existed before there really was a rural Utah. From the first, strong urbanizing influences contributed to its dominance. Utah immigrants have always had an urban turn.

133

Rootstock Mormons hailed from New England and New York, America's most urbanized region. To this was added their experience at Nauvoo, the largest city in Illinois by 1844, while the "City of Zion" ideal exerted an urbanizing influence until at least 1900. Abroad the gospel's net gathered converts of a distinctly urban cast—especially the tens of thousands from Great Britain, most of whom came from industrial centers.

But the Mormon gathering was only one dimension of the city's strength. Political activity was concentrated there during the long Mormon conflict. After 1870 the city became increasingly important as a distribution center, with almost all imports and many exports passing through it. Banks developed slowly, although several were established after 1870. Some failed in the Panic of 1873, but Walker Brothers and others continued to extend their business, providing support for shaky local banks as well as financing businesses and farms throughout the state. Mineral deposits at Bingham, Alta, Park City, and Tooele—all within a forty-mile radius of the city—concentrated mining's development at Salt Lake City as at no other regional capital of the West. Streetcar systems first drawn by horse and after 1890 powered electrically extended through Salt Lake City's business district and suburbs. By the early decades of this century the Wasatch Front was tied together from Springville to the Idaho border, as Simon Bamberger and David Eccles took the lead in building more miles of interurban railroads than existed in all other mountain states combined. Electricity became available by 1880 as a myriad of competing power and light companies utilized Utah's ample coal and water power, meeting needs first in Salt Lake City and Ogden and then broadening to include Provo and Logan and all intervening communities.

Transportation too tended to emphasize the importance of the Wasatch metropolis. Travel conditions in Weber Canyon had sent the first migration to Salt Lake City's site. Other pioneer developments, including the opening of the California Corridor, continued that trend. The transcontinental railroad built its line north of the Great Salt Lake, making Ogden the "junction city," and for a time Ogden controlled through traffic as well as northern Utah. Rather than being a "geographical rebuke" to

Salt Lake City, however, Ogden's emergence after 1869 was more as a twin city than as a serious challenge.[1] Turn-of-the-century developments continued to emphasize the twin-cities relationship of the two railroad centers as the Oregon Short Line and the Lucin Cutoff extended from Ogden and the Western Pacific and Los Angeles and Salt Lake railroads bolstered Salt Lake City's role. By the 1930s the freight tonnage moved through Utah greatly exceeded that of transcontinental lines to the north and south, although southern lines carried more passengers. Railroads became the biggest single employer in the two cities.

Ogden did not share the same prominence where highways were concerned. "Like the legs of a spider," eight roads led to Salt Lake City by 1930: three from the east, three from the Pacific Coast, and two from Arizona and Montana.[2] By World War II they carried far more freight and passengers than did railroads.

Culture too, blessed Salt Lake City. Its Salt Lake Theater was long a landmark. Publishing focused there, with the *Salt Lake Tribune,* the *Deseret News,* and the *Salt Lake Telegram* accounting for 84 percent of the daily circulation in Utah and distributing 50,000 papers within the city and 70,000 elsewhere by the 1930s. During this period the percentage of the state's total population served by the *Tribune* was exceeded only by dailies in states of limited area such as Delaware, Rhode Island, and Maryland. Virtually all of Utah's magazines were published at Salt Lake City as well. Mormon periodicals had a combined circulation of 85,000 by the 1930s, while the *Utah Farmer, Irrigation Age,* and the *National Woolgrower* together with the *Western Mineral Survey* and various other special-interest publications were or had been published there.

Only in education was Salt Lake City's predominance limited by early developments elsewhere in Utah. At Salt Lake the University of Deseret had little more than a nominal existence for

---

1. Chauncey D. Harris, *Salt Lake City, A Regional Capitol,* private edition (Chicago: University of Chicago, 1940), p. 109.

2. Harris, *Salt Lake City,* p. 52.

years before coming to new life as the University of Utah under John R. Park's presidency after 1898. By the end of World War I the University enjoyed an enrollment of 4,100 students and boasted schools of medicine, law, engineering, and mining as well as a broad and varied offering in the liberal arts. In 1897 the Presbyterian Church started Westminster College, which later became an interdenominational institution. In Provo Brigham Young Academy was established in 1875 and under the leadership of Karl G. Maeser attracted an increasing enrollment by 1900. At Logan Brigham Young College functioned until 1925 and the Utah State Agricultural College became the state's land-grant school after 1888.

Various other private and church schools appeared after 1870. Coming to Utah in 1873, the Reverend Lawrence Scanlon of the Roman Catholic Church instituted St. Mary's Academy, All Hallows College, and St. Ann's Orphanage in Salt Lake City and Sacred Heart Academy in Ogden. Protestant mission schools and academies were also established to meet educational needs resulting from Mormon–gentile conflict over control of educational policy. With the easing of the polygamy question after 1890, something of an educational renaissance took place. The Mormon Church opened academies at regional headquarters towns and gave its full support to public education. A generation of men and women inspired by Park, Scanlon, Maeser, and John A. Widtsoe carried the benefits of education to communities long denied its benefits. Advocates of a new gospel, they exercised an influence scarcely less important than business and religion and contributed to a steady procession of students to Utah's colleges and to out-of-state graduate schools. Another evidence of the high hopes placed in education in the years after the turn of the century was the appointment of Mormon scientist-educators James E. Talmage and John A. Widtsoe to the Quorum of the Twelve Apostles, where they enjoyed prestige and power rarely shared by educators when church leadership became more aware of education's challenges.

The reach of education to the state's rural areas points up the fact that to understand Utah one must go beyond Salt Lake and the metropolitan region in many directions. Standing-up Country; Utah's Dixie; Uinta Basin; Canyonlands: these are place names for the Colorado Plateau which lies not only beyond Salt Lake City but beyond the Great Basin itself. For decades the Colorado Plateau was little appreciated, and to this day many Utahns view its potentials only in terms of its contributions to the state's metropolitan areas. The result has been the development of a different Utah—one to which Indians were removed, from which water was diverted, and into which livestock and mining frontiers extended from five adjacent states. It was a Utah in which the Mormon question was muted and where ethnic and racial minorities played a more important role and a Utah in which solitude and grandeur have finally come to their own.

With the exception of Utah's Dixie, which lay on the California Corridor, the Plateau country was a hinterland to pioneer Mormons—a "vast contiguity of waste . . . valueless excepting for nomadic purposes, hunting grounds for Indians and to hold the world together." [3] A brief and abortive attempt was made in 1855 to establish the Elk Mountain Mission at Moab. Determined efforts to hold the southwest corner of Wyoming failed. Otherwise the plateau half of Utah long lay beyond the perimeters of Mormon Country. When attention did turn that way, it was as the byproduct of Mormon migration to other states and as a pre-emptive response to invasion from beyond Utah's borders.

Settlement passed over the Wasatch Plateau into eastern Utah's Castle Valley after 1880. Directed—according to Castle Valley tradition—by church calls posted in the ward chapels of Sanpete Valley, the literate migrated, leaving their nonreading brethren behind. At Moab and Vernal independent Mormons joined wandering gentiles to create chest-thumping outward-looking communities, which found their interests in an expansive economy and their heroes among those who became wealthy and among the cowboys and badmen in which the Colorado Plateau abounded. In a last colonizing mission, Mormons who were sent to settle Bluff on the San Juan River turned di-

3. *Deseret News*, September 25, 1861.

saster to victory in the famed Hole-in-the-Rock trek through the
canyonlands. Later they staved off starvation as the river
washed away their tiny parcel of farmground, and finally found
a passing prosperity in livestock. Unlike Moab, Bluff and its
daughter communities looked inward. Thrice cleansed—once in
the waters of baptism, once by the spirit, and once at the Hole-
in-the-Rock—they found their deepest meanings in the mission
to claim the San Juan region for the church. Their closest associations were in the pioneer brotherhood, and their heroes in the
persons of Benjamin Perkins, who had blasted the road across
the canyons, and in Bishop Jens Nielsen, who persisted at
Bluff, vowing he would never leave until carried to the town's
hilltop graveyard.

Settlers were not the first occupants of the Plateau. They invaded a wonderland of ancient Anasazi cultures whose ruins
hang high against canyon walls or lie in miles of brush-grown
mounds along the twisting bottoms of Montezuma Creek and
other desert watercourses. The first modern invaders took casual
note of the ancient communities that have come to be known as
Hovenweep, Pancho House, and Fourteen Windows House. In
time men of science classified the Anasazi according to location
and lifestyle as the Fremont, Mesa Verde, Kayenta, and Virgin
River cultures. From beginnings in the centuries after Christ,
these people developed an agricultural civilization that disappeared suddenly around 1300 A.D. Thereafter the forefathers to
the various Paiute, Ute, and Navajo stocks continued to follow
primitive patterns until after 1800, when the acquisition of the
horse and opening of the Old Spanish Trail brought change.

After the Old Spanish Trail's brief day, the plateau country
was subjected to a period of reconnaissance and survey. To tie
California to the nation, Congress initiated a series of railroad
surveys in 1853. One of them under Lt. John W. Gunnison and
a related independent expedition led by John C. Frémont
crossed the Colorado Plateau. Later, during the Utah War, efforts to open southern routes into Utah resulted in an exploration
of the Colorado River by Lt. Joseph C. Ives and an effort to
reopen the Old Spanish Trail by Capt. John N. Macomb. After
the Civil War three great western surveys also worked the

Colorado Plateau. In these the Utah work of Ferdinand V. Hayden and George M. Wheeler was overshadowed by the monumental achievements of John Wesley Powell. After much-publicized explorations of the canyons of the Green and Colorado rivers in 1869 and 1871, Powell conducted a reconnaissance of the Plateau which was not completed until 1879 and supervised the publication of ground-breaking works in geology by G. K. Gilbert and Clarence E. Dutton. The photography of Jack Hillers, the paintings and sketches of Thomas Moran and William Henry Holmes, and the fine descriptive writing of Frederick Dellenbaugh were early whispers of what grew to be a loud acclaim for the region's beauty. Powell himself generalized brilliantly about the character of plateau geology and, in his *Report on the Arid Lands of the United States, With a More Detailed Account of the Lands of Utah,* advanced a theory for resource utilization in the arid West and proposed drastic reforms in the public land laws that pertained to such regions.

Although the Colorado Plateau attracted geologists and other scientists, the public tended to see it as Utah's "great American desert" where Indians could be isolated at little or no cost to whites. Abraham Lincoln created an Indian reservation in its Uinta Basin in 1861. This action was followed in 1865 by treaty arrangements to remove all Utes from the Great Basin, which triggered Utah's Black Hawk War of the mid-1860s. An Indian agency was established in 1868 and the Uintah Utes were attached to it. White River and Uncompaghre Utes were also moved to the Uintah Reservation in the 1880s as result of the Meeker Massacre and vigorous Indian removal efforts in Colorado. In the years that followed, the Utes experienced the general misfortunes of Indian administration. In 1895, 1390 individual land allotments were made, totaling 103,205 acres. Two years later the Uintah Forest Reserve was created with a loss of over a million acres to the reservation, and in 1905 an additional million acres were taken for white homesteading.

Meanwhile the southeast portion of the Colorado Plateau had become a catchall for Indians displaced by advancing whites. When Anglo-Americans arrived, Utes dominated the area. As time passed they hunted the La Sal and Abajo mountains and

moved restlessly between the Uintah Reservation and southern
Colorado. Prompted by confused federal policy and Indian removal pressures, the entire tribe left Colorado's Southern Ute
Reservation and during the winter of 1894 appeared in San Juan
County, where they suffered from cold and hunger while whites
determined they had to return to Colorado. Navajos, too, came
and went. After 1865 their occupation south of the San Juan
River took on permanent characteristics when Hoskaninni and
others hid in Monument Valley during Kit Carson's Navajo
campaigns. In 1884 President Chester Arthur made Utah south
of the San Juan River part of the Navajo Reservation. Later the
Aneth extension north of the river was added. A small population of Paiutes also occupied Utah's Four Corners area. Of un-
certain lineage, they were rarely distinguished from Utes but
had connections with the Paiutes of western Utah. Although the
southeast part of the state was not one of the nation's great bat-
tlefields, few areas suffered a more protracted history of friction
between Indians and whites. The Pinhook Battle of 1881, the
Monument Valley killings in 1881 and 1884, the Abajo Mountain and White Canyon skirmishes of 1884 and 1887, and the
twentieth-century escapades of Polk and Posey—or, as Forbes
Parkhill has called them, "the last of the Indian Wars"—
marked four decades of nagging discord.[4]

Even more than history, nature has set Utah's Colorado Plateau apart. Not only is it colorful, remote, and romantic, but in
it all time is joined. Man is part of the eons that have gone
before as he views its canyons and gorges and contemplates its
geology. Indeed a grand time tunnel exists, progressing from
geological epochs out-of-mind, to the age of reptiles, to the
prehistory of the Anasazi, to a hint of Spanish influence in place
names, to pioneer and frontier doings, and finally to man of
today. Here man is in perspective. It is a land of time enough.
Moreover it is a land of space and solitude—solitude that exerts
much the same pull that drew anchorite monks to the banks of
the Nile or Christ to the desert for reflection and fasting. In it

   4. Forbes Parkhill, *The Last of the Indian Wars* (New York: Crowell-Collier Publishing Co., 1962).

the mystical beats strong, imponderables lie easy, and man's soul is rejuvenated.

The appeal of the Colorado Plateau's other Utah has grown from the recognition of a few to become the heritage of a nation. Pioneers viewed it with a pragmatic mix of antipathy and awe. Powell found it a geological mother lode where the bosom of the earth lay open, revealing the moods and processes from which life had risen. And a small but influential fraternity of archeologists, geologists, Indian traders, and river runners dramatized its romance and color. Discovered, accepted, then promoted, the Colorado Plateau boasted ten of Utah's twelve national parks and monuments by 1970. The parks and monuments themselves reveal the triple influence of scenery, prehistory, and geology. Zion National Park, for example, was recognized from the first for the magnificence of its scenery and was for years called Joseph's Glory after one pioneer promoter. Not untypical were the words of Frederick Dellenbaugh as he undertook to describe the Great White Throne in Zion's Canyon: "Niagara," he wrote, "has the beauty of energy; the Grand Canyon of immensity; the Yellowstone of singularity; the Yosemite of altitude; the ocean of power; *this Great Temple, of eternity*." [5] At Hovenweep National Monument it was prehistory that kindled excitement. First discovered in 1854, Hovenweep attracted the admiration of F. V. Hayden's surveyors in the 1870s and was thoroughly studied by the Archaelogical Institute of America in 1907. In 1922 J. Walter Fewkes, of the Bureau of American Ethnology, became obsessed with Hovenweep's towers and succeeded in having five sites on the Utah-Colorado border set apart as a monument the following year. On the other hand, the Uinta Basin's Dinosaur National Monument provides an open book for the study of natural history and geology. Earl Douglass, a man with a yen for the badlands and an itch to know, discovered the site in 1909. His excavation of some 350 tons of dinosaur fossils for the Carnegie Museum attracted national attention and resulted in the site's designation as a national monument. In addition to its giant fossils, Dinosaur Monument provides one of the world's best opportunities to ponder the vastness of time, as its eroded canyons encompass an even greater time span than does the Grand Canyon.

The plateau country's magic has also been good business. The potential of natural wonders to put Utah on the map and fill its tills with tourist money has been an element in park promotion since Utah artist H. L. A. Culmer and Salt Lake City Commercial Club President Edwin F. Holmes first dramatized the Natural Bridges by a trip to explore, photograph, and paint the new-found wonders in 1905. Possibly no factor was more important in the development of highways from north to south than was interest in southern Utah's parks and in their economic exploitation. Chamber of Commerce groups, governors, senators, and occasionally even presidents aided in the promotion.

In the early years, national forests assumed travel promotion functions later carried on by the State Travel Council and by the parks themselves. With administrative jurisdiction over the Natural Bridges, the La Sal Forest issued travel guides that used colorful names to divert attention from the primitive character of southeastern Utah's roads. In 1917 travelers were directed south from Salt Lake City via the Midland Trail to Thompson, thence over the Sandrock Trail to Moab, from which they could proceed south over the Rainbow route. By 1929 names had changed but color and optimism still dominated the La Sal Forest promotional literature. Travelers could now follow the Arrow Head Trail to Thompson, pick up the Navajo Trail to Blanding, and if hardy indeed could travel west by an impossible path called the Old Mormon Trail to the Natural Bridges in the heart of the canyonlands.

The pattern has persisted. Highways, accommodations, the multi-million-dollar tourist industry, and the very image Utah seeks to portray have grown in no small part from the appeal of its second self. Thus the Colorado Plateau is a different world, once forgotten, feared, and avoided but forever enchanted. With no city over 10,000 and with special concentrations of minorities, it is also one of the state's most rural regions.

Rural communities have contributed richly to Utah's heritage and to the strength of its people. This has been achieved under conditions that have often been adverse. The distribution of wealth has always favored the urban areas. Opportunities and services have been limited. Schools developed slowly. Libraries and other cultural facilities lagged far behind Salt Lake City and other centers, with the result that in many localities pre-World War II young people grew up under conditions that differed only superficially from those of frontier times.

Indeed, rural lag was in many ways the product of frontier processes. It was a new country and its people paid the price. Scores of mining camps and boom towns existed briefly, then failed, joining the passing parade of ghost towns. The enthusiasm for irrigation and real estate development before World War I brought dozens of villages into tenuous existence. Like Valley City near Moab and New Castle west of Cedar City, they made pretentious beginnings and then waited, the new lumber of misplaced hotels and homes weathering first and finally deteriorating entirely in desert winds.

Add to the normal lag of frontiers the fact that Mormon lag was in a real way deliberate and creative. Village life had represented both the maximum expression of Mormon withdrawal from the world and the means of Mormon expansion. As Mormon headquarters, Salt Lake City made concessions to the world reluctantly until 1890, thereafter with increasing enthusiasm. Insulated by the mother city as well as by some of the nation's most impenetrable natural barriers, village Utah became the residuary of primitive Mormonism. In the small communities the customs and values of Mormonism as a peculiar culture survived for many decades.

Nevertheless the expectations of country Utahns provided a common denominator with the broader life. In their mining promotions Cass Hite and Marion Fowler were prophets of expectation. Union organizers at Tucker and Castlegate looked to the better way, as did the growing membership of the Grange and Farm Bureau. Commercial clubs superimposed themselves upon the authority structures of church and municipality to set up the city parks, dance pavilions, and amusement centers which fairly swept rural Utah in the first third of the twentieth century. Lodges and benevolent societies showed a surprising appeal especially in mining and railroad towns. Even Mt. Pleasant in the heart of Sanpete County, where Mormons accounted for over 90 percent of the population, boasted at least five lodges by 1900. Veterans' societies and civic clubs also multiplied.

Journalism did much to enliven the country experience. In a 1938 study, Cecil Alter identified 585 Utah newspapers. More than 150 of these issued from Salt Lake City and Ogden, but the product of the hinterland was still impressive. Some of the earliest were manuscript sheets copied by hand to meet local needs for literary expression. Far more were vehicles of promotion. Some inevitably were given to excess. Not unusual was an editorial in a Carbon County paper which concluded that Price's prospects far overshadowed those of Los Angeles. Perhaps it was significant that the writer's fortunes had brought him to his editorial desk in Price from a large Los Angeles paper via a Salt Lake City daily.

That people took the local papers seriously is apparent. "Real news" tended to hurt feelings and alienate readers. News tips were often "loaded with dynamite" and editors suspected contributors of wanting to "take whacks at their enemies." [6] On occasion "fighting editors" were warned by church leaders, and many pursued favorite causes with a determination that lost reader support. A few were run out of town or kept from mailing their papers. Others were beaten, and in 1915 an editor was knifed by a fellow editor when a journalistic vendetta got out of hand.

Fortunately editors more often tended to the tongue-in-cheek, and statewide dialogues were carried on as they chided one another and made use of a neighbor's copy to meet deadlines. An especially intriguing development was the *Heber Herald* of the 1890s which was published by a precocious lad of eleven named Abram Hatch. "Filling both ears" at Heber's "Whittling

---

6. J. Cecil Alter, *Early Utah Journalism: A Half Century of Forensic Warfare, Waged by the West's Most Militant Press* (Salt Lake City: Utah State Historical Society, 1938), p. 93.

Club," the young editor "hurried back across the street and set it in type." [7] The paper mixed boyish pleasantries (albeit in adult prose) about the problems of editorializing when one was "bossed around by a big brother" and the unfairness of a curfew law that failed to "make the Old Folks stay at home too" with more serious comments about public drunkenness and the practice of dragging dead animals through ditches from which many of the townspeople continued to take their drinking water.[8] At the tiny southern Utah town of Kanab, which held the reputation of being "a good place to start a newspaper, but a poor place to continue one," two unsuppressible high school boys bought the defunct *Clipper* in 1903. In their inexperience they washed type in a tub and mixed b's, d's, p's and q's so that for months "God became 'Gob,' 'Gop,' or Goq.' " [9] Always dependent upon "ready print" pages, the *Clipper* and other country papers tended increasingly to the "diet of froth and folly" served up by the news services.[10] As rural population diminished during the 1930s so did the number of the local sheets.

A variety of theatrical experiences also enlivened country life. Road-worn circuses with a few pathetic animals worked the most remote byways, and in even the most rock-ribbed Mormon communities the summer tents of itinerant evangelists drew large audiences. As movies and other modern entertainment came to dominate the tastes of urban audiences, traveling troupes and chautauquas made their last stand in such out-of-the-way areas as Emery County.

Emery County apparently provided its own entertainment before 1900. Thereafter, magicians, animal shows, and healers that attracted attention with wild claims of universal cures came and went. One medicine man was noted for his frequent arrests for practicing medicine without a license and his noisy argu-

7. Alter, *Early Utah Journalism*, p. 86.

8. Alter, *Early Utah Journalism*, p. 84.

9. Alter, *Early Utah Journalism*, pp. 92–93.

10. John Sword Hunter Smith, "Localized Aspects of the Urban-Rural Conflict in the United States: Sanpete County, Utah," unpublished master's thesis, University of Utah, 1972, p. 87.

ments that "doctors are born not made." [11] By 1910 minstrel shows, as well as touring stock companies, visited the county regularly. Among the more engaging oddities were an Oriental magician named "Cunning Cunningham" and "Dante the Conjurer," whose magic produced a packed house but failed to bring forth the star himself.[12] In 1917 the Chautauqua circuit opened for the first time. During the next decade it flourished, as civic groups and commercial clubs radiated enthusiasm about its "upbuilding" character, and audiences displayed an unflinching capacity to sit through its performances. By the midtwenties Luke Cosgrave, forty-year veteran trouper, called Castle Valley "the last refuge for the traveling show." With "the face of the past turning away," even Cosgrave finally took a night train for Hollywood and the "door was closed" on a significant phase of rural living.[13] Thereafter local theatrical groups and school shows continued, but even these yielded to the entertainment marts of urban centers as traveling movies, radios, and later local movie theaters penetrated rural areas. Some L.D.S. wards made movies available on "a budget ticket" that admitted entire families to eight or ten movies monthly for as little as $3.50. Only television in recent years has had a greater effect on family entertainment.

Cultural specialties characterized various localities. In San Juan, what may be termed a "Hole-in-the-Rock mystique" was constantly burnished. Elsewhere diarists left records in such plentitude and detail as to guarantee their communities a flourishing future among historians. One of the West's truly remarkable schools of local study developed in Utah's Dixie when Nels Anderson, Juanita Brooks, Karl Larson, and LeRoy Hafen made the region's history (including the Mountain Meadows Massacre) well known. In Sanpete County citizens found fun and function in the difficulties posed by shared Scandinavian patronyms. Nicknames ran the full gamut. Chris Tallerass was

11. *Emery County Progress,* December 15, 1900.

12. Elmo G. Geary, "A Study of Dramatics in Castle Valley from 1875 to 1925," unpublished master's thesis, Brigham Young University, 1953, pp. 243–244.

13. Luke Cosgrave, *Theater Tonight* (Hollywood: House Warven, 1952) pp. 195–199.

broad of posterior. Sorrel Pete drove a sorrel team and sported a red beard. Bottle John had an affinity for drink. And the great number of Peters led to such "euphoneous titles as 'Perty Pete,' 'Shingle Pete,' 'Little Pete,' and 'Tossy Pete' " and a dozen more.[14] A "badman" folklore that flourished among northeastern Utah residents attracted historian Charles Kelly, whose *Outlaw Trail* gave the cult its chronicle in 1938. In Carbon County the name of the outlaw Butch Cassidy—for whom an uneasy and contested grave site is marked in the Price Cemetery—came near being the universal response to the word "history" as the locality reveled in the "Robin Hood" romance surrounding the famed badman.

But the family may well have provided rural Utah with its greatest strength and its greatest ironies. In the state as a whole families were large and the death rate low. In rural districts families were even larger, and increase in poorer families with limited education topped the list. As the new century progressed, questions of people and what to do with them posed a growing problem. Seasonal unemployment was the norm in many villages. In Springville crowds of men and boys—called "whittling deacons" by one observer—gathered on the "sunnyside of Reynold's store." [15] At Clarkston's two stores, "men stood in groups to while away the long hours of winter," their remarks and stares complicating passage for women and children.[16] In 1923 sociologist G. Lowry Nelson found that at Escalante "winter comes like a soothing night," lulling farmers and stockmen "into pleasant indolence." [17] Some adults found it possible to go to school. Others worked homesteads in the summer and coal mines in the winter. Of the latter sort were a dozen or so unmarried men who ranched in eastern Utah's rugged Range Creek country. In a region so remote as to deny almost

14. Hector Lee and Royal Madsen, "Nicknames of the Ephraimites," *Western Humanities Review* 3 (January 1949): 13.

15. Diary of Aaron Johnson, December 30, 1907, Utah State Historical Society.

16. Ann Godfrey Hansen, "Isolated Personal Reminiscences of Clarkston, Utah, A Pioneer Town," Utah State University Library Archives, p. 41.

17. G. Lowry Nelson, *The Mormon Village* (Salt Lake City: University of Utah Press, 1952), p. 107.

all outside contact, they made the John Downard ranch at Rock Creek on the Green River something of a summer rendezvous, gathering now and then to enjoy Mrs. Downard's cooking and relieve the lonely tedium of ranch life. In the fall they left their stock to shift for itself and hired on at Sunnyside and other mines. Teaching, merchandising, politics, and peddling also provided off-season employment for country folk.

In southwestern Utah around the turn of the century, Dode Brooks, a teen-aged girl, carried a "peddling kit" filled with straight pins, needles, shoelaces, and ribbons from town to town, visiting as she made her leisurely rounds. Occasionally blacksmith Russell Chandler joined her in a wagon driven by her youngest brother. Arriving in a town, Chandler would stand in the back of the wagon and chant a song "without a tune: 'chain-lengths, open links, bolts & screws, bars and clevises! Come and get-em! Bring anything in exchange!' " When sales were good Chandler went home with a stock of provisions and Dode Brooks with a jubilant song: "Hurrah, hurrah, hurray, I've made twenty dollars today!" [18] At Clarkston and many other towns, peddlers gave variety to life in the first decades of the century. Children watched for extra riders in the white-topped mail-and-stage buggy or spotted peddler wagons long before they reached town. The Watkins Man they followed like a Pied Piper. Most knew well the tearful pitch of a Syrian woman who year after year made a few sales by assuring buyers her proceeds would be used to bring her two children to America. "Old Pete's" three-horse hookup marked the fruit wagon, while a weeping little fellow known as the "Cry Man" sold almanacs and an occasional novel.

But peddling was as much an indication that development was not keeping pace with the growing population as it was an economic activity. By 1900 a state built upon the gathering began a diaspora that continued in absolute numbers until after 1940 and continues to deplete farm and rural populations in the 1970s. The census of 1910 showed a net migration from the

18. Juanita Brooks, *Uncle Will Tells His Story* (Salt Lake City: Taggart & Company, 1970), p. 53.

state of 1200 people during the previous decade. That number grew to nearly 92,000 between 1930 and 1940. The dispersion was widespread, but Utahns went mainly to California and other mountain states, where they numbered 75,000 and 67,000 respectively by 1940. The lion's share of this outward movement came from the hinterlands as, in a paradoxical reversal of Mormon Zionism, "Utah's best crop"—its sons and daughters—took to the roads.

These statistics fail to take full measure of the migration from the countryside. Farm populations reached a maximum of 132,000 in 1910 but fell to 94,000 in 1940. In the same period urban populations increased by almost 100,000 to nearly a third of a million and nonfarm rural populations increased by one third to 150,000. Few of these migrants found their way into businesses that required heavy capital investment. On the other hand, they did have certain resources to invest. The aging population that remained behind provided both motivation and a start toward social mobility. They sacrificed capital inprovements that they and earlier generations had achieved to send their young people to school, thereby preparing them for success in the world outside.

Thus it was an old story—a story told in virtually every rural locality in America—but only in South Dakota and Oklahoma was the retreat from the country proportionately larger than in Utah. However, the Utah experience was not *The Grapes of Wrath*. Far from a rout, it was an ordered withdrawal. Education and preparation bought by those who remained behind opened the way. At Bear Lake, David L. Wright probed its irony and ruefully measured its cost when he wrote the following:

> . . . they talk gently
> of sons and grandsons making more money in a month
> than they in a year;
> . . . saying nothing of . . . their sacrifices for offsprings
> whose fortunes had to be sought apart from the heritage,
> in worlds of stone and steel—
> Selling cows, sheep, ancestral lands
> to send them through universities,

reducing poverty to want;
wise, these old, to see the cast
of the world's change did not lie with villages,
though hurting somewhat that it were not so,
hurting, even yet, for the progeny rarely returns and,
returning, gives scarce evidence of honoring the heritage.[19]

The wholesale migration stopped with World War II. But the Depression, defense spending, and the proliferation of government agencies had hastened the exodus from country to city. Finally legislative reapportionment officially stripped the hinterlands of the vestiges of power long lost. The experience of a resident of Price summarizes the city-country dilemma. In the 1960s he left the College of Eastern Utah and his home and friends of many years to seek a Ph.D. at the University of Utah. Having traveled the road to Salt Lake City almost weekly for years, he was amazed when his many connections drew him home to Price only twice in two years. The experience led him to note that, the realities of distance notwithstanding, it was farther from Salt Lake City to Price than from Price to Salt Lake City. The double irony was that it was farther from Salt Lake City to Washington, D.C., or for that matter the outside world than it was from the outside world to Salt Lake City—a fact which the influx of ethnic minorities had long since proven.

The growth of minority groups accompanied the move to metropolitan areas. A new wave of immigration after 1900 created a segment of society which cared little about Utah's Mormon–gentile polarity. Concerned with values and needs of their own, the new minorities found themselves excluded from many social and political functions and for decades were admitted only to pick-and-shovel jobs. Diverse in background and character, they lived to themselves, provoked hostility among their neighbors, and suffered persecution and poverty. Yet many found opportunity and in time were fully accepted in Utah life.

Minorities existed from the first, but to 1900 their numbers were extremely small and their impact negligible. By contrast,

19. David L. Wright, "River Saints: A Mormon Chronicle," multilithed (Utah State University Library, n.d.), pp. 24–25.

they have played important and enriching roles in the twentieth century. Their experience has been complex and dynamic—yet does admit of a few generalizations. People of a dozen or more national and racial backgrounds were involved. In the broadest terms the first two decades of the century were the classic era of minorities, with immigration running high and the cultural impact reaching a climax. The 1920s were an era of leveling off as earlier immigrants adopted American ways and the great flood of immigration was slowed to a trickle by restrictive federal legislation. During the Depression, movement reversed itself as minorities joined the general exodus from Utah. World War II altered the order once again, bringing a quick influx which continued in the postwar years.

The first two decades of the century were in the main the time of southeastern European immigrants—Italians, Slavs, and Greeks—although an influx of Orientals and Mexican-Americans provided secondary themes. The Balkan and Mediterranean immigrants had much in common yet differed significantly. In addition to national divisions, numerous local and cultural subdivisions existed which made for internal frictions and complicated adaptation to America. For almost all, Utah was initially no more than "a stop on a tedious journey out of poverty" that was expected to end with return to the old country.[20] Theirs was a migration of young men for whom state and local perimeters meant nothing and jobs everything. All three peoples were imbued with loyalty for homeland and a deep sense of nationalism. In Europe the Slavs and Italians had long been part of an itinerant work force exposed to radical influences and ridicule.

Beginning about 1895, they came—the Italians first, the Slavs hard behind, and the Greeks after 1903. The vast migration that had saturated eastern labor markets brought the Italians and Slavs to Utah. Most appear to have entered the state via the Denver and Rio Grande Railway. They concentrated first in Carbon County, moving later to Bingham and then into the

---

20. Helen Zeese Papanikolas, "Introduction," in Papanikolas, ed., *The Peoples of Utah* (Salt Lake City: Utah State Historical Society, 1976), p. 4.

urban industries of Salt Lake City and Ogden. Agents of Leonidas Skliris, "Czar of the Greeks," recruited his countrymen
throughout the West and from as far away as Omaha and Chicago, to make Utah a center of Greek populations. It is difficult
to know their numbers. They came and went, moving ahead of
census takers who in 1900 counted no more than 170 Italians in
Salt Lake County. Three years later the Pleasant Valley Coal
Company reported 848 Italians and 232 Slavs on its work force;
census takers in 1910 counted a statewide population of 3,117
Italians and 4,099 Greeks.

Once in the state the immigrants gathered to themselves,
locating according to family, regional, and national relationships. In Salt Lake City Greeks congregated near the
railroad yards. Italians at Sunnyside tented in "Ragtown." In
Bingham the Piedmontese were called "Short Towns," after
their stocky builds and their area of town. Yugoslavs formed
family clusters at Bingham and Midvale and in Carbon County
towns. In a subtle blend of their past and America's industrial
civilization, each society adapted its own institutions to Utah
conditions. Coffee houses, Greek and Italian stores, boarding
houses, national lodges, and "Godfathers" made life tolerable.

The newcomers failed to appreciate many Utah axioms, including the sense of religious and secular mission that actuated
most Americans. For them religion was a source of comfort and
a benign influence but scarcely a force to nurture and promote
until it filled the world, as Mormons believed. Similarly, the
American dream that expressed itself during World War I in
"make the world safe for Democracy" meant little. Prohibition
was beyond their ken, its morality incomprehensible. Government was viewed with a jaundiced eye, while courts and law
often represented repressive power, not protection.

Not surprisingly the new immigrants took recourse in their
own values and traditions. They renewed old-country vendettas.
Labor agents and interpreters exploited their countrymen, in effect selling their "pound of flesh." A southern Italian society
called the "Black Hands" extorted and occasionally murdered,
and labor organizers and anarchists stirred unrest. Thoughts of
home were strong. Some sent the money they had come to earn.

Others returned to fight wars and to take wives. Still others left Utah for more promising opportunities elsewhere in America. But some remained.

As naturalization progressed, the population shifted from a young male society to one of increasing age in which women and families played an important role. For years women were rare, particularly among the Slavs and Greeks. In 1903 there were no Greek women in the state; by 1910, fewer than a dozen. In south Slav communities the arrival of the first woman was a celebrated event. Joseph Mikié of Midvale recalled: "They had saloon there in Midvale and some Serb used to run saloon there. First woman come there. His wife come there . . . God, well, you know, we crazy. See her, first woman from . . . Yugoslavia." In a strange reversal of European dowry customs, Mikié and his friends gathered $800 and in the enthusiasm of the moment gave it to this first pioneer as a wedding present.[21]

In lieu of home life and associations with women, young workers turned to conversation and gambling. "At long intervals" they could see wandering shows from home or "a tarnished Greek performer, Madame Sophia," who danced and sang, according to one report, "with the grace of an elephant and the voice of a wolf."[22] There was little opportunity for association with local girls, many of whom shared the feeling of their elders that "intermarriage with foreigners was . . . as bad as death."[23] However, one immigrant's report that Bingham was a "town of 22 saloons and 600 sporting girls" suggests that feminine association was not entirely lacking.[24]

As years passed, many of the immigrants sent home for "picture brides." Relatives or friends still in the homeland sometimes made the selection. Among the Greeks, money was pooled and agent bachelors dispatched to bring "a bevy of

---

21. Joseph Stipanovich, "Falcons in Flight: The Yugoslavs," in *The Peoples of Utah*, p. 368.

22. Papanikolas, *Toil and Rage*, p. 138.

23. Papanikolas, *Toil and Rage*, p. 139.

24. Philip F. Notarianni, "Italianita in Utah: The Immigrant Experience," in Papanikolas, *The Peoples of Utah*, p. 308.

young women." [25] Occasionally girls came alone marked with tags to identify them to future husbands at railroad stations or were left at remote sidings to face a strange and hostile world.

With marriage came children, and with children came changed plans. The original intent to send money home and save a nest egg with which to re-establish life in the old country was now abandoned. Life became less a matter of moving from camp to camp and more one of stable communities with Catholic or Greek Orthodox churches. Immigrants looked increasingly two ways as children went to American schools, supplemented the mother tongue with English, and penetrated the social barriers thrown up against them.

Barriers were formidable. The southeastern Europeans met prejudice and suspicion on every hand. Various devices kept them in place; unwritten laws governed economic opportunities. Housing convenants and tacit understanding limited where they could live, and their status was fixed by an array of values and ideas. To anti-papism and other hackneyed fears as old as Protestantism were added Mormon doctrines of "chosen people" and "the curse." Teachings of hereditary inferiority and survival of the fittest were widely accepted. Newspapers were filled with lurid accounts of gambling, fighting, and socialism, as Utah's own brand of yellow journalism appealed to the sentiments of readers and played on national fears. Hostility took on special virulence during strikes, and group was pitted against group as strikebreakers were recruited. World War I brought added distrust, when immigrants were slow to share the burdens of battle and refused mandatory classes in Americanism. Asking why "Hundreds of Red-blooded" Americans had to "Submit to the Blatant . . . Effrontery of South European Domination," editorials fanned antiforeign sentiment to a peak in the strike of 1922.[26] The Ku Klux Klan was organized in 1924, functioning in south Salt Lake and Carbon County, as citizens made social regulation their business.

In spite of continuing opposition, the 1920s were in a way a

---

25. Papanikolas, *Toil and Rage*, p. 141.
26. Quoted in Notarianni, "Italianita in Utah," p. 323.

golden age for Balkan and Mediterranean minorities. While it was often vocal and sometimes violent, opposition decreased. With their children maturing, many of the immigrants gave up their determination to return to the old country and became American citizens. Opportunity increased. Some farmed, raising produce for coal camps and smelter towns. Affinity for the pastoral life led some into sheep ranching, and many found upward mobility in business. The young went to school, and significant numbers entered the professions. World War II found most of Utah's southeastern European community fully assimilated, their votes solicited, and their sons fighting for their adopted country.

But assimilation rarely meant loss of identity. Each of the three major groups retained elements of its native culture. The Greek language continued to be taught. Newspapers were published in the languages of all three and native customs persisted, including festivities marking old-country holidays and the healing arts of folk doctors and midwives. They were less provincial in outlook than Mormons and less dominated by the profit ethic than the sons and daughters of the American frontier, and their ties with the old world and with ethnic groups throughout the United States added a significant dimension to the Utah experience.

Meantime other minorities played less obtrusive but significant roles. The experience of blacks came near being the experience of American blacks elsewhere. Work on the railroads and in the mines was sometimes available—little else. Restrictive housing covenants limited black populations to declining urban areas. Utah newspapers wrote approvingly of lynchings in neighboring states, and in 1925 Robert Marshall was hanged on a cottonwood tree that for years stretched over Highway 50–6 south of Price. Seeming progress was often subverted. Mignon Richmond, for example, graduated from Utah State Agricultural College in 1921 but for years found no teaching opportunity. Black entertainers drew large crowds but could not use public accommodations, although by determined effort Robert E. Freed was able to open the entertainment park at Lagoon to blacks by 1940. The Mormon Church's denial of the priesthood to blacks remains a problem because it implies an inferior status that is at variance with human and civil rights.

By comparison, Jewish immigrants met few restraints. Newcomers continued to reach the state after 1900 but as in earlier years came in a trickle. Having suffered much in the old country, they were "animated by Horatio Alger motives . . . plus a resolve to find a permanent . . . home." [27] For most this meant life as shopkeepers in Salt Lake City or Ogden. "Parents and grandparents put a few dollars together, rented a tiny shop, persuaded wholesalers to take credit risks, and a new luggage, furniture, or dry goods establishment came into being." For newcomers jobs were available, "not through the State Employment Service but down the street at some fellow Jew's store." [28] For one group of Jewish refugees Utah meant the agricultural colony of Clarion in Central Utah. Arriving in 1910, Clarion settlers were supported by promoters, including Governor William Spry, and a colonization fund of $150,000. Clarion, however, succumbed to adverse conditions and by 1915 had gone the way of Valley City, New Castle, and other defunct towns. Simon Bamberger became Utah's fourth state governor in 1916. Feisty and redheaded, Bamberger had struck it rich at Eureka, invested in coal mines, built railroads, and served as a state senator. As governor, Bamberger provided one of Utah's most forward-looking and effective administrations. Other Jews have distinguished themselves in a wide variety of professional and cultural circles as well as in public and business life. They have suffered little from overt anti-Semitism. While Utah Jews may "remain more than a mite removed from the mainstream of American life," their business activities and their connections with the Jewish community elsewhere have broadened the confines of Utah's Zion and have placed the state in touch with elements otherwise beyond its ken. [29]

Japanese movement into the state paralleled that of the Balkan and Mediterranean peoples. By 1910 Japanese numbered

27. Jack Goodman, "Jews in Zion," in Papanikolas, *The Peoples of Utah*, p. 212.
28. Goodman, "Jews in Zion," p. 212.
29. Goodman, "Jews in Zion," p. 215.

2,111 and by 1920 nearly 3,000. They came to work in the mines or railroads, and often at the most dangerous and disagreeable jobs, for the lowest pay. Some found their way into farming. Not unusual was Ichii Fuckui. Arriving in 1907, he worked for $1.50 per day as a "gandy dancer" on the Union Pacific railroad at Evanston, Wyoming. By World War I he had moved to Ogden but continued to work on the railroad. Shortly thereafter he wrote home for a picture bride, married, and by 1920 had acquired land in Box Elder County, where he and his family became known for their industry and sugar beet culture. Other Japanese stayed with the railroad. Jinzaburo Matsumiya worked as a section foreman out of Jericho, returned to Japan for a wife, and for years was something of an institution in that remote western Utah community. Much more important was Edward Daigoro Hashimoto, who founded E. D. Hashimoto Company in Salt Lake City in 1902. The Hashimoto Company provided railroads with Japanese section hands, imported Japanese food, handled payrolls, money orders, and legal work for Japanese workers, and in time expanded into banking and sugar beets. Known as "Daigoro Sama," or Great Man, among the Japanese, and as "Salt Lake City's Mikado" by Americans, Daigoro was revered by his countrymen and the associate of notables throughout the United States.[30] The Japanese were law-abiding and "led hard-working, predictable lives."[31] They made respectable positions for themselves and rarely experienced the same hostility as the southeastern Europeans, although latent fears later proved explosive. Their numbers increased throughout the 1920s but over a thousand joined in the general exodus of the Depression years.

The Japanese attack on Pearl Harbor in 1941 revealed the transparent nature of the good will Utah's hard-working Japanese people enjoyed. The anti-foreign discrimination that southeastern Europeans had felt in World War I now fell on them with fury supplemented by fear. Utah's support of the wartime

---

30. Helen Z. Papanikolas and Alice Kasai, "Japanese Life in Utah," in Papanikolas, *The Peoples of Utah*, p. 337.

31. Papanikolas and Kasai, "Japanese Life," p. 343.

frenzy was general. Newspapers fulminated, public accommodations posted ''no Japs wanted here'' signs, Japanese employees were fired, and long-time residents were subjected to repeated inspections. Yet United States Senator Elbert D. Thomas, who had filled a Mormon mission in Japan, and a few other prominent Utahns expressed sympathy for the Japanese and exerted influence in their behalf. Humor helped soften the blow of Pearl Harbor in the case of Dr. Edward Ichiro Hashimoto, ''son of the Mikado,'' who on the day after the attack is said to have

> entered his gross anatomy class at the University of Utah Medical School . . . to a profound silence. ''What are you fellows staring at?'' he said. ''I'm Irish. I was home in Dublin at the time!'' With relief and delight, Dr. Hashimoto's students relaxed. Known for being able to draw human figures with both hands . . . the doctor was called, from then on, the ''Ambidextrous Irishman.'' [32]

But World War II spelled the tragedy of evacuation for many Utah Japanese when Topaz, ''the Jewel of the Desert,'' was established as a relocation center in Milford County.[33] There in desolation and alkali dust some 8,000 Japanese from throughout the West were subjected to indignity and hardship. Elsewhere in the state Japanese had comparative freedom but faced overt hostility and loss of economic rights. At the war's end many evacuees stayed in Utah, increasing in number until by 1970 people of Japanese ancestry were estimated at 4,700.

Mexicans constitute one of Utah's oldest minorities but for decades came and went, making few permanent communities. In the years after 1900 stockmen in southeastern Utah began to employ men from New Mexico. By World War I a homestead *colonia* had been established at Allen's Canyon in the Abajo Mountains, and New Mexican families continued to work for stock outfits including the La Sal Livestock Company, where some like Fernin Lopez and Marijildo Valdez became trusted lieutenants. *Colonias* also developed at Tremonton, Delta, and Spanish Fork to which came not only New Mexicans but, after

---

32. Papanikolas and Kasai, ''Japanese Life,'' p. 353.
33. Papanikolas and Kasai, ''Japanese Life,'' p. 357.

the Revolution began in 1910, immigrants from Mexico to work in the sugar-beet fields. Non-agricultural employment was rarely available to Mexicans before 1920, but a few did work at mines. Bingham even produced a significant folk hero in the "strange case of Rafael Lopez," who in 1913 shot and killed one Juan Valdez, gave dozens of deputies the slip, and disappeared into the maze of tunnels that laced Bingham Canyon.[34] During the 1920s Mexican population in Utah increased to 4,000. Men came from Mexico and families from Colorado and New Mexico to replace southeastern Europeans and Japanese who were leaving the section gangs and less desirable jobs in the mines. Other classes reclaimed industrial jobs during the Depression, although Mexicans continued to do much of the "stoop" work in agriculture. By 1940 the identifiable Mexican population had dwindled to 1,000. Since the beginning of World War II, Spanish-speaking populations have increased to 43,000 and include Puerto Ricans, Central and South Americans, and Basques, as well as Mexicans and Mexican-Americans. Politically active since 1960, this group has dealt increasingly with questions of human rights and economic opportunities.

What then has been the general meaning of the "other Utahs"? In the most obvious and direct sense, each of the three dualities dealt with in this chapter has meant diversity and complexity. More significantly, all have conformed to the national experience and multiplied the points at which the local tradition interlocks with the broader American community. A frontier state that began as a peculiar society had not only come to conform politically and economically but was drawn to the nation as well by the influences of its geographical regions, by its urban–rural playoffs, and by its minorities. The Colorado Plateau hardly belonged to pioneer Utah, but state boundaries and late-coming settlement worked to hold the region, while influences from neighboring states and a physical character that charmed a nation made it clear that the Great Basin's rim demarked "two Utahs" and helped form the union that held the

---

34. Wallace Stegner, *Mormon Country* (New York: Bonanza Books, 1942), p. 269.

state to the nation. Salt Lake City came increasingly to dominate the countryside. To loss of status that paralleled the dilemma of rural America everywhere, the migration from rural Utah added the double irony of a failing Mormon hinterland and the fact that Salt Lake City itself was part of a countryside whose emigrants fed a national metropolis. Finally, the new minorities brought new challenges. Mormon–gentile polarity meant little. Jobs, labor movements, and anti-foreign sentiment meant much. In forging the bonds that held minorities to Utah, local influences were eclipsed by national considerations including markets, professional norms, wars, and—at last—federal human rights legislation. Thus the dimensions of Utah's other self represented a significant element in the state's progress from frontier to mainstream America and from a peculiar to a pluralistic society. Politics in the twentieth century reveal similar influences.

7

Twentieth-Century Politics

*T*HE quest for community that dominated the last years of the territory has continued to be the great theme of twentieth-century politics. In this search for stability and security, Utahns have hewed to the center and followed well-marked national paths. The two national parties have found a remarkable balance from which they have easily dominated third parties and other insurgencies. A nagging awareness of the numerical majority of the Mormons and memory of the bitter battle over the church's proper role in government have overshadowed the entire political process. Occasionally echoes of the church conflict have opened old wounds. More often they have emphasized the utility of partisan loyalty and national issues as stabilizing influences. The church has made no pretense to govern, yet as the institutional representative of about seventy percent of the state's population it has been interested in a wide variety of issues and the Mormon vote has always been a key factor. With millennialism receding as a practical force, the policy of "superior virtue" adopted in the earlier period has been perpetuated, leading Mormons to espouse patriotism, respectability, and what may be termed the economic-political establishment. National developments have had profound influences upon the course of state politics. Reform, wars and international relations, depression, and post-World War II prosperity have carried the state deeper into the national matrix while absentee ownership and opportunity have often drawn Utah's affluent and powerful to the economic and power centers of the nation.

If Reconstruction meant a single party for the American South, Utah's reconstruction meant a two-party system. Events in the decades following statehood produced an affinity for the two-party tradition that has been quite as dominant as the influence of the Democratic Party in the solid South. Utahns regarded the establishment of two strong parties as a barrier against the resurgence of the old Mormon problem, and the issue was of paramount concern during most of the state's first quarter-century. In subsequent years the two parties have remained strong, alternating in power on a remarkably even basis.

After statehood, top Mormon leaders continued the delicate task of defusing their own participation in politics. Prompted by the backstage voice of George Q. Cannon, Wilford Woodruff, church president until 1897, and Lorenzo Snow, the last of the old-line Mormon presidents, who served until 1901, advanced the development of two-party politics in various ways. Together with politicians in and out of the church, they arrived at an unwritten agreement by which top political offices were parceled out more or less evenly between Mormons and non-Mormons—an arrangement which, in light of the overwhelming numerical superiority of Latter-day Saint voters, tended to place the church in the political background. Woodruff and Snow also contributed to an emerging consensus as to what kind of Mormon and what kind of gentile could expect widespread electoral support, thus fostering a middle-of-the-road tradition when they encouraged moderates rather than firebrands of the old conflict to run for political position. Moreover, the two aging presidents appear to have supported the establishment of a strong Republican Party. Because it had long been regarded by Mormons as the party of oppression, the rehabilitation of the Grand Old Party took considerable doing, but sufficient progress had been made by 1895 to secure Republican support for statehood. Hiram Clawson, John Henry Smith, and other prominent church figures were allowed to spread Republicanism through the church—political gumshoeing, one prominent Democrat called it—and were encouraged in their political aspirations. Snow apparently pledged his support to national Republican leaders and backed Thomas Kearns, Park City miner and Roman Catholic, in his successful bid for the Senate in 1900.

More important in the shift of Mormons to the Republican Party was Joseph F. Smith, a tall, austere nephew of Joseph Smith who guided the church throughout the remaining years of this formative period. As an apostle and counselor to Woodruff and Snow, Smith had recognized that when Mormons combined "against . . . political majorities" as they had done under the old People's Party, "they became a disturbing element." Thus convinced, he became the church's most vocal and influential advocate of "division in politics on national party lines." Reflecting the waning influence of millennialism on Mormon expectations, he had written a cousin, Jesse N. Smith, in 1891 that "our lot is cast in the world, and we must . . . unite on a proper division in the politics of the day." For him this meant "leaning to the winning" or the Republican side.[1]

During the first years the politics of statehood were confused and halting, reflecting the newness of party lines, past tensions, and the Populist sentiments then widespread in the West. Heber M. Wells, a Utah-born Republican and son of old Mormon stalwart Daniel H. Wells, was elected the first state governor. The first congressional delegation was divided between Mormon and non-Mormon and between the Democratic and Republican parties.

However, memory of the long strife between the Republicans and the Mormons together with "free silver" and other Populist causes resulted in a show of Democratic strength that some feared would perpetuate the old Mormon–gentile cleavage along national party lines or—almost as bad for a state seeking full respectability—fasten Utah into a permanent minority framework, as many regarded the Democratic Party to be. In 1896 Democrat William Jennings Bryan's capture of 82 percent of the Utah vote in a presidential election that went nationally to William McKinley supported fears that the state would perpetuate its off-

---

1. Letter of September 14, 1891, made available to the author by S. George Ellsworth, Logan, Utah; original in the Church Historical Department.

beat ways. Utah Democrats won overwhelmingly again in the off-year elections of 1898 but presented a front so riddled by factions that the legislature failed to designate a senator in what has been known as the "election that failed." [2] Even the unity of the Mormon hierarchy broke down as it dealt with questions of partisan division, and two Democrats, Apostle Moses Thatcher and B. H. Roberts, another church officer, were reproved for running for political office without approval from their church superiors. Acknowledging error, Roberts continued in his church position and survived as a pillar of the Democratic Party, although the members of the House of Representatives to which he was elected in 1898 chose not to seat him because he was a polygamist. Thatcher, who argued he was within his rights, was dropped from the Quorum of the Twelve and broken as a politician.

Otherwise Utah's Democratic Party remained strong, maintaining wide appeal through its support of silver and protective tariffs on sugar and wool and offering moderate candidates known for their sound connections and respectability. Joseph Rawlins stood out in his term as senator. William H. King's election to the House of Representatives in 1896 launched a distinguished political career that saw him hold a Senate seat from 1917 to 1941. But perhaps the epitome of Utah Democracy was James H. Moyle. A loyal Mormon as well as a lawyer and businessman, he ran for high office often, held his party together, and served as the lightning rod of conscience when Republican Mormons tended to overstep the bounds of political propriety with reference to the role of church and state. A party man to the core, he was the key to the effectiveness of the Democrats in opposition during the first two decades of statehood.

After several lean years in the late 1890s, the Republican Party effectively challenged the Democrats after 1900. Its success depended in large measure upon the efforts of Reed Smoot, Mormon apostle and Utah senator from 1903 to 1933. Thin and humorless, Smoot began as a local businessman in Provo and

2. Stewart L. Grow, "Utah's Senatorial Election of 1899: The Election That Failed," *Utah Historical Quarterly* 39 (Winter 1971): 30–39.

became a national figure of considerable prominence. Quite without glamour, he "staged no rebellions . . . coined no phrases" and offered no new ideas, but he "worked without stint," won elections, and became a pillar of big business and party regularity. For years the myth that Utah was "a pocket borough" belonging to Reed Smoot and his silent partner Joseph F. Smith was one of the "minor fables of American politics." [3] Nevertheless, the church president–apostle–senator team maintained its control only by the sparest margin and in the long run served more to establish a viable two-party system than to perpetuate a Republican juggernaut.

Indeed for several years it appeared that an apostle-senator was not to be. Presidents William McKinley and Theodore Roosevelt warned Smoot not to run, evidently believing his candidacy would breach the accommodations undergirding statehood. Nevertheless, Smoot was elected senator in 1902. Petitions urging that he be refused his seat led to hearings that drew on from March 1904 to April 1906 and probed Smoot's private life as well as the inner workings of the church. Reviving much of the old bitterness and titillating the nation's current passion for muckraking, the Smoot hearings upstaged even such sensational exposés as Lincoln Steffens's *Shame of the Cities* and Upton Sinclair's *The Jungle*. However, the hearings served as a symbolic cleansing; and nonpolygamist Smoot, in a statement attributed to Senator Boies Penrose, was absolved as a "polygamist who doesn't 'polyg.' " [4]

The Smoot hearings also provided an opportunity for the church to reaffirm its respectability. As Bernard DeVoto has noted, "Israel had" long since come to "terms with finance" and as a result was developing "not in the direction . . . of the United Order or the Kingdom of God but in the direction of Standard Oil." [5] The period of the Smoot hearings saw further

3. Milton R. Merrill, *Reed Smoot: Utah Politician*, Monograph Series, Vol. 1 (Logan: Utah State Agricultural College, 1953), p. 5.

4. O. N. Malmquist, *The First 100 Years: A History of the Salt Lake Tribune 1871–1971* (Salt Lake City: Utah State Historical Society, 1971), p. 229.

5. Bernard DeVoto, *Forays and Rebuttals* (Boston: Little, Brown & Co., 1936), p. 122.

consolidation of the Mormon union with business, when
H. O. Havemeyer of the American Sugar Refining Company
acquired control of Utah and Idaho Sugar Company and E. H.
Harriman purchased Utah Light and Railway Company. These
corporations, reputedly the largest in the state, set up interlock-
ing directorate arrangements that seated the church president
and members of the quorum of apostles on the company boards.

Perhaps even more revealing were Mormon efforts to portray
themselves as unblemished patriots. The church issued a new
manifesto against polygamy in 1904 and excommunicated two
apostles who advocated plurality. Mormon leaders taught patriotism almost as a religious principle, emphatically disclaiming
lingering ideas that the "Kingdom of God that is to be" pertained "to the present." Indeed, they officially proclaimed in
1907: "Our allegiance and loyalty to our country are strengthened by the fact that while awaiting the advent of Messiah's
Kingdom, we are under a commandment from God to be subject
to the powers that be until He comes whose right it is to
reign." [6] Conventional Americanism had become the order of
the day. The church had made an about-face from the "near-
nationalism" of the 1850s. Faith in God's earthly kingdom was
still intact, but by indefinitely postponing their expectation of
the millennium Mormons had come to see America as a permanent and God-ordained protector rather than as a passing phase
in the kingdom's development. In its practical effects, this shift
bolstered the various attributes of American nationalism with a
sense of religious mission that has remained unflagging and re-
silient.

And yet Joseph F. Smith wielded great political power. He
was Israel's head—a fact Smoot acknowledged in all situations.
In turn, Smith was a bulwark of power for the senator. His influence was a key ingredient in Smoot's first election and in the
bitter 1904 struggle by which the senior Utah senator, Thomas
Kearns, was displaced by George Sutherland, a more acceptable
gentile. Smith let it "be known that he believed there was

6. Clark, *Messages of the First Presidency,* v. 4, pp. 79, 154.

divine purpose in keeping an apostle in the Senate." [7] Perhaps even more important, he helped Smoot put together a well-disciplined party machine that for more than a decade was the controlling element in Utah politics. But limits to Smith's political influence were apparent in the continuing crises of the era.

Ousted from the Senate, Thomas Kearns joined other disgruntled gentiles to form the American Party along lines very similar to the old Liberal Party. With the Kearns-owned *Salt Lake Tribune* as its public voice, the American Party controlled elections in Salt Lake City and Ogden from 1905 to 1911. The American Party also represented a major Republican split that pressed the Smoot machine to its limits and constantly threatened to repoliticize the Mormon question and shatter the delicate lines of party regularity that were emerging.

That the Republican Party withstood the dual test of the American Party's urban challenge and the statewide strength of the Democrats was doubtless the result of Smoot's machine—the Federal Bunch—and his regularity in the national party. Teddy Roosevelt had given his support to Smoot during the Senate hearings. Smoot responded with unflinching loyalty to the party under both T. R. and William Howard Taft. As a state boss he used his influence with Joseph F. Smith to demand total fidelity from the Mormon "boys" of the machine and wooed gentiles by shrewd distribution of political positions and patronage and by his fullhearted support of business interests. Many thought he had the power to send "a cigar store Indian" to the United States Senate.[8] Indeed his power was great. Over the years he helped make Sutherland senator, replaced Governor Heber M. Wells with businessman John C. Cutler in 1904; coldly dismissed Cutler in 1908 for William Spry, a more persuasive vote-getter; helped wrest Salt Lake City from the American Party in 1911; and in 1912 highlighted a great Utah tradi-

---

7. James Henry Moyle, *Mormon Democrat: The Religious and Political Memoirs of James Henry Moyle,* ed. Gene A. Sessions (Salt Lake City: Historical Department, Church of Jesus Christ of Latter-day Saints, 1975), p. 215.

8. *Salt Lake Herald,* January 8, 1905, as quoted in Merrill, *Reed Smoot,* p. 50.

tion for party regularity and preference for the incumbent when he faced down Teddy Roosevelt's Bull Moose insurgency to make Utah one of two states supporting incumbent William Howard Taft.

But it was the prohibition issue that revealed the degree to which Smoot and his supporter in the church presidency were committed to the twin ideals of party regularity and suppression of the old division along Mormon–gentile lines. No issue ever had greater appeal for Mormons than prohibition. It seemed a heaven-sent political expression of the abstinence proclaimed by Joseph Smith's Word of Wisdom revelation which, after the demise of polygamy, increasingly became the hallmark of Mormon peculiarity.[9] Thus when the breath of progressive reform quickened the latent forces of prohibition nationally in 1908, Mormons were eager to put Utah in the fore. Leaders including Smoot, Heber J. Grant, and other apostles came on hard, passing a resolution in general conference and otherwise supporting prohibition. However, Smoot backed off immediately. Not only did he sense the threat that prohibition posed to Utah's small but flourishing liquor industry and the disapproval of the national party, but he also recognized that under existing circumstances many would regard a prohibition law as legislation by church fiat. In Smooth's view, the whole thing would play into the hands of the American Party and tend to reorient state politics on the old Mormon–gentile lines as well as bring about his own defeat. In the ensuing frenzy, Smoot was charged with corrupt bargains and apostasy. Governor Spry, who could not flee to Washington, had no idea "his people could be so cruel" and in bitter jest expressed fear "that burning at the stake would be in order in six months." [10] Fury peaked during the 1909 session of the legislature, when a prohibition law was averted by the narrowest majority. Smoot engineered the defeat. That this act failed to destroy him politically is attributable to Joseph F. Smith's silent approval and covert support. But Smith's departure to "the more salubrious surroundings of Honolulu," where

9. *Doctrine and Covenants* 89.
10. Merrill, *Reed Smoot*, p. 20.

the "Hawaiian Saints needed his ministrations," suggests that the heat of the battle had affected even the church president.[11]

Although the prohibition issue continued to fester, Smoot and his cohorts successfully kept it from erupting until 1915, when Governor Spry vetoed a prohibition bill in a way that antagonized many voters. Utah ignored Smoot's late return to the prohibition fold in 1916, voted with the nation to return Woodrow Wilson to the presidency, and elected Simon Bamberger its first Democratic governor. In a flurry of legislation, Utah Democrats passed prohibition and a series of progressive laws. The year was an unmitigated disaster for the Republicans. Smoot, who did not face re-election, survived. Otherwise, it was a clean wipeout: William King took away Sutherland's senatorial seat, and the Smoot machine was swept away.

Soon thereafter death also cast its ballot. Both Joseph F. Smith and Thomas Kearns died in 1918. With them passed the surviving links to the two poles of the old order. Kearns's *Tribune* soon abandoned its "give-'em-hell" tactics to become a restrained voice of all the people—conservative, pro-business, and often Republican, but never again a screaming fount of anti-Mormonism. With Smith gone, Mormon leadership felt less compelled to "steady the political ark." [12] Heber J. Grant, who succeeded to the church presidency, continued to support Smoot, but the Mormon hierarchy since that time has rarely involved itself in politics with the directness that characterized the Smith period.

On the other hand, two-party politics has persisted. Utah followed the nation in turning from "nostrums to normalcy" in 1920, voting for Republican Warren G. Harding in the presidential election, returning Smoot to the Senate, and electing Republican Charles R. Mabey governor. Democrats dominated the years that followed, first at the state level and after 1932 in national elections. During post-World War II years Republicans came on strong again, without dominating the field. In all, the

---

11. Merrill, *Reed Smoot*, p. 23.

12. G. Homer Durham, "A Political Interpretation of Mormon History," *Pacific Historical Review* (June 1944): 148.

state's voting record adds up to a remarkably even division between Democrat and Republican and suggests a preference for incumbents and a tendency to follow national trends that reflects the state's quest for the center. Six of eleven governors have been Republican, five Democratic. In eighty years of statehood, each party has governed forty years. Since 1900 six Republican senators have served for a total of eighty-four years; four Democrats have held the post for sixty-six years. The state has tended to re-elect governors and senators. Seven governors have enjoyed two terms; Calvin Rampton (1965–1977) was elected three times; and only three governors have served but one term. One senator was elected five times; two have had four terms; two, three terms; two, two; and only two have served for one term. Although it has been apparently self-regulating since the days of the Smoot–Smith partnership, Utah's two-party system has maintained a remarkable balance.

By a similar token Utah has been slow to respond to reform movements and political change. While the state has demonstrated some affinity for reform and has introduced some innovations, it has generally done so only through the established parties and after strong precedents have been set elsewhere. The Populist protest of the 1890s, which seared Kansas and sent David H. Waite, the Lincoln of the Rockies, to the governor's mansion in neighboring Colorado, was by contrast listless and tame in Utah. Such force as it did muster came from mining communities and the urban unemployed. Utah farmers apparently cared not at all. However, a handful of ill-matched bedfellows, inveighing against the paradox of poverty amidst plenty and looking hopefully to "free silver" to restore prosperity in Utah's mines, managed to patch together a Populist slate for several elections before 1900. Activity peaked in 1896 with the election of four state legislators. But the Populists made the mistake that year of joining with the Democrats to support William Jennings Bryan and elect an Ogden mayor. Thereafter the party quickly collapsed, broken, according to one Populist, by the "fornication of fusion" but in a more fundamental way the victim of apathy.[13]

13. Warren Foster in *Living Issues* (Salt Lake City), September 16, 1898.

Although the progressive reforms of the early 1900s were more respectable nationally, Utahns received them with a similar lack of enthusiasm. Their chief impact came through party channels and gradual change rather than through the frontal attack of insurgencies or the third-party movements that shook cities and states elsewhere. Arguing that the American dream of democracy and equality had failed, Progressives pointed to monopoly in business and corruption in government as chief culprits. They sponsored a wide array of reforms including laws enlarging the regulatory and social functions of government, humanitarian legislation, and popular government measures such as the direct primary and initiative and referendum. The muckraking literature by which Progressives stirred public opinion nationally took a different and limiting turn in Utah, focusing less on monopoly and corruption and more on irregularities of the Mormon Church. As it turned out, the old Mormon bugaboo had passed its zenith as an issue and, worse yet from the standpoint of reform, tended to division along the Mormon–gentile lines of the earlier conflict rather than leading to progressive programs. It was not that Utahns utterly rejected progressive proposals, but they were slow to put them into effect until after 1916. Then the Democratic Party, under Simon Bamberger's leadership, enacted a wide range of laws promoting popular government and regulating labor relations, industry, and public utilities.

In addition the state showed a mixed reaction to the constitutional amendments of the era. Utah's congressional delegation failed to support amendments providing for direct election of senators and federal income tax, as did the state legislature. Prohibition was accepted only after the nation generally took up its cause. Woman's suffrage, on the other hand, had not only been written into the state constitution but received wide support, enjoying even the backing of conservative George Sutherland, who became "the acknowledged leader" of the U.S. Senate forces "fighting in behalf of the women" during pre-World War I years.[14]

---

14. Joel Francis Paschal, *Mr. Justice Sutherland: A Man Against the State* (Princeton, N.J.: Princeton University Press, 1951), p. 92.

Utah's tendency to introduce reform only after change had been well established elsewhere curtailed the role of third parties sharply. Progressive supporters of Teddy Roosevelt and Socialist groups put together third-party movements briefly in 1912 but ran well in only a few mining areas. The American Party, which was probably the most powerful third-party movement in the history of the state, not only had little interest in reform but was actually defeated in Salt Lake City when reforms substituted a commission form of government for the mayor-council system. Equally telling as an index of Utah's attitude toward third parties was the widespread misgiving when Parley P. Christensen of Salt Lake City emerged in 1920 as the presidential candidate of the national Farmer-Labor Party, an amorphous collection of Progressive splinter groups. Scornfully writing that the "joke is on Utah," the *Salt Lake Tribune* lamented that a malcontent defender of the IWW was in position to upstage Senators Smoot and King as Utah's spokesman and buried word of his activities in its back pages.[15] Other newspapers treated Christensen more kindly, but he gained only a trifling 3 percent of the Utah vote.

Nevertheless, the state did respond to national trends in its own way. This may be observed in the enactment of progressive programs and in the popularity of Woodrow Wilson, whether as a man of peace, war leader, or architect of the League of Nations. Utah's response to the League is particularly pertinent. The vast majority of the state's population supported the League as Wilson presented it, as they had his war policy. Many, including rank-and-file Mormons and the majority of the church's leadership, saw Wilson as a "great political seer . . . raised up of the Lord" and worked fervently for passage of the League.[16] A smaller but influential group opposed it with equal fervor. Among opponents was J. Reuben Clark, later Under Secretary of State and early advocate of nonintervention in Latin America. To Clark the League represented an entangling alliance that

15. *Salt Lake Tribune*, July 16, 1920; and Gaylon L. Caldwell, "Utah's First Presidential Candidate," *Utah Historical Quarterly* 28 (October 1960): 336.
16. Moyle, *Mormon Democrat*, p. 342.

could only reduce American sovereignty and interfere with its destiny. For similar reasons, Reed Smoot was wary of the League and followed Henry Cabot Lodge and other Republicans in the fight that ultimately defeated it. As the fight for the League subsided in 1920, Utah shifted away from the nostrums and changes of reform with an eagerness that, added to its slow conversion to progressive measures, suggests a fundamental inclination to the sure precedent and the safe path in politics. Republican Warren G. Harding received an overwhelming majority of the Utah vote, and Smoot was elected to the Senate for a fifth term.

In the decades that followed, two impulses suggest the continuation of Utah's quest for the center. A group of established figures strongly supported the status quo, calling for isolationism in foreign policy and support of business nationally and opposing government intervention to achieve social reforms. Most of this group had penetrated professional and power structures in the years around the turn of the century and had attained or were nearing the peak of their influence. At their head was Reed Smoot. During the 1920s he enjoyed great national prestige and a reputation of being quite beyond all ordinary political threats in Utah. Hailed as the state's "most distinguished native citizen," he became "Watchdog of the Treasury," chairman of the Committee on Finance of the United States Senate, and a member of the Debt Funding Commission. "He hobnobbed with Presidents and Wall Street bankers and Andrew Mellon" but still found time to grind out the almost unlimited statistics and schedules required to put together the Smoot–Hawley tariff. For him, property was a sacred constitutional right, profit America's driving force. Government's responsibility was to protect and stimulate business. Regulatory legislation was undesirable. "His role was not to create a new society, but to defend the one presently functioning." [17]

Several others in this established group attained national recognition. Senator William King, prompted by hard times in

17. Milton R. Merrill, "Reed Smoot, Apostle in Politics," *Western Humanities Review* 9 (1954–1955): 12.

Utah's sugar industry, had long opposed imperialistic adventures in Latin America's "sugar republics" on the grounds that they interfered with protective tariffs. He also believed that many New Deal reforms were dangerous extensions of federal power. James H. Moyle and William Spry continued careers launched earlier—Moyle as Under Secretary of the Treasury in Wilson's administration and Spry as Land Commissioner in the 1920s. Moyle introduced changes in the procedures of the Treasury that contributed to its general overhaul in the early twenties, but neither he nor Spry could be regarded as a representative of change. Under Secretary of State J. Reuben Clark, on the other hand, called for change, but Clark recommended alterations that would restore America to its former isolation and stay the flow of federal regulations and controls. As governor and as Secretary of War, Democrat George H. Dern was known by fellow Democrats as a "distinct progressive" but, as one of them later wrote, "there was nothing . . . in his administration . . . that indicated reform or originality. He just went along satisfactorily without making mistakes. He was conservative rather than radical, but his ideas and reading were in full sympathy with the progressives and the President [Franklin D. Roosevelt]." [18]

The Utahn who made the most important national contribution may well have been Associate Justice George Sutherland, a "great spokesman for the tradition of individualism," whose career in the United States Supreme Court (1922–1938) has been described as "a man against the state." [19] Unsung at home and the herald of a lost cause nationally, Sutherland had grown up in Utah's early mining and railroading era and partook deeply of Herbert Spencer's notion that social progress is the inevitable consequence of an unending "struggle between man and man." The pioneer Mormon passion for independence and self-help also influenced non-Mormon Sutherland, as did the teachings of limited government emanating from the University of Michigan Law School, which was "riding the crest of a na-

18. Moyle, *Mormon Democrat*, p. 332.
19. Paschal, *Mr. Justice Sutherland*, p. 244.

tionwide fame" when he and James H. Moyle roomed together there in the 1880s.[20] After one term in the House of Representatives, Sutherland was elected to the Senate in 1904. During his two terms there he "bewailed the mania for passing laws" and opposed Wilson's reform program.[21] Yet his was not a reactionary influence, but rather one of calculated and paced change. "It is important," he told the Senate in 1911, "that we should advance, but the vital thing is not that we should simply get somewhere—anywhere—quickly, but that we should arrive at a definite goal with the torch of sanity and safety still ablaze." [22] Sutherland was appointed to the Supreme Court by Harding in 1922 and quickly became one of its chief spokesmen. Indeed, his biographer has written, "while he was on the Court, no other justice spoke for the majority in so many cases. . . . If the Constitution is what the judges say it is, Sutherland was its chief author during his incumbency." [23] With Sutherland writing its majority opinions, the Court struck down one legislative innovation after another during the 1920s, binding Congress with the shackles of rugged individualism and limited government. The Depression's hurricane of catastrophe did little to moderate his position, and he continued to play a leading role among the "nine old men of the court" who so greatly compli cated the course of the New Deal. His reluctance to give over limited government's "torch of sanity" for unbridled experimentation in new programs was completely consistent with the Utah that produced him. Like the state, he found the "blaze of safety" in the most solidly established programs and doctrines.[24]

A second theme influencing politics after World War I was an expression of dissatisfaction by a society that had generally lacked the opportunities enjoyed by Sutherland and his generation. In no small part this was a matter of economic depression. Hard times began in 1920. Agriculture, mining, and manufac-

20. Paschal, *Mr. Justice Sutherland*, pp. 15, 125.
21. Paschal, *Mr. Justice Sutherland*, p. 73.
22. Paschal, *Mr. Justice Sutherland*, pp. 62–63.
23. Paschal, *Mr. Justice Sutherland*, p. xii.
24. Paschal, *Mr. Justice Sutherland*, pp. 62–63.

turing each suffered a serious decline. Unemployment was high and economic distress widespread. Mining rebounded after 1923, but agriculture remained depressed until the World War II years, and manufacturing failed to reach its pre-1920 strength until 1950. Weakened by the long recession of the 1920s, Utah's economy was plunged into deeper distress by the Great Depression. Drought in the early 1930s complicated an already tragic situation and by 1932 no fewer than 61,500 people—35.8 percent of the work force—were unemployed.

The election of Democrats at the state level as early as 1924 gave some evidence of dissatisfaction, although Utah followed its wonted pattern of voting with the nation in presidential elections. The state supported Republicans Calvin Coolidge in 1924 and Herbert Hoover in 1928. By 1932 Utahns had had enough and abandoned the Republicans entirely, giving Franklin D. Roosevelt 56 percent of their vote and favoring obscure University of Utah Professor Elbert Thomas over the untouchable Reed Smoot, who in the early hours of election returns "suspected that someone was playing a ghastly joke" on him.[25] Newly elected Governor Henry H. Blood mobilized state government and cooperated with New Deal programs in an effort to meet the needs of Utah's people. George Dern, governor for eight years after 1925, became Roosevelt's Secretary of War. Generally Utah's response to the Depression exemplified the state's political tradition: stirrings of unrest in the 1920s, a swing to the Democrats with the nation in 1932, but always a solid middle-of-the-road performance in meeting crises.

For a year or so early in the 1930s, however, protest stirred deeply, and pessimism sapped the vitals of many. The causes for which Senator William King had spent his life seemed in jeopardy. Indeed he saw little to hope for and told his son that Utah had passed its heyday. The young man reported to a friend:

> He said that the outlook was very gloomy for Utah. It would always
> be a 3rd rate state, and I would never see the day when it had
> 1,000,000 people. He said that it was drying up. The Utah Lake is

25. Malmquist, *The First 100 Years,* p. 329.

little more than a mud puddle, (smaller than it has ever been) and rain is falling less and less every year. He said that it was becoming more and more difficult to support the population, and that people were becoming more discouraged now than ever. . . . Why . . . in the land of plenty, with its huge mountains, rich in mineral resources, with its beautiful orchards, with its prairies, with its cattle, and its trees, why should there be such want and destitution? Why, in a state whose people preach progression and industry, should there be such despondency. Surely the chosen people of God, those who have the light of the restored gospel, those who have something bigger to live for than any one else, surely they shouldn't be wandering in the morass of despair.[26]

The young were hit hard. Many left the state, but some had no place to go. A few like Warwick Lamoreaux thought the "day of public ownership" was near. A devout Mormon, Lamoreaux wondered "why is the church so silent," and lamented his poverty—"I have been poor for so long that I don't know what purchasing power feels like." He became the youngest member of the state legislature, where he denounced capitalism as being "the very image of selfishness" and pointed up the "need for christianizing our economics." Ultimately, he sought the Democratic congressional nomination. Together with Communists whom he distrusted, a handful of fascists who commended him on having a philosophy, and various consumers' leagues, unemployed councils, and workers' organizations, Lamoreaux debated, demonstrated, and worked for reform. However, even in Lamoreaux's case power had a moderating influence, as he and others of his circle talked not of themselves for governor but of Herbert Maw, a hardworking, reform-oriented Democrat who was finally elected in 1940.[27]

In Carbon County labor unrest produced an upheaval that finally broke the iron hand the coal companies held over county politics and resulted in the unionizing of the coal industry. Interestingly, the breakthrough was produced by the unlikely combination of national labor legislation and the threat of the National

26. David S. King to Warwick Lamoreaux, June 1, 1934, entered in Warwick Lamoreaux Diary, June 1, 1934, xerox, Utah State University Archives.
27. Warwick Lamoreaux Diary, entries for 1934.

Miners Union, a Communist-dominated group that enlisted more than 2,000 men in 1933 and called a widespread strike. Thus threatened, the company managers turned to the long-dormant United Mine Workers, who launched an organizing drive of their own. The National Guard was called in, as it had been in 1903 and 1922, and many of the United Mine Workers were deputized. In time the NMU campaign was broken up. The UMW remained in possession of the field, and Carbon County was changed from a company-controlled Republican fiefdom to Utah's most solidly Democratic county.

Throughout the remaining years of the 1930s and the early 1940s Governors Blood and Maw and Senator Thomas worked in the full tradition of the New Deal. Administrative paraphernalia increased, and federal programs distributed nearly $98 million, or $342 per capita, placing Utah (along with other Western states) among the most heavily subsidized states in the nation.

But dependence was anathema to Mormons, and the church "used all of the moral suasion it had . . . to induce its members to abandon the generosities of government." [28] To meet the dual threat of Depression and government dole, the church developed its own relief program after 1935. Based on principles of thrift, human dignity, and self-sufficiency, the Welfare Program perpetuated themes as old as Mormon Utah and continues to carry a significant portion of the state's total social welfare effort. J. Reuben Clark, who was appointed to the first presidency of the church in 1934, was particularly adamant in his opposition to the New Deal and according to the faithful but Democratic James H. Moyle, thought Roosevelt "to be an evil genius . . . undermining the cornerstones" of freedom "and putting in vital danger the Constitution, the most sacred thing in our national life." [29] Clark grew in influence as aging President Heber J. Grant took a less active role, thus reinforcing already strong anti-New Deal sentiment. Church leaders came out in open opposition in the campaign of 1936, and the

28. Moyle, *Mormon Democrat*, p. 335.
29. Moyle, *Mormon Democrat*, p. 343.

church newspaper, the *Deseret News,* unlimbered its heaviest guns on Roosevelt. The *News* endorsed Alfred M. Landon and editorialized that while one candidate regarded the Constitution as "of 'horse and buggy' days," the other "stands for the Constitution and for the American system of government." Then the *News* concluded: "Church members who believe the revelations and the words of the Prophet must stand for the Constitution. Every patriot, loving his country and its institutions, should feel duty bound to vote to protect it." [30] The election results made it clear that the day when church preference and doctrines of limited government controlled Utah was past. Roosevelt took 70 percent of the vote. More than any other phenomenon of the era, this vote points to the ascendancy of economic and national issues over religion and local considerations in formulating popular political conduct.

Since 1940 Utah's affinity for middle-of-the-road politics has continued. As a New Dealer and something of a liberal in his social philosophy, Senator Elbert D. Thomas drew heavy fire and was finally defeated by Wallace Bennett in 1950 in a campaign notorious for its smear tactics. Bennett served for twenty-four years, making business and the economy his chief concerns. Ezra Taft Benson, a Mormon apostle with long experience in the Farm Bureau and farm cooperative movement, served two terms as Dwight Eisenhower's Secretary of Agriculture. Operating under the premise that "a planned and subsidized economy weakens initiative, discourages industry, destroys character and demoralizes the people—and surely is not good for America," he had much in common with J. Reuben Clark and more than a little with Smoot and Sutherland.[31] At the gubernatorial level, J. Bracken Lee, one-time mayor of Price in Carbon County, presented himself as a Republican and drew conservative support. Nevertheless he managed to be something of a maverick and the most colorful political figure of

30. *Deseret News,* October 31, 1936.
31. "Remarks by Ezra T. Benson," in Wayne D. Rasmussen, ed., *Agriculture in the United States: A Documentary History,* 4 vols. (New York: Random House, 1975), 4:3043.

the era. He assailed income tax, government expenses, and higher education and became a formidable force quite aside from the party—a fact proven by his showing as an independent senatorial candidate and by his repeated elections as mayor of Salt Lake City. Republican George D. Clyde, on the other hand, was fully regular as governor, following generally conservative policy. Democrat Calvin Rampton, who was governor from 1965 to 1977, operated on the basis of fiscal responsibility and pushed industrial development, tourism, and the defense industry.

All—governors, senators, presidential appointees, and voices of dissent alike—fit in the center-seeking, slow-to-change mold of Utah politics. From 1900 to the Bicentennial year Utah responded to the lure of the center, opting for the ideals of limited government and free enterprise and following established trends. The two-party system has obscured disruptive local issues and worked with remarkable balance. Yet Utahns have ignored few of the trends that have swept the country, and national programs have made their way into the state as they have other areas. In practice, fear of expanding government and shrinking individual initiative has rarely impeded governmental programs. Once a symbol of withdrawal and escape, the state has come to be a political heartland quite as surely as it is America's most inward-oriented physiographical region.

8

The Mid-Century Years

ALTHOUGH World War II and numerous other forces
revitalized Utah's economy in the years after the Depression,
the state continued to operate under serious natural restraints.
Remoteness, resources resistant to development, and the chronic
shortage of water remained serious liabilities. Absentee ownership continued but concerned Utahns less than in previous decades. The unprecedented growth of California, the overwhelming influence of the federal government, and defense spending
were all important outside influences.

One index of the strengthened economy was an upsurge in
population from 500,000 people in 1940 to 1.2 million in 1974.
No such numerical growth had occurred previously, but the
growth rate still lagged behind the Mountain West and the Western states generally. To an unparalleled extent, growth was the
product of natural increase. Birthrates ran consistently about 40
percent above the national average and death rates substantially
below. Only a small portion of the growth resulted from in-
migration, which produced a net gain of about 11,000 persons
per decade in the 1940s and 1950s and a similar net loss in the
1960s. By 1970, 336,976 persons born in Utah lived in other
states. Conversely, only 257,218 Utahns had been born elsewhere, so that the state sustained a net loss through interstate
movement of nearly 80,000 over the years.

The restlessness of Utahns was also apparent in the decrease in rural population during every post-Depression decade. Urban population, on the other hand, soared from slightly more than 300,000 to nearly 900,000 and by the mid-1970s claimed more than 80 percent of the state's inhabitants. Chief beneficiaries of the rural uprooting were the four Wasatch Front counties, where population grew by 65 percent between 1950 and 1970. Davis County, a bedroom community to Salt Lake City, increased 163 percent.

Wealth, like population, found its way to the countries bordering the Great Salt Lake. People there enjoyed above-average incomes, and industry and property were concentrated there. By contrast, the rest of the state confronted chronic economic problems. This was especially true in the southern counties, where the income of many residents fell below the poverty level.

Both expatriate Utahns and country folk recently moved to the city reveal a strong homing instinct. An unmeasured but recognizable portion of the in-migration consists of former citizens who have returned to retire or to fill prime administrative and professional positions opened to them by achievements out of state. Examples of the latter phenomenon are Dallin Oakes and Glen Taggart, respective presidents of Brigham Young University and Utah State University. Many second-generation emigrants return for educational purposes, in response to the persisting echoes of Zion's call, or in attempts to exchange metropolitan complexity for the simpler, more natural existence of Utah's mountains and deserts. While no strong reverse path from city to country is yet apparent, rural ideals and the convenience of outdoor recreation result in a stated preference for country life on the part of many Utahns.

The forces that produced population change also altered economic and production profiles. Agriculture and mining lost the dominant positions they long held, employing no more than 4 and 3 percent of the state's work force respectively by the 1970s. The number of farm operators fell from a maximum of 30,000 in 1934 to 12,700 in 1975. In addition, more than 60 percent of the latter number had off-farm jobs that involved substantial portions of their time. Canning, sugar processing, and other farm-related manufacturing diminished, and by 1974 only one cannery and one sugar plant survived where upwards of two dozen had operated in each industry before the Depression. Although total acreages of farm land nearly doubled between 1940 and 1975, prime lands with good water rights were increasingly devoted to subdivisions and made into highways along the Wasatch Front and through the fertile valleys. By 1975 a flourishing export industry of truck crops had virtually ceased, and grocers throughout the state imported much of their garden produce.

Although its percentage of the work force fell dramatically, mineral production increased from $100 million in 1940 to nearly $1 billion in 1974. As impressive as the increase may seem, Utah's 1974 production accounted for only 1.7 percent of the national total, in contrast to nearly 3 percent during the 1940s. With the giant Bingham pit of the Kennecott Copper Company processing ores that yielded as little as 11¢ per ton, copper continued to be the leading metal, producing $357 million or about 15 percent of the national total in 1974. This contrasted to production approaching 30 percent of the national total during the Korean War. After 1957 oil became a significant element in Utah's minerals economy, with nearly 40 million barrels of petroleum coming from the Aneth field in San Juan County in 1959. Thereafter petroleum production fluctuated from 23 million barrels in 1968 to nearly 40 million in 1974. More dramatic were the uranium strikes of the early 1950s that triggered a mining bonanza reminiscent of the old West, complete with prospectors, speculative crazes, boom towns, and quick-rich mining lords. Charles Steen was foremost among the latter. He made a fabulously rich strike, constructed reduction plants, built mansions in Moab and near Reno, Nevada, had a fling at state politics, and diversified his enterprises, only to face financial collapse. Coal production, long depressed in spite of the presence of some of the largest deposits in the nation, began a comeback after 1973 when the energy crisis turned attention to fossil fuels.

Rapid growth in other sectors of the economy offset the decline in older industries. Government employment increased fivefold, from 21,550 in 1940 to 108,000 in 1974, to become the biggest employer in the state. More than 11 percent of the total population was employed by the government, making Utah the leader in the forty-eight continental states, with a ratio about half again above the national average. Professional and related services, too, have increased dramatically, accounting for 20 percent of the people employed by the 1970s. Trade, manufacturing, and transportation—all supported by federal defense spending—are also major employers. During World War II the buildup of military installations resulted in the employment of approximately 100,000 persons. Since that time, this number has fluctuated downward with the fortunes of national defense. By 1960 Utah ranked third nationally in defense-generated employment; the state was first by 1962. In the years that followed, the state continued its reliance on defense-related enterprises.

Tourism has become an increasingly important resource in Utah, which bills itself "discovery country." A rich historical and cultural heritage, Indian societies and dramatic evidences of prehistoric cultures, more national parks than any state save California, high mountains and beautiful streams, canyonlands and Lake Powell's 1,800 miles of scenic shore line, "the greatest snow on earth," and one of the nation's great deer herds make Utah's list of recreation attractions impressive indeed. Each year nearly 5 million nonresident tourists visit the state, and citizens by the hundreds of thousands pursue outdoor recreation with a zest and enthusiasm that puts an army of 200,000 deer hunters in the field each fall, maintains a horse population that consumes more than 20 percent of the state's hay production, and makes recreation vehicles a major industry. Skiing, one of the most appealing tourist attractions, hinges on the urban communities of the Wasatch Front and depends partially upon public transportation. Other outdoor recreations, as well as prehistory, Indian cultures, and much of Utah's heritage, center in the hinterland. Indeed, 57 percent of summer tourist expenditures occur in the state's 25 rural counties. Among the advantages cited for tourism is its character as a clean industry in which environmental damage is limited.

In recent years there has also been a changing and expanding concern for environmental considerations. From territorial times questions of the environment demanded attention. Early Mormons made marked concessions to the Great Basin's environment of scarcity, seeking to utilize fuel and wood resources to the fullest and to make the desert blossom by bringing water to the land. Unfortunately their concern for the environment did not extend to grazing resources, and by the 1890s Utah suffered from repeated floods, serious water pollution, and erosion that lowered water tables and dumped untold tons of debris and mud into the valleys and villages. The Mormon mandate to redeem the wasteland also yielded to more exploitive impulses during the period of accommodation that followed 1890. In the same period private capital failed signally in its efforts to harness larger streams and bring water from the Colorado River drainage into the Great Basin. Thus deterioration of grazing resources, changing attitudes, and the inability of private companies to reclaim unutilized water set the stage for the development of the conservation and reclamation movements in Utah in the years after 1900.

Beginning with the creation of the Uintah Forest Reserve in 1897, some 9 million acres were placed under the Forest Service's jurisdiction by 1910. Regional headquarters were established at Ogden, and the Forest Service imposed drastic reductions in the number of livestock grazed on Utah's mountains and limited the destructive practice of trailing stock to and from neighboring states. Until the 1930s Forest Service efforts were largely preventive. Thereafter a new flood of federal money became available, and the Soil Conservation Service and the Taylor Grazing Act strengthened the federal government's conservation forces, making effective management of the public domain possible.

Reclamation, too, has been a continuing force in twentieth-century Utah. Where conservationists undertook to apply multiple-use practices to achieve maximum long-range service from renewable resources, the Bureau of Reclamation, founded in 1902, undertook to bring new resources into production. It authorized the Strawberry Project in east-central Utah during 1905 to convey Colorado River water to Utah Valley. By 1922 the Strawberry Project had placed 16,000 new acres under irrigation and provided additional water for 26,000 acres. In 1927 construction began on the Echo Reservoir, the major feature of the Weber River Project. During the Depression seven additional projects were undertaken at a cost of nearly $30 million. These were in turn dwarfed by the post-World War II Colorado River Storage Basin Project, whose great reservoirs at Flaming Gorge and Glen Canyon fall largely within Utah. Reclaiming no land, these mammoth projects focus upon the storage and distribution of the Upper Colorado Basin waters and upon hydroelectric power and recreation. The Central Utah Project, still in development, will utilize most of the water allotted to Utah under the Colorado River Compact of 1922 and the Upper Colorado Basin Compact of 1948, by which the seven Colorado Basin states have adjusted their interest in the river.

Not surprisingly, a number of Utah politicians have made reclamation their stock in trade. Reed Smoot was chairman of the National Conservation Commission's Committee on Forest Reservations but helped block reclamation projects from 1913 to 1919. Elbert D. Thomas was instrumental in securing Depression projects for the state, while Democratic Senator Frank E. Moss emerged more recently as an important figure in reclamation politics. But by far the most ardent senatorial champion of reclamation that Utah has produced was Arthur V. Watkins. During the 1940s and '50s he worked with a fervor opponents called evangelical and fanatic and influenced many of the decisions leading to the Colorado River Storage Project and the Central Utah Project.

A marked change in mood regarding the environment has occurred since 1960. Scarcity of key resources has always been a recognized fact of life, but the growing recognition that scarcity rather than abundance was the national norm brought a new concern, a new vocabulary, and a new pessimism in Utah as it did elsewhere. Water remains the key. Rainfall is limited, as it has always been. Rivers are widely scattered and carry relatively little water. Urban growth, recreation, and industry now add their needs to those of agriculture. In part the growing pressure on water is a matter of supply. In part it is a matter of location, and in a very real way it is a matter of the claims of other

Colorado River Basin states. Interstate compacts carefully mete out Utah's share. Of this amount the Central Utah Project is slated to transfer a major portion across the rim of the Great Basin to the Wasatch Front metropolis for industrial and domestic purposes. In addition optimists expect some 75,000 acres of new land to be irrigated and supplemental water to be provided for 87,000 acres.

Although the productive capacity of Utah land is sharply limited, interest in development is keen, and subdivisions and ranchette promotions dot the hinterlands. Former Utahns and out-of-staters—particularly from California—make investments, secure retirement or vacation hideaways, or hedge against urban disaster by buying land in rural Utah. Together with the energy boom, such factors have created land and real estate values that have little relation to productive capacity. A little-recognized dimension to the "multiple-use" approach to uncultivated lands is their value to environmental enhancement—especially to air and water quality. Amounting to nearly 50 million acres, Utah's uncultivated land may yet make a contribution to pollution control and the total environmental balance that will outweigh all other values.

Lauded in local myth and values as a region removed from the world's problems, Utah has nevertheless been subjected to serious forms of pollution. By 1900 municipal waters were often unsafe because of animal filth. A smoke belt from smelters and refineries at Murray, Magna, and Garfield had wiped the east front of the Oquirrh Mountains clean of foliage and affected farm production throughout Salt Lake Valley. In the 1950s fluorine poisoning resulted in the loss of millions of dollars in livestock and had unknown human effects in Utah County, as fallout from United States Steel's Geneva plant infected water and crops.

Pollution has reached new dimensions in recent decades. Industry is concentrated in the valley fold of the Wasatch Front. No mass transportation system exists, and Utahns are only less addicted to automobiles than their California neighbors. When winds and atmospheric conditions are right, the resulting pollutants blow away. When temperature inversions turn Utah's valleys into giant exhaust tanks, residents gasp in some of the nation's filthiest air. In recent years the problem has moved to the hinterland, as coal-burning power plants and other industrial developments seek energy sources. Plants built in the late 1960s at Huntington in Emery County and on Black Mesa in neighboring Arizona provoked deep distress among environmentalists, but the controversy came to a peak with the proposal to build a giant plant stoked by strip-mined coal from the Kaiparowits Plateau in the mid-1970s. Environmentalists argued that the proposed Kaiparowits plant, in the heart of scenic southern Utah, would fill the air with smoke, scar a fragile landscape, and pollute and divert woefully scarce water. In short, they argued, the plant would totally and utterly despoil one of industrial man's last natural refuges. Supporters, on the other hand, pointed out that the Kaiparowits Project would bring thousands of jobs into the region and greatly bolster Utah's lagging rural economy. The project was abandoned in the spring of 1976, with the environmentalists apparent winners. Similarly, oil shale—"the rock that burns"—has produced little more than controversy at this point.[1] Northeast Utah embraces substantial portions of a vast shale deposit holding nearly a trillion barrels of potential crude oil—some sixty times America's proven oil reserves. But with this potential for prosperity lies the threat of strip mining, water shortage, and disastrous social impact.

Utah's official and business community has apparently favored steam generation of electricity and oil-shale development, as well as industrial growth generally. Although this sector of society has by no means ignored social and environmental concerns, it has tended to measure opportunity and economic gains rather than environmental costs. In a real way it seems willing to make Utah an "energy colony." By contrast, some neighboring states appear to be less ready to welcome development that exploits their environment to meet needs extraneous to their own societies. Utah developers are apparently following the state's twentieth-century tradition of keeping to firmly fixed pre-

1. James Bishop, Jr., "Oil Shale: Bonanza or Bust for the Rockies?" *National Wildlife* 12 (June–July 1974): 11.

cedent. For all its currency, environmentalism is recent, and in the energy crisis, as in earlier crises, safety lies in the established way. Thus growth and economic need still make more serious demands on state and business planners than do social and environmental impacts. Environmental concerns, however threatening, are nevertheless somewhat nebulous in character and at least create problems more acceptable than those implicit in a growing population coupled with a lagging economy.

In the private sector the same sort of calculus reveals itself in what environmental planners suggest is a division between long-time residents and recent immigrants. By subjective assessment, the former appear less conscious of environmental deterioration and more sensitive to economic need and local control of policy. For example, in Kane County, site of the proposed Kaiparowits development, a population of 3,000 ranchers and townspeople strongly supported the project, evinced little concern for environmental impact, and expressed sharp resentment that outside influences should oppose their point of view. Theirs was essentially a modern expression of an earlier mentality that held that pioneering, proximity, and local interest bequeathed a special knowledge of what was best for the country and demanded a disproportionately large role in its government. This line of reasoning, though characteristically American, pays little heed to broader environmental consequences and to the fact that most of the land in Kane County, as elsewhere in Utah, is public domain and therefore related legally as well as psychologically and aesthetically to the American public at large.

Matters of cultural heritage have also brought about some divergence in viewpoint. Few states have a stronger sense of the past than does Utah. The Mormons have been particularly keen in representing their heritage. However, the formula by which they have presented it is relatively narrow and, with significant exceptions, has emanated from the church itself rather than from its people. This, coupled with the fact that the physical remnants of Utah's past are not old enough to be venerable, just awkwardly obsolete, has caused a number of sharp controversies. At Heber, in central Utah, preservationists fought successfully in the middle 1960s to save the Wasatch Tabernacle of the

Latter-day Saints. In neighboring Coalville, the razing of the tabernacle in 1971 resulted in adverse public opinion in Utah and elsewhere. Since then the church has authorized adaptive restoration of the Farmington Stakehouse and created an effective Historic Arts Committee that is working to define and broaden appreciation of the church's heritage.

The Utah Historical Society, supported by the Historic Preservation Act of 1966, has taken the lead in public preservation. An active committee continually reviews and designates historic sites for nomination to the National Park Service's National Register of Historic Places. A controversy over the First Church of Christ Scientist illustrates the attitude of at least one public official toward historic preservation. Chagrined when nomination of the church to the National Register without the owner's consent appeared inevitable, Governor Calvin Rampton reorganized the review committee and shifted responsibility for historic preservation from the Director of the Historical Society to his government superior, the Director of the Department of Development Services.

Over the years environmental considerations have expanded from conservation and reclamation to include an array of complex relationships that touch the lives of all Utahns. Almost nothing is without some sort of impact. As the concern for preservation and heritage suggests, matters of culture and education are thus interwoven in a social mosaic of increasing complexity.

By 1940 Utah had established an enviable educational system. With balanced higher education, a manageable number of public school districts, and a unified finance system, it was sometimes said to outclass "all other states in overall performance." [2] By great effort the state continued to lead the nation in many educational areas during the postwar decades. Recent studies, for example, indicate that it surpasses all states in producing scientists and scholars trained at the Ph.D. level.[3] In every census since 1940 the state has led the nation in the

2. Utah Foundation, *Research Report* (July 1973), p. 150.

3. Kenneth Hardy, "Social Origins of American Scientists and Scholars," *Science* 185 (August 9, 1974): 497–506.

average years of schooling completed by its adult population. In 1970 it also led in percent of adult population who had completed high school and ranked third after Colorado and Alaska in the proportion who had completed four years of college.

This achievement is the more remarkable in view of the burdens it has entailed. Throughout the entire period, the state has had a relatively youthful population and a limited tax base. In 1970 public school enrollments amounted to nearly 30 percent of the population, or to 633 school-age children for every 1,000 persons of working age, which represented a burden 26 percent heavier than the national average.

With huge budgets, centralized organization, a large professional staff, and access to the young in a state where families are large and important, the public school became increasingly important in the hierarchy of local institutions. While this expressed itself throughout the state, it was most noticeable in smaller communities where school districts grew rapidly and municipal governments did little more than hold their own.

College enrollments have almost quadrupled since 1953, with 93 percent of Utah's college students attending schools in the state, while nonresidents comprise at least 32 percent of all students enrolled in Utah colleges. Private colleges account for one third or more of the total, with most of the private enrollment accruing to Brigham Young University, which after 1950 became one of the nation's largest private institutions of higher education.

Among the achievements of Utah's educational system has been the notable contribution made by the colleges and universities to the arts and humanities. In a state where changing times have complicated the problems implicit in small, scattered populations, higher education has created outposts of activity and a climate of appreciation. Names little known outside Utah saw local opportunity and turned it into a richer life. Harold R. Clark established one of the great concert series in the United States at Brigham Young University, and B. F. Larson became a leading light in the visual arts, assembling a broadly oriented and gifted faculty and one of the state's best collections of art. At the University of Utah LeRoy J. Robertson distinguished himself as one of the nation's great composers and Lee Green Richards took the lead in the art department, bringing such notable figures as La Conte Stewart and Alvin Gittins. Everett Thorpe and Calvin Fletcher made lasting contributions in art at Utah State University, as have Harrison Groutage and Gaell Lindstrom in more recent years. At Southern Utah State College in Cedar City Fred Adams introduced the Shakespeare Festival, which has become one of the finest Shakespearean performances nationally and provides a welcome change of pace to Southern Utah's canyonlands and pioneer heritage. Since the 1920s when the old Salt Lake Theater was torn down amidst a protest that reverberates yet, the role of higher education in maintaining a viable theater tradition has been particularly significant. This situation continues to the present despite much talk of re-establishing the commercial theater on the tradition of the old Salt Lake Theater, which has been celebrated in the construction of the Pioneer Memorial Theater at the University of Utah.

Beyond the influence of higher education, the state of the arts is what James L. Haseltine, former Director of the Salt Lake Art Center, aptly termed one of innocence. Referring especially to the visual arts, he noted a total lack of the "promotional, congratulatory and cannibalistic mechanisms" of the great art centers.[4] Yet innocence is not without life and promise. Good work is done. Good artists return. In sculpture the great work of Cyrus E. Dallin and Mahonri Young played mainly an illustrative and documentary role. More recently Philip Morton's "assemblages of weathered wood, iron, and leather have the feel and smell of the Old West in a thoroughly contemporary manner."[5] Lee Deffebach, Tony Smith, and other painters have also made significant contributions in recent years. Many Utah artists have reached a state of maturity that enables them to tackle commissions for architecture, and the success of murals and sculpture in public and business buildings throughout the

4. James L. Haseltine, "A Song of Innocence," *Report on the Fine Arts in Utah 1968* (Salt Lake City: Bureau of Economic and Business Research, 1968), p. 32.
5. Haseltine, "Song of Innocence," p. 33.

state heralds a local renaissance, as does the opening of several new commercial galleries.

The literary arts, too, have functioned in something of a state of innocence or, perhaps more rightly, in a condition of unfulfilled promise. Themes abound: romantic setting, heroic conquest, great achievement, tragic counterpoint, and deep-seated conflict—the stuff from which great literature emerges. Yet few Utahns have risen to the challenge. Literary success has often been achieved by expatriates, most notably Bernard DeVoto and Wallace Stegner.

In the realm of western and Utah history the achievement has been somewhat more significant. DeVoto and Stegner have written sound and appealing works in which the Utah experience has been important. Another expatriate was Dale Morgan, who, after brilliant beginnings with the Utah Writers' Project of the New Deal, became caught up in the mountain-man and fur-trade history of the West and moved to the Bancroft Library at the University of California, where he produced numerous works of outstanding value. Juanita Brooks's *Mountain Meadows Massacre* has few peers in Utah history, while Fawn Brodie's *No Man Knows My History* led to her excommunication from the Mormon Church but has been widely acknowledged for its insight into Joseph Smith and the early Mormon experience. Of this group only Juanita Brooks has remained in Utah. In recent years Leonard J. Arrington, who won national acclaim with his *Great Basin Kingdom,* has headed a broadened and awakened school of Mormon history and has become historian of the Mormon Church, bringing new vigor to its historical publishing.

The Mormon Church has also played a significant role in the broader expressions of the arts. In recent years as in the past, it has stressed what might be called participatory arts. Church architecture has emphasized utility and function more than majesty. By a similar token the church has fostered art forms that encourage activity in both the doing and the beholding. Utah's most widespread programs of theater and dance have risen from church youth activities. By contrast, church programs have given short shrift to the literary and visual arts, with their more limited opportunities for group involvement. The Tabernacle Choir is perhaps the greatest artistic achievement of the Mormon Church. Founded in 1847, the choir has now some 375 volunteer members. Great directors, appreciative church audiences, broadcasting history that dates back to 1929, acclaim on tour, an unusual home base, and the support of the renowned Tabernacle organ and several of the nation's finest organists have combined to make the choir one of the state's most important attractions. In total, the church's impact on the fine arts has been considerable, although its emphasis has been on utility and group involvement rather than upon art for the sake of art.

Meantime the Mormon cultural area broadened from a Utah Zion to "the church world-wide," as the outward vision of the church expressed itself in new ways after 1940. Temples were built on the West Coast, near Washington, D.C., and in England, Switzerland, and New Zealand. A missionary force composed primarily of young men increased from about 2,000 in 1947 to some 20,000 in 1976, as a Mormon brand of ecumenicism ignored church councils to approach individuals directly. "The church world-wide" encouraged converts to stay at home, as the gathering became a matter of associating with other Mormons in local wards (congregations), and Zion became more a state of mind and less a "place by God prepared." The flood of missionaries that went out and returned to Utah has given the state a distinctly cosmopolitan cast, although the strong focus of missionaries on the business of proselyting places distinct limits on the cultural impact of their travels. By the 1970s vigorous educational and health programs in the Pacific and in Latin America caused the church to withdraw support from an extensive hospital program in Utah to concentrate its means on areas of greater need. Similarly the rituals of Mormon heritage, which focused upon the valleys of the mountains and America, are undergoing some change, although numerous public addresses and official publications during the Bicentennial year emphasized the "America–promised land" theme. The missionary program and other efforts to promulgate the Mormon heritage have resulted in a vigorous and grassroots dissemination of a particular brand of Americanism from Utah.

Utah's tradition of broad participation has contributed to premium rewards in the Ballet West and the Utah Symphony. While the symphony and the ballet are recent developments, they take advantage of an urge for statewide appeal and broad exposure that artistically speaking dates back at least to 1899. In that year the efforts of Alice Merrill Horne resulted in the founding of the Utah Arts Institute, which acquired a fine collection of Utah paintings and showed them widely in outlying hamlets and towns during the early years of this century. In time the Art Institute became the Fine Arts Institute, which continues to emphasize an outreach tradition. The same impulse for broad exposure became a special watchword with Maurice Abravanel, who as director of the Utah Symphony after 1947 was described as the "most significant artistic figure of the state's second century" and credited with changing "the cultural face of Salt Lake City and Utah." [6] Under Abravanel's brilliant direction, the Utah Symphony became one of the finest and most traveled orchestras in America. In addition to bimonthly concerts in Salt Lake City, the symphony made repeated trips over the 400-mile length of Utah and into neighboring states. Abravanel's programming emphasized the masters but included the new and the popular and attempted always to awaken appreciation in his audiences.

Something of the same happy chord of broad involvement and brilliant direction appeared in the gratifying success of the Ballet West. The ballet came to its own as a dance form in Utah only after 1941, when Willam Christensen left the San Francisco Ballet to work with C. Lowell Lees at the University of Utah. They first established a highly successful student performing program, then the Utah Civic Ballet; and finally the Ballet West came into being. Gifted leadership; cooperation of community, state, and university; and the support of thousands of

6. Lowell M. Durham, "The Abravanel Years," *Utah Academy Proceedings* 43 (1966): 1–12.

Utah citizens have made possible a period of continuous ballet growth and development.

The state must give part of the credit for the success of the Utah Symphony and the Ballet West to the Utah centennial in 1947. In addition, the national cultural awakening that came as the country anticipated its Bicentennial has constituted an important influence. Particularly significant are programs funded by the National Endowment for the Arts and the National Endowment for the Humanities and under the Historic Preservation Act of 1966. Still to be measured are the more direct effects of the Bicentennial celebration itself. However, with prospects already assured for a multimillion-dollar arts center in Salt Lake City and lesser programs elsewhere in the state, the promise for a flowering of the arts in Utah has rarely been brighter.

In the Bicentennial year, Utah looks back on a period that, compared to the pre-World War II decades, has been relatively prosperous and has provided a high standard of living and an opportunity for growth. Yet by numerous standards the state's economy has lagged, and developments have entailed serious erosion of local autonomy. Before the energy crisis of the 1970s directed national attention to the shortage of fuels, Utah's economy was sluggish and its unemployment rate high. In spite of some dislocations from the inflation and recession of the mid-seventies, the revival of its economy has run ahead of the nation, suggesting that demand for resources may be interjecting new resiliency into the economy. Whether revitalization will actually mean more opportunity or not, it surely implies a continuation of federal influences, outside financing, social mobility, and a future in which the forces working on all Americans, if indeed not upon all mankind, will influence Utahns.

9

Toward Century Three

AT the two-hundred-year mark, the dual process of becoming that began so appropriately for Utah with the Dominguez–Escalante Expedition and the Declaration of Independence in 1776 still continues. Now, as then, forces recognizably national have combined in the making of the state. The interior provinces of the continent were explored and became a frontier territory, then a testing ground for American federalism, and finally a state absorbed in the national experience. Utah's course through two centuries has been traced in the foregoing chapters. Broader questions and summations remain. What has Utah's experience meant in the context of the continuing American Revolution? What can be said of the character of its people? And what are the state's prospects as it looks, with the nation, to the third century?

In several ways Utah's path has been different. Primary among the signposts that have marked its course are the Great Basin environment and the social interaction between Mormons and other Utahns. In a nation where 50 percent of the population lives within fifty miles of the sea and most of the remainder within fifty miles of a river articulating to the sea, the Great Basin was and remains an anomaly. The most isolated region in a nation where isolationism has been a watchword, it has nevertheless been pathway to the Orient, highroad to empire, and crossroads of the West. It has been heartland and interior, a land

197

of escape and new beginning. Physically, it is a region of maximum deviation—a region especially uninviting to individuals. Rainfall varies from sparse to nearly nonexistent. Other resources are scattered, inaccessible, and remote from markets and shipping centers.

The Basin of the Great Salt Lake was the first heartland of the Rocky Mountain fur trade. Thereafter it became a barrier impeding access to other places, as the Old Spanish Trail and variations of the Oregon and California trails were worked out. For the Mormons the Basin was a gathering place, a halfway house on the road to glory, and a home to a recluse people where oasis farming required a minimum of countering loyalties and remoteness prevented interference with polygamy. Through central planning and group action, the Mormons redeemed an environment that lay beyond the interest and capacity of individual frontiersmen and in the process added a significant set of practices to the methods by which America claimed the West. Although the Mormon approach to the Utah environment was cooperative, it produced a sense of self-reliance that dovetailed nicely with the sentiments of laissez faire and rugged individualism during the period of Mormon accommodation at the turn of the century. Self-reliance has persisted as a major Utah value during the twentieth century, although it has sometimes expressed itself more emphatically in rhetoric than in practice.

The Utah environment has also shaped economic developments in significant and lasting ways. Big money and sophisticated technology have been necessary in all but the most primary industrial developments. The impact of this first became apparent in railroading, when the best local efforts were unable to control a territorial railroad system. Later the Harrimans, the Havemeyers, the Guggenheims, and a parade of other wealthy absentee owners moved at will to take over resources and industry whose development defied local abilities. Local entrepreneurs who did survive often left the state to become absentee owners themselves, or remained to become "token locals" on boards of directors of outside-dominated corporations. In addition, the scattered and low-grade character of Utah resources slowed the development of the mineral and livestock frontiers and contributed to diverse themes in ethnic, labor, and native American history.

While the federal government first invaded Utah over the Mormon question, the environment has caused a far more extensive federal invasion. Basically this invasion rose out of the question of who was to control Utah's resources. Because of the country's nature, relatively small acreages passed into private hands through the homestead and purchase provisions of Congress. Upwards of three quarters of the land remained in the public domain, used and controlled by private interests who felt that customary usage and proximity provided the best bases for control and utilization. With conservationists claiming a growing government obligation to manage publicly owned resources after 1900, two major lines of invasion opened. The first of these followed the trace cut by the Forest Service, which had confronted frontier areas of Utah with the idea that regulation was necessary and through the years trained people in the ways and thinking of resource managers. Later came the "resource-creating" Bureau of Reclamation, which has injected central resource planning and vast amounts of money. More recently an entire host of management agencies, along with private energy-development and nature-conservation interests, has entered the decision-making arena.

In spite of the passage of years and the interplay of various economic and social forces, the most useful summary of Utah's social and political considerations still begins at that point where the Mormon society has met the broader national society. Because of this interplay, Utah has been a "Unique West." With nationwide attention focused on polygamy and the often overlapping affairs of church and state, it was known as a "different" territory. Vigorous missionary programs and the travel and sensational literature of the time helped to spread the image of peculiarity. The imprint of the Mormon village upon the landscape also contributed to the state's image. In spite of landscape patterns formed by homesteads beyond the village confines, dry farms on the ancient terraces of Lake Bonneville, and mining, ranching, and railroading terrains, the village landscape was and to some degree remains the best reminder of early Mormon traditions.

In its constitutional development, Utah provided the most searching examination America has ever given to the meanings of the religious adjustments that grew out of what Sidney E. Mead has called the "Revolutionary Epoch." [1] In its way, Joseph Smith's establishment of the Mormon Church rejected the separation of church and state and the "agreement to disagree" that freedom of religion implied. The Mormon preference for divine revelation over the will of the majority and the church's reworking of America's secular destiny in favor of the earthly kingdom of God also countered the religious adjustments of the Revolution. The tensions thus created were resolved, but the process of adjustment spread over a century and fell into three major phases.

The first reaction against Mormon nonconformity took place in Missouri and Illinois. Non-Mormon majorities invoked "higher law" to justify extralegal or vigilante action to defeat a threat that defied legal and political expedients.

The second phase occurred in Utah, where isolation, the nation's preoccupation with larger issues, the Mormon majority, and changing times made possible the abandonment of the social violence implicit in the "higher law" for political solutions to the same problems. For a half-century the wheels of the federal government ground ponderously, as the American people first decided that Mormonism did indeed break with standard American practices and then slowly created the legal and political machinery and judicial precedent to force conformity. The process so defined the limits of religious freedom as to deny constitutional protection to practices considered morally offensive by the larger community. Similarly, a single-issue church party that took its direction from church leaders and Mormon views of a religious rather than a secular national destiny were judged to breach the principle of separation of church and state.

1. Sidney E. Mead, *The Lively Experiment: The Shaping of Christianity in America* (New York: Harper and Row, 1963), p. 52.

The third period saw the Mormon question depoliticized. Mormons agreed to take the church out of politics, and the federal government agreed to dismantle its coercive machinery and give Utah statehood. A result of this adjustment was a firm commitment to the two-party system as the best means of broadening and balancing Utah politics and defusing Mormon–gentile relations. An added dimension of patriotism among Mormons has risen from this settlement. Mormon teachings have accepted the religious principles of the Revolutionary Epoch not only as the matrix out of which the Kingdom of God would arise but as the long-range guarantors of religious freedom necessary to protect the church through an indeterminate period of secular dominance. In time the church approved the religious adjustments of the Revolution, modified the conflicting elements of Mormon belief and practice, and postponed the time framework of Mormon millennialism.

Although the experiences by which the constitutional questions implicit in the Mormon problem were resolved lacked the transcending importance that the slave issue and Civil War held for America, they nevertheless laid an indelible mark on Utah and the nation. Religion has been one of the great motivating forces of Western civilization. The explosive force of the Muslim expansion, the Crusades, the Reformation, and the rivalry between Protestant England and Catholic Spain represented a crucial theme in Old World tradition. Looked at one way, the Mormon conflict was the echo of this thundering issue; penetrating the consciousness of Americans, it reminded them how thoroughly the Revolution had done its work, how completely its adjustments had disarmed religion's explosive potential for conflict, and attested how, without the bloody truncating of the Soviet Union's overthrow of the church, the American Revolution had preserved for all citizens the broadening practices and ennobling sentiments of religion. Examined from a slightly different vantage point, the Utah experience was evidence that those issues that marked the course of great civilizations marked America. At no great cost, the nation had mastered the contradictions of sword and cross, thus taking its rightful place among history's great powers in this as in other respects.

To a degree Utah is still undergoing the third period of adjustment. Mormon–gentile tensions no longer relate directly to the religious adjustments of the American Revolution, but the question of religion still touches the state's deepest sense of group consciousness. Utah society forms groups along such conventional lines as political persuasion, profession, education, place of origin, age group, ethnic background, and level of income. Nevertheless, the Mormon–non-Mormon division cuts through and influences all other grouping arrangements. Like the subsurface portion of an iceberg, its dimensions are difficult to measure. They express themselves publicly and politically only in such issues as Sunday closing, liquor by the drink, and the Equal Rights Amendment. Even in such situations Utahns exhibit a self-conscious determination not to let the Mormon issue become the dominating issue of politics. In the place of disruptive political struggle, tension now vents itself in group loyalties, in a thousand private adjustments, and by the more or less constant awareness that this particular social division, like death and taxes, is a significant fact of life in Utah. One effect of this consciousness has been to make religious association generally viable and dynamic, while another has been the identification of groups of dissent both within the Mormon society and among the state's citizens generally. While such groups sometimes express themselves politically, the general effect of group alignment has been not only to withdraw issues from the public arena but to divert the thoughts and efforts of people from the political arena. Offsetting such influences is the strong sense of public responsibility that characterizes Utahns and the tendency to look to government for all kinds of services and resolution of almost all problems.

In many of its expressions, group loyalty is an affirmative expression of equality. In Utah, as elsewhere, the ideal of equality holds a strong place in the expressed value system. Yet equality "Utah-style" has its limits. Masculine influence has remained dominant. Mormon pioneering made Utah women co-equal with men more than on other frontiers, and even polygamy, with its strange way of placing economic responsibility upon women, worked to enhance their status. Still, twentieth-century Utah has not found female equality a compelling need. Business, politics, and the great popularity of hunting and outdoor sports revere masculine dominance, as does the Mormon Priesthood, which is open to conforming males. The Priesthood also excludes blacks, who, with other minorities, suffer most of the social and economic handicaps found elsewhere. Public education functions without overt discrimination and for decades has been a means of social mobility as well as the highroad on which Utahns with liberal and professional training have been able to seek opportunities elsewhere. Yet Utahns generally suffer from a form of "educational colonialism." Remoteness and social connections place beyond the reach of most residents the educational superstructure of prep schools, Ivy League, and interinstitutional fraternity which control many of America's social and power perquisites.

By a number of standards, Utahns fail to demonstrate strong tendencies toward individualism. Natural conditions have rewarded cooperative action, corporate power, and technological development. After early Mormon experimentation led to social conflict and bitterness, conformity has had a special dimension, as Utahns, in an attempt to avoid reawakening the old divisiveness, have sought values acceptable to all. Reform causes have rarely flourished until they have been widely accepted elsewhere. University campuses have served as educational centers and places of social aggregation rather than hotbeds of debate. Except for occasional neo-homesteaders in the canyonlands, Utah has produced few communes and fewer intellectual colonies. Even in personal manners, the urge to conform commonly stifles individualism, with the result that society follows well-fixed norms in dress and conduct and in its moral codes. Change, however, has its individualistic overtones; and generation gap, protest, increasing crime, and desire for a new order have disturbed and challenged Utah, as well as the rest of the nation, in recent decades. Attitudes of welfare-statism at the public level and insistent immediatism on the part of wage earners and others who demand pay increases have increasingly supplanted independence and self-reliance. Nevertheless many continue to express their individualism in distrust for big and distant government. To people of this persuasion, local government still seems less complex, less foreign, and more responsive to individual rights in a world run amuck with giant bureaus and outside interests.

In spite of a number of radically disrupting forces, the Utah family remains a viable institution. Challenges to family bonds are as old as man's memory. No aspect of Indian society has suffered more tragic shock than the family. An uprooted masculine society manned the state's mining frontier and, to a lesser degree, the early livestock industry. More than tradition acknowledges Mormon Utah was built on disrupted homes, as one or two from a family were gathered out of Europe or the eastern part of the United States. The revering traditions that arose about converts who left father, mother, child, or brother raised an implicit justification for family ruptures that countered a strong family orientation within the church and may still contribute to a Utah divorce rate that is exceeded by few states. Church callings and polygamy also tended to loosen family bonds. Women and children were left to shift for themselves for long periods as men filled missions or gave heavily of their time to church duties. Polygamy scattered families, encouraged matriarchal loyalties, and resulted in a number of divisive influences as well as some that made for close unions. Education, professions, mobility, and war have uprooted families, as have attitudes about self-fulfillment. Nevertheless, family bonds in Utah bind the community. This results partly from traditional American influences and partly from a recent Mormon emphasis on the importance of the family in teaching moral values and providing meaningful and intimate associations.

As the third century begins, the area that was a vague confusion of myth to Dominguez and Escalante and completely beyond the consciousness of the founding fathers has been thoroughly assimilated into the mainstream of American society. Frontier conditions that sharply limited economic options, services, and government have been supplanted by a system that now seeks to meet needs rising out of a national arena. Government has exploded, and energy needs threaten a new colonialism. The nation's news is Utah's news, as are the nation's fears.

Yet most Utahns would concur that life in Utah has a character recognizably its own and that its distinctions are worth perpetuating, both for what they mean to the state's people and for what they add to the nation. Most of them would still regard federalism, with its division of powers between the states and the nation, as not merely a necessary administrative arrangement but a dynamic system for generating new programs and a richer national culture as well as a means of achieving Utah's needs. Most would agree that federalism functions fairly well in Utah. Yet few would deny the existence of threats to liberty and to the balance of power between the nation and the state upon which federalism rests. In the face of danger, many recognize that in the history of the state lie the seeds of a vital and continuing federalism. As the American Revolution moves into the third century, it may be hoped that Utah's heritage will continue to contribute to pluralism and liberty within the American union.

Suggestions for Further Reading

An abundant literature is available for the reader who would pursue the story of nineteenth-century Utah. Works that give general coverage include J. Cecil Alter, *Utah, the Storied Domain, A Documentary History* . . . (3 vols., Chicago: American Historical Society, 1932); Andrew Love Neff, *History of Utah 1847 to 1860* (Salt Lake City: Deseret News Press, 1940); and H. H. Bancroft, *History of Utah 1540 to 1886* (San Francisco: The History Company, 1889). William H. Mulder and A. R. Mortensen, eds., *Among the Mormons: Historic Accounts by Contemporary Observers* (New York: Alfred A. Knopf, 1958), consists of carefully selected extracts from contemporary views held together by readable editorial comments. In addition the body of literature that reflects the interest of nineteenth-century travelers and commentators is enormous. Outstanding is Sir Richard F. Burton, *The City of the Saints and Across the Rocky Mountains to California* (New York: Harper & Brothers, Publishers, 1862). Horace Greeley, *An Overland Journey from New York to San Francisco* . . . (New York: C. M. Saxton, Barker & Co., 1860), and Philip S. Robinson, *Sinners and Saints* . . . *Three Months Among the Mormons* (Boston: Roberts Brothers, 1883), also provide balanced profiles of Utah society and word pictures of its natural setting.

Studies of exploration and discovery reflect the geographic riddles posed by the Great Basin. Bringing Spanish exploration into focus is Herbert Eugene Bolton, *Pageant in the Wilderness: The Story of the Escalante Expedition to the Interior Basin, 1776* (Salt Lake City: Utah State Historical Society, 1950). The roles of the mountain men and early government explorers are delineated in Dale Morgan, *The Great Salt Lake* (New York: Bobbs-Merrill Company, 1947). Less directly concerned with Utah but excellent for the broader discovery of the Great Basin is Gloria Griffin Cline, *Exploring the Great Basin* (Norman: University of Oklahoma Press, 1963). Wallace Stegner, *Beyond the Hundredth Meridian: The Exploration of the Grand Canyon and the Second Opening of the West* (New York: Houghton Mifflin, 1953), and Richard A. Bartlett, *Great Surveys of the American West* (Norman: University of Oklahoma Press, 1962), bring to focus the work of John Wesley Powell, F. V. Hayden, and others in unlocking the last secrets of Utah's canyonlands. Mormon literature abounds. Balanced treatments are less numerous. Brigham H. Roberts, *Comprehensive History of the Church of Jesus Christ of Latter-day Saints, Century I* (6 vols., Salt Lake City: Deseret News Press, 1930) is a balanced and sound official history of the church. Excellent for grasping the broad lines of Mormon history as well as the rudiments of their theology and social organization is Thomas F. O'Dea, *The Mormons* (Chicago: University of Chicago Press, 1957). Only less notable is Fawn M. Brodie, *No Man Knows My History* (New York: Alfred A. Knopf, 1946), which is considered the standard work on Joseph Smith. No satisfactory biography of Brigham Young exists, but M. Robert Werner, *Brigham Young* (New York: Harcourt, Brace & Company, 1925), is still serviceable. Robert Bruce Flanders, *Nauvoo: Kingdom on the Mississippi* (Urbana: University of Illinois Press, 1965), marks a highpoint in the study of Mormon experience in the Midwest, while the *Autobiography of Parley Parker Pratt* (Salt Lake City: Deseret Book Company, 1938) represents a benchmark in the personal narratives of persecutions, conversions, and early Mormon life. Klaus J. Hansen, *Quest for Empire: The Political Kingdom of God and the Council of Fifty in Mormon History* (East Lansing: Michigan State University Press, 1970), discusses Mormon millennialism and the strange turn it gave to nationalism among mid-nineteenth-century Mormons. Leonard J. Arrington, *Great Basin Kingdom, An Economic History of the Latter-day Saints, 1830–1900* (Cambridge: Harvard University Press, 1958), stands together with Nels Anderson, *Desert Saints, the Mormon Frontier in Utah* (Chicago: University of Chicago Press, 1942), at the top of the literature on frontier Utah.

Trail literature dealing with the Mormon exodus is also considerable. A classic primary account is *William Clayton's Journal* (Salt Lake City: The Deseret News Press, 1921), while Wallace Stegner traces the long stretch of the trail in *The Gathering of Zion: The Story of the Mormon Trail* (New York: McGraw-Hill Book Company, 1964) and LeRoy R. Hafen and Ann W. Hafen describe handcart migration and the tragic emphasis it lent Mormon trail lore in *Handcarts to Zion: The Story of a Unique Western Migration, 1856–1860* . . . (Glendale: The Arthur H. Clark Company, 1960). The Mormon gathering as missionary effort and folk movement is described in two excellent books: William Mulder, *Homeward to Zion: The Mormon Migration from Scandinavia* (Minneapolis: University of Minnesota Press, 1957), and P. A. M. Taylor, *Expectations Westward: The Mormons and the Emigration of their British Converts* . . . (Edinburgh: Oliver & Boyd, 1965).

Territorial politics have been the object of considerable attention. Dale Morgan, "The State of Deseret" (Vol. 8, *Utah Historical Quarterly,* 1940), a book-length treatment, details the Mormon effort to lay the groundwork for a political system that could succeed to power at Christ's second advent. Norman F. Furniss, *The Mormon Conflict, 1850–1859* (New Haven; Yale University Press, 1960), studies the Utah War, while Juanita Brooks looks penetratingly at the tragedy that grew from it in *The Mountain Meadows Massacre* (Palo Alto: Stanford University Press, 1950). Howard R. Lamar provides an excellent political overview of the entire territorial experience in *The Far Southwest 1846–1912: A Territorial History* (New Haven: Yale University Press, 1966).

By contrast, historical literature dealing with twentieth-century Utah is sparse and spotty. In the absence of book-length treatises, the articles appearing in the *Utah Historical Quarterly* are especially valuable. UHQ began publication in 1928 with an emphasis upon pioneer, exploration, and Indian accounts but in recent years has become increasingly an outlet for articles on the twentieth century including those of Leonard Arrington and various collaborators on mining and defense spending since World War II. A brief overview of twentieth century politics is provided by Frank H. Jonas, "Utah the Different State," in Frank H. Jonas, ed., *Politics in the American West* (Salt Lake City: University of Utah Press, 1969). A view of twentieth-century politics from the vantage of the *Salt Lake Tribune* appears in O. N. Malmquist, *The First 100 Years: A History of the Salt Lake Tribune, 1871–1971* (Salt Lake City: Utah State Historical Society, 1971). The national role of one Utah senator is the subject of M. R. Merrill, *Reed Smoot: Utah Politician* (Logan: Utah State University Press, 1953), while Joel F. Paschal, *Mr. Justice Sutherland: A Man*

Against the State (Princeton, N.J.: Princeton University Press, 1951), deals with George Sutherland's contributions to the conservative court of the 1922–1938 era. Helen Z. Papanikolas's *Toil and Rage in a New Land: The Greek Immigration in Utah* (Salt Lake City: Utah State Historical Society, 1970) traces the history of Utah's Greeks from 1900, and a recent milepost is her role as editor of *The People of Utah* (Salt Lake City: Utah State Historical Society, 1976), in which the state's ethnic groups are treated. G. Lowry Nelson, *The Mormon Village* (Salt Lake City: University of Utah Press, 1952), and Juanita Brooks, *Uncle Will Tells His Own Story* (Salt Lake City: Taggart & Company, 1970), do much to chronicle the continuing importance of rural Utah, while C. Gregory Crampton's *Standing Up Country: The Canyon Lands of Utah and Arizona* (New York: Alfred A. Knopf, 1964) points to a growing recognition of the importance of the Colorado Plateau and the canyonlands in the Utah experience.

Index